SCANDALON

Running From Shame and Finding God's Scandalous Love

SCANDALON

Running From Shame and Finding God's Scandalous Love

A Memoir

by Susan Elaine Jenkins

CLADACH
Publishing

PUBLISHED BY CLADACH PUBLISHING
Greeley, CO 80634 www.cladach.com
All rights reserved.

Scripture quotations, unless otherwise noted, are taken from the Holy
Bible, New International Version, NIV. Copyright 1973, 1978, 1984 by
International Bible Society. Used by permission of Zondervan Publishing
House. All rights reserved.

Although based on facts, as verified by the author, many names mentioned
in this memoir have been changed.

Cover Art: iStockphoto

Library of Congress Cataloging-in-Publication Data
Jenkins, Susan Elaine, 1955-
Scandalon : running from shame and finding God's scandalous love : a
memoir / by Susan Elaine Jenkins.
p. cm.
ISBN 0-9818929-0-6 (pbk.)
1. Jenkins, Susan Elaine, 1955- 2. Jenkins, Susan Elaine, 1955
— Travel—China. 3. Divorced women—California—Biography. 4.
Abused women—California—Biography. 5. Women teachers—China—
Biography. 6. Women teachers—California—Biography. 7. Christian
biography. 8. China—Biography. 9. California—Biography. I. Title.
CT275.J5537A3 2009
979.4'054092--dc22   [B]   2009015593

ISBN-13: 9780981892900
ISBN-10: 0981892906

Printed in the United States of America

To Dad ~
for your amazing generosity of spirit as I share this story.
I love you so much. You are proof that it's never too late to
allow love to have its way in our lives. Thank you for your
consistent acceptance and grace. Your presence lights up a
room; even four year olds knock at your door, asking you to
come out to play with them! I adore you.

To Mom ~
so recently passed on to heaven, for reading the manuscript
and giving your sweet blessing "that others would be
helped." As you told me one week before you went to be with
Jesus, "We will have an eternity to laugh together and talk
heart-to-heart." See you later, Mom.

Foreword

This is a book about a survivor, a very real and courageous survivor . . . a story of betrayal and devastation . . . a journey from humiliation to hope and healing.

The Greeks had a word for this type of journey—*scandalon*. It means "to cause to fall, to offend, to bring disgrace."

The author's perilous journey is one of sizzling honesty. You might be amazed that she has been able to put her pain into words, to share her brokenness with us.

She reveals her personal calamity in hopes that she might help other hurting people. These reflections of transparent pain are both admirable and cathartic. This book is a gift to anyone who has been victimized, manipulated or abused. It is a recorded journey of shattered dreams, authentic intimacy and thankfully, healing. And, perhaps, as you journey through these often-tortured recollections—you might discover a bit of yourself in her story.

It is a profound symbol of restoration that a pastor has been requested to write the foreword. Without giving the story away, I can tell you that your heart will be warmed, afflicted and enticed as you journey across the great Pacific between Asia and America in a catharsis of tragedy and torment. Some of the recollection of the journey sizzles and shakes. However, the intention is not for voyeurism, but for healing—perhaps yours.

Join in the journey.

Pastor David Spaite
Visalia, California
January, 2009

scan-dal (skan´ dl) n. 1. Any act or set of circumstances that brings about disgrace or offends the morality of the social community; a public disgrace. 2. The reaction caused by such an act or set of circumstances, outrage: shame. 3. Any talk damaging to the character; malicious gossip 4. Damage to behavior; a disgrace. 5. One whose conduct brings about disgrace or defamation. (*The American Heritage Dictionary of the English Language*, 1980)

Not just one, but a series of scandals hit my life, either of my own, or of someone else's making. Wherever you've been or whatever you've experienced, you might find a bit of yourself in my story.

I began writing—in a magnificent house in Pebble Beach, California—shortly after the worst scandal came to a crisis. Daniel, a warrior in my life, whom I knew from church, gave me his keys and said, "The house is yours. I don't need it—I'll be traveling all summer. Use it whenever you need to."

So I found myself at his massive kitchen table, watching the surf change from sky blue to aqua to navy and white. Daniel would call occasionally and ask, "What color is the ocean today?" Then he'd describe the eagles flying overhead from his mountain climb, the big catch of his deep-sea fishing off the coast of Canada, or the cuisine at a Beijing business banquet.

I typed. When the issues became too difficult to deal with, I turned off the rented computer, zipped on a sweatshirt, and walked in the salty air. It was seven miles to the town of Pacific Grove, where a small bookstore served coffee and homemade cakes. Another mile or so brought me to the Asilomar conference grounds. There I would settle into an oversized, knotty pine chair beside the stone fireplace, cozy on chilly summer evenings. After more writing or a game of ping pong, I was ready for a sound sleep, occasionally disturbed by the barking seals on Seal Rock.

When summer ended and it was time to go back to school, I packed up the computer, put the pages in a file folder and went about the painful task of getting on with life. I began practicing the art of "covering up," a skill I developed for emotional safety and survival.

As the years unfolded, the task of writing my story took much longer than I had anticipated. The condition of my heart delayed the journey. You see, I wanted to be loved by—and accepted by—everyone. I craved attention. Besides, anger and fear were getting in my way. Both emotions gnawed at the remnants of my wounded soul. The process of trying to describe my ordeal seemed too complex a task; so, in my attempt to hide the pain, the pages of my story kept going back into a cardboard box to rot and gather dust.

I expected the haunting memories to float away and to make sure they did, I employed the use of several destructive crutches. I tried sleeping, taking pills, disengaging, eating, shopping, and finally moving halfway across the world in a frantic effort to get away from the pain. No matter how far I ran, the memories followed. They were like a festering, seeping wound. Hiding and covering up could not begin to heal me.

Even after an exciting and audacious move to China, the painful shame lodged like a stone cold monument in my heart.

You I have called out from beyond the stars, from below the earth, from My own imagination, to find your life within My heart. From end to end, your life will I hold together. Nothing can happen to you outside My knowledge.

I was raised as a pastor's daughter in a vibrant denomination that taught the necessity of being saved and living a holy life. Our family life was built around the weekly line-up of church activities—Sunday services, prayer meetings, choir rehearsals, and Wednesday night potlucks with tuna noodle casseroles, jello with whipped topping, and macaroni salads. There were missionary society meetings, revival services, visitation programs and fund-raising campaigns. Our family sat around the TV on Saturday nights, folding Sunday bulletins. Many times my mother entertained newcomers on Sunday evening and a good portion of Saturday was consumed with cleaning the house for company. There were never-ending tasks of washing windows, dusting baseboards, arranging flowers and baking cakes. I learned to do things without complaining. I learned to talk with people—interesting people, dull people, those I admired and those I tolerated. Connecting with others was something we did.

In spite of the life skills and excellent biblical understanding that I absorbed from my family and church, some unhealthy messages were picked up along the way. Somehow, I was convinced that if I "fell" or "backslid," if I ever really messed up, I wouldn't be good enough for God. If scandal landed in my life, that would be it for me spiritually; my journey with God would be over. However unfounded, this fear would open the door to a fierce spiritual battle in my adult life.

Whatever misconceptions I took in, it was within the arms of that church fellowship that I first discovered the love of an intimate God. During those wonderful years, He wrote His words onto the walls of my heart. It was the most natural thing in the world that as my young heart focused on believing Him, I learned to discern God's voice in earnest and sincere prayer.

Much later, the murkiness that had moved between my soul and the peace of God began to slowly ease from the corners of my heart while I was living in the northern Chinese provincial city of Tianjin. The shadowy images that lurked in my dreams were exposed and the veil hiding the lies and pain began to lift. I learned that, incredibly, no matter what scandals haunt our lives, God desires to completely "out-scandal" every possible scenario in our pasts. He is by far the most scandalous Lover of all.

Your small, trusting heart already recognizes the perfect breath of all that is most Holy. I see you and walk with you.

*T*ianjin is an enormous city covered with a pinkish haze. On most Friday afternoons I'd come to a café for a cup of coffee, to unwind and write in my journal. It's an Italian restaurant, owned by a Canadian-Chinese businesswoman who knows nothing about food but everything about making money. The Chinese cooks meticulously follow Italian recipes and the expatriates flock from all over the city, bringing their families and friends, languages, newspapers and gossip. The Chinese waitresses enjoy their jobs. They sit at the tables to join in the conversations and practice their English.

One September night the air was intermittently hot and rainy, the sizzling brick-lined street sending up clouds of steam. Every balcony jutting awkwardly from its accompanying apartment was swollen with strings of leeks and corn, heaps of cabbage and odd bits of clothing dangling from sagging ropes. I could see grandmothers squatting over plastic bowls of swirling gray water, rinsing vegetables for dinner; mothers arriving home from work, carrying small plastic bags of vegetables or meat bought at the neighborhood market; fathers rolling their shirts halfway up their torsos, lighting cigarettes and bouncing their child on their knees; sleepy schoolchildren arriving home to sip sugary snack drinks through straws before practicing their piano lessons or beginning their extensive homework assignments. Grandfathers in loose, cotton pajamas shuffled along the street in flat, plastic shoes, under the shadow of weeping willows, nodding greetings or stopping to chat with friends. Some were already pulling up tiny wooden stools to play their nightly game of chess or mahjong on the wet street under yellow lights.

As I sipped my cup of rich black coffee, I began to write in my journal, finding words to describe the slow end of a typical work day in China and reminded of the first time I was in Guangzhou, then known as Canton.

Swish, swish. Bicycles, black and small and packed close. Swish. Dusk filters through the leaves, falling slowly into the old. The ancient. Do you like it? This is China.

My first glimpse of the Cantonese people was from a bus, with forty-nine other young American men and women on a world study tour. I was astonished to see hundreds of people bicycling home from their factory jobs—all dressed in white cotton shirts, baggy "Chairman Mao" trousers, and flat shoes.

That was 1980—there were no skyscrapers, towering hotels, sprawling office complexes, traffic lights, freeway overpasses, or myriads of tiny taxi cabs pushing through rush hour commutes. Instead, bicycles creaked through quiet streets unblemished by the blazing neon lights of today.

Back then, a hush blanketed the city in the evening. Giggling and curious teenagers pressed their noses against our skin, touched our hair as we walked by and asked us to take their pictures. We found everything strange and quaint—from the wisps of doled-out toilet paper to the strict schedule ("The bus will leave at 7:37 tomorrow"), to the "watcher" that was assigned to sit at a tiny desk on our hotel floor and . . . watch us. There were polite smiles and efforts made to impress the American students.

We had come to China via railway from Hong Kong. There we had crawled into a cave-like opening that led us to the Walled City. We saw dark corridors underground, with urine-stained walls, where refugees shared the windowless space with rats big as cats, and criminals watched for their chance. It was only eight years after Richard Nixon's historic trip to Peking, when he met with Chairman Mao, the Great Helmsman, chatting amiably over tea and posing for a photograph that shook the world.

In those days the train journey took us through green farm-land. Water buffalo grazed near streams. Bent-backed farmers stood knee-deep in rice fields. Cooking fires dotted the country-side and groups of peasants gathered near glowing lanterns while children played with sticks.

I could practically hear the whisper of China beckoning, "Come in, come in. We've been closed for a long, long time, but the gates are creaking open, the dust is falling away, and we want you to come in, come in."

As I rode in the brand-new train, seated beside my brilliant friend, Linda, on blue upholstered chairs with primly crocheted antimacassars, I penned in an Italian red-leather journal: "China is breathtakingly beautiful. People stream from small mountains carrying baskets of produce, as others rhythmically work the Asian earth, their conical hats shielding their eyes from the sun. Everything looks as if it's been here forever. I'm falling in love with this place."

We spent the next seven days visiting Canton, Peking, and Shanghai. We toured factories, climbed the Great Wall, bought delicate tea sets and exchanged addresses with people who had never before seen a Caucasian person. We studied history and attended opera and ballet. We held babies, snapped photos of panda bears, and ate some of the best food we had ever tasted.

I met a twenty-year-old man. He asked quietly and shyly, "What is your work? What is your unit?"

"My unit? We don't have units in America. I am a teacher. Next year will be my third year of teaching."

"You are very fortunate to select your work." His clear-black eyes, bright behind cheap plastic lenses, glinted.

"You didn't get to choose your area of study?"

"No, no." It was hard to hear him, as he lowered his chin and his words floated into the July dampness. "Impossible. I had to give up my studies and now I am a box packer."

I leaned forward. "A what? Did you say a box packer?"

"Yes, now I must pack boxes in a factory. All my life I will be a box packer." He spat his words with bitterness.

"What were you hoping to do, may I ask?"

"I wanted to teach English. You are very lucky."

It was the Fourth of July. Our tour guide stood on top of a chair and waved a tiny United States flag. Gradually we stopped talking and put down our morning tea to sing *The Star Spangled Banner*. We were young and homesick.

On Sunday, our last day in China, the tour guide took us to church, one of the three recognized churches in Shanghai. The service was held in an old church building. The tour guide, who seemed tense on this outing, eventually showed us to our seats in the balcony with a view of the enormous sanctuary below. Goose bumps rose on my skin as I looked down at the people crammed into the church pews. Perhaps a thousand people were packed into that cavernous space. There were only a few hymnals, and I didn't see any Bibles. Instead of a cross, an enormous portrait of Chairman Mao was displayed behind the pulpit.

Still, I felt the presence of the Lord. Tears flowed from my eyes as I watched these people, all dressed in drab colors, raising their hands in praise to God. We sang "Wonderful Words of Life," the Chinese louder than our English of course, but all lifted in praise together. People who had suffered atrocities that were unspeakable were weeping in relief, grief and hope.

After a lengthy service, the grim tour guide checked off our numbers as we formed a queue, lining up to board the bus. The rain was falling and people were squeezing close to us, pressed in by others behind them, reaching out to shake our hands.

And, unlike other places we had visited in China, these Christian believers were speaking to us. Weeping and smiling, they grasped our arms, their faces transformed with a joy that I knew came from a living and speaking God.

How good it is to sing praises to our God, how pleasant and fitting to praise him! ... He heals the brokenhearted and binds up their wounds (Ps. 147:1, 3).

*W*e brought into China small Bibles given to us by a Hong Kong church. We hid bundles of them in our luggage, between T-shirts and flip flops. We prayed open-eyed as we went through customs, chatting casually about the weather and the food.

There was a touch on my arm, a woman's eyes pleading, asking, "Do you have Bible?"

"I can't give you a Bible, but please write your address on this paper. Someone will bring you one later." Her hand shook as she drew the precise, vertical characters.

When our plane lifted off the runway in Shanghai and headed toward Vernasi and Calcutta, I heard that Voice I had learned early to know: "You'll be back, Susan."

One Divine Heart within one human heart—speaking, moving, living.

*S*eventeen years later I returned to the exotic land of China. Only this time I came with boxes of school supplies, three suitcases, and a laptop computer—coming to live and to teach. I had signed a two-year contract, thinking, "I can surely get out of this if I have to. I will stay for one year; I can handle that."

I arrived in a state of personal brokenness and depression. I had "messed up" so badly, I thought God had forgotten about me, that whatever purposes He had desired for my life had been crushed to nothing. I expected simply to try to sweep up the broken pieces and salvage what I could of my life. China was as good as any other place, I reasoned. Why not? I had lost everything already; what else was there to lose?

I never imagined I would be here for more than a decade. I never imagined that here, in this country broken by its tumultuous history, God would gently gather my broken parts and lovingly heal me—that He would choose this unlikely place to remind me of His first whispers of love.

And I never imagined He would use the people in China—those I met and worked with, those I came to help—to teach me about His love and faithfulness.

All that comes about in your life is and will always be within My imagination. Trust Me.

*I*n 1997, long before the shining new Beijing airport had been built, it seemed as if the international flights were about to land in the fields alongside the farmers. But to my relief, the 777 rolled to a stop on the runway. I scrambled for my carry-on bags along with the other two hundred and fifty passengers.

I stood in line at the luggage cart window and the clerk stared at me, holding out her hand and mumbling, "One yuan." I tried to explain that I didn't yet have any Chinese money. She gazed at me sullenly, opened her hand and repeated the request. "One yuan." The gentleman behind me stepped up, reached into his pocket for the yuan fee and, with his son, helped me load all my boxes and suitcases in a chaotic tumble on the cart. Sweaty and exhausted, I pushed the hair out of my eyes and tried to smooth wrinkles from my linen pantsuit, feeling not at all ready to meet my new school principal and his family waiting outside.

After introductions, Mr. Chung, the beaming driver employed by the school, sped along the freeway to the city of Tianjin near the Yellow Sea. In spite of the darkness and heat, the narrow streets teemed with life—women sitting on small benches, nursing babies, their pant legs rolled up to just under their knees; men slinging back beer and gathered together in small huddles; young lovers strolling hand-in-hand, oblivious to curious gazes of passengers so close they could reach out and touch them. Several students stood resting against lampposts, faces frowning in concentration over flimsy paperbacks.

Mr. Chung slammed on the brakes and joined the slow crawl of drivers trying to get a closer look at an accident. People descended from darkened steps to see what had happened. A man lay on his back in the road, his bicycle smashed by a motorcycle. He was motionless and his genitals were exposed through the opening in his thin trousers. I turned away. It was too close, too intimate. I was horrified and embarrassed.

People were everywhere on the streets. Many were sleeping on beds made of plywood, newspapers, and straw—or curled up in dusty wheelbarrows filled with rubbish. Others were stretched out in long, endless rows, skinny legs knotting together, arms wrapped around each other. Some slept propped up against bicycles; others curled inside doorways or cardboard boxes.

I muttered, "These people sleep everywhere, don't they?"

Craig, my new principal, nodded. "Yes, they sleep wherever they can get comfortable. It's too hot in their houses tonight. And personal space and privacy are not yet big concepts in China." His wife laughed in agreement. His two children rustled and shifted in their sleep beside me.

We drove past the school building and another mile or two into the dirt drive of the Peace Apartments, where I would live for the next three years. We fumbled with luggage and boxes as we negotiated steps in the darkness. I could feel the silent gazes of knots of people on the other side of the drive. It wouldn't be until the next day that I would see the row of temporary housing covered with sheets of tin for the migrant construction workers. The air was thicker than I had remembered from 1980—heavier, wetter, and even hotter. The smells were the same, with an added layer—that of new construction and development.

We stepped into the lobby, glass doors opened by smiling security officers in blue. Our shoes left footprints on the dusty floor. All about lay heaps of discarded rubbish—beams, metal poles, pipes, broken tiles, nails.

As we ascended to the twelfth floor, Craig explained that three other teachers and I would be sharing one floor in four separate flats. He apologized for the temporary mess. He unlocked the door of my apartment. Mr. Chung and others in blue delivered my boxes and luggage, and I was home, turning on lights and taking a tour of the two bedroom flat. The tiny kitchen had a sink that looked almost scary to use—stuck in a dark corner and filled with bits of construction debris. The bathroom had exposed piping and a covered balcony that, as Craig suggested, could be used for hanging laundry. The bedrooms were carpeted and the sitting room floor was a shiny hardwood. Before he left, Mr. Chung turned on the air conditioner. I gratefully said good-bye and shut the door.

I wanted to call my parents to let them know I had arrived. But how? I picked up the cranberry-red telephone sitting on a side table. How does one call America? I tried a few times, then went downstairs to ask the smiling men in blue uniforms. They were surprised to see me again so soon. After a long and painful attempt at conversation in Mandarin, I realized that one of them spoke English. He falteringly explained how to place a long-distance telephone call to America.

At the time my parents were divorced and living on opposite ends of California. I called Mom first, and at the sound of her voice I felt instantly comforted. Then I phoned Dad, and he was amazed that I could be calling from halfway around the world. He confided, "I cried when that big bird in the sky took off, Susan. I was afraid I'd never see you again."

"No, Dad, I'm okay! It's okay here . . . I think."

Finally I called my younger brother, Paul, and my eight-year-old niece answered. In her breathy, somewhat dramatic voice she asked, "Aunt Susan? You're in China? Right now, right this minute?"

"Yes, Lauren."

"Okay, Aunt Susan. Look out the window and tell me exactly what you see."

"I see . . . um, buildings. Only tall buildings in all directions, Lauren."

Her voice fell. "Oh."

I added, "But maybe later I'll be able to see more. It's about four o'clock in the morning right now."

"Okay, call back later and tell me what you see then. Bye, Aunt Susan." *Click.*

Every trip to China has left me feeling somewhat dizzy and disoriented upon arrival, but that first time was the most difficult. I felt like I was suspended in air, or maybe just turned upside down. The exhaustion was bone deep. I wriggled out of the damp linen suit, showered, then collapsed on the floral polyester sheet of the queen-sized bed.

I'm always with you. Your heart will leap at the sound of My whisper and this will be joy to you. Even in strange lands you will know Me.

*T*he next morning we new teachers had our first orientation session. One teacher asked, "Craig, what are some of the basic points to remember about behavior here?"

Craig laughed. "Well, you can spit anywhere you want."

We laughed and I thought, *What a fun group of people. I can barely believe I'm going to be paid to do something I love doing in such an adventurous location.*

We had lunch at a surprisingly Western restaurant that catered to expatriates. Halfway through the meal of burgers, soggy coleslaw and limp fries, I felt sick. Excusing myself, I found the bathroom, where I stood in shock for a moment, taking in the filth and stench. The toilet was a hole in the floor. It was not the first I'd seen, but at that moment, with the jet lag and upset stomach, it was too much. I stumbled back to the table. Caroline, Craig's Chinese-American wife, took one look at my green face, thrust taxi fare into my hands, and scribbled the name of my apartment building on a piece of paper for me.

The driver sped out among the clatter of bicyclists and fruit and vegetable stands. The taxi zoomed along, making a path through the people walking in the middle of the narrow streets. I was getting a closer look at this city. It seemed to be dotted with one partially finished skyscraper after another. Zealous investors had begun to build monstrous projects, only to abandon them as funds were depleted. Peasant workers were bussed back to the countryside. The discarded slabs of cement, twisted chunks of metal and other remnants of construction work had become part of the landscape in these peaceful neighborhoods. A part of me resonated with the incongruent scene. The people apparently ignored the half-finished, hulking monuments that loomed over their lives; fortunes lost and dreams gone awry seemed an accepted fact of life here.

Someday I will get married and have a beautiful wedding. Ivory lace, pink taffeta and flowers from a garden. I will have a baby and live in a white house in the country. We will be happy. Someday. Love and children in a small white house.

9 gave my heart to the Lord at the age of four in an old-fashioned revival meeting. My dad was the guest preacher at a church in the mountains of Southern California; and while I can't remember many details, I recall the moment when the peace of Jesus Christ filled my heart and made me cry with joy. I remember being tucked into bed later that evening between the pastor's daughters and feeling that, without a doubt, Jesus loved me. God loved me. Something happened within me that night.

I was taught about God in church by loving, dedicated people who gave up sitting in the "big" church, where it was air-conditioned and comfortable, to trudge over to the "children's church," where the Bible was patiently and lovingly unfolded to us. In those small, stuffy rooms, I began to absorb the glory of God.

The most memorable of my children's church teachers was my own mother. Her animated storytelling captured the attention of everyone in the room. I'd gaze at her proudly, beautiful in lemon, pink or black suits and high heels, her dark hair in a bouffant style. She wore very little make-up, as she had naturally rosy cheeks, full lips and straight white teeth. Her chiseled jaw line and high cheekbones reflected her part-Indian heritage; her soft brown eyes were expressive.

I sat in chiffon dresses with puffed sleeves and ribbon bows over white petticoats that were scratchy and stiff. My legs dangled from the small chairs, ending in white lace-edged anklets and patent leather Mary Jane shoes. My hair was done in pin curls and ribbons and I carried a dime for the offering in my tiny purse. My two brothers' hair was slicked back with Bryll Cream as once a week they exchanged their baseball uniforms for proper suits with clip-on ties.

Mother's voice changed to fit the characters and we were transported in time to the Nile River, hiding on the muddy banks alongside Moses's mother, watching the baby boy floating away in a basket of bulrushes. We were part of the taunting crowd hurling insults and making a fool of Noah as he faithfully built the ark. Or Mother became Hannah, desperately praying for a baby in the temple while Eli watched in secret. And she was the shepherd counting the ninety-nine sheep and not resting until the one lost lamb had been found.

The Bible stories were larger than life—almost unbelievable—yet we believed in the God of miracles who had turned a walking-stick into a snake and a desert bush into a flame of fire. I knew that the Red Sea parted and that Jonah spent three days inside the belly of a great fish. My curiosity, imagination and passion for God was ignited in those basement Sunday school rooms. During the week, when I went to school or played in the neighborhood with friends, a consciousness of God's presence remained with me. He wasn't just a story or a picture to color after the Sunday school lesson. He was a person. He liked me to talk with him and tell Him things that were on my six-year-old mind, then my ten-year-old heart, and, later, within my thirteen-year-old soul. He listened. He responded. He laughed and He cried. Not in words I heard with my ears, but in words I sensed in my heart. He was a peaceful presence who brought joy beyond explanation. He was a gentle inner warmth that accompanied me on the playground, to camp, and at home. I never felt alone.

Find your desires in Me.

On our second day in Tianjin, the newly-arrived teachers took a trip to the medical center for physical exams. After we passed through the door marked ALIENS, we had blood tests, blood pressure tests, ultrasounds, and X-rays, and our eyes, ears, noses and throats were checked. The tests were performed in small cubicles with flimsy partitions; we could see each other's heads and shoulders as we bobbed up and down, in and out of the examination spaces. The nurses kept us moving briskly. They shouted back and forth to each other, laughing as they recorded our weights.

My favorite part was the eye exam. I've had poor vision since third grade. Because I usually wear contacts, most people don't realize just how poor my vision is. But on this one day and each year thereafter in China, I look forward to this test, the day I magically get to have perfect vision. I take out my contacts, keeping my glasses close at hand, and the examiner begins the test. If I turn my hand in the wrong direction, indicating which way the E is facing, she firmly shakes her head until I finally "get it right." Then she smiles happily and with a flourish marks the box that says PERFECT VISION. And I get to enjoy a fleeting, satisfying moment of being an alien with perfect vision.

Two weeks after this first physical, I noticed a ping pong table in the room next to the lobby. I love to play ping pong, so I approached the blue-clad security guard and asked, "May I please play?" I pointed to the little room across from his desk.

His face turned bright red as he dialed the telephone. Another security officer trotted out from a back room with two paddles and a ball. I was pleased, but noticed the first security guard writing detailed notes in a large, black notebook. (Later I learned that everything about us was recorded in that book, from what we bought at the store to the names and addresses of our dinner guests.) After some hesitation, they finally relinquished the paddles and ball to me. Then I realized I had no partner.

I invited both guards to play with me, first one then the other, but they shook their heads, saying, "No, no, no."

I looked around again. There was no one else in the lobby. However, about thirty peasants crowded outside the windows staring at me, their weathered faces pressed up to the grimy windows. I walked outside into the heat and, with hand gestures, invited the nearest young man to play ping pong with me. Somewhat bewildered, but visibly delighted, he accepted the paddle and followed me into the gloomy entryway. His friends outside were clapping and cheering, slapping one another on the back and shouting, "Look, look! He's going to play ping pong with a Big Nose Ghostie!"

The tall, handsome security guards stood frozen behind the desk, their smiles gone. They watched silently as the peasant worker and I began to play; then one of them picked up the telephone again.

In less than two minutes, a third security officer appeared, the one who spoke English, sweat pouring from his worried face. "Excuse me, Madam, what are you doing?"

I smiled blissfully as I slammed the ball across the table. "Playing ping pong!"

"Uh, excuse me, pardon me, Madam, but you cannot play ping pong with this man."

I wiped the dripping sweat from my face, preparing to serve the ball. "Why not?"

The peasant man let the ball go by; the joy of the game had disappeared from his face. He noiselessly and carefully set the paddle down on top of the ball as the security guard explained. "This man is a peasant from the countryside. He is a worker."

I laughed nervously. "Well, I'm a worker, too. I go to work every day, as you've noticed, I'm sure."

He said, "Yes, Madam, we know you are a teacher. But this man cannot come into this building.

"He comes into this building to paint the apartments. Why can't he play ping pong if I invite him?"

The brown peasant man, bones visible through his thin clothes, quietly melted away. So did the crowd of curious onlookers peering in through the smudged windows.

The officer continued, "I'm very sorry, Madam." He fiddled nervously and apologetically at his tie. "Uh, why don't you go upstairs now and have a rest?"

"Oh, I don't want a rest. Not yet. I just began playing!"

Another man marched into the dismally-lit, airless room, wearing a tailored suit. He walked up to the security officer and whispered in his red ears. Then, both motioned to the first guard and they began a loud conversation in Mandarin which lasted at least ten minutes.

At last, the English-speaking guard turned to me triumphantly. "Good news! We have found someone to play ping pong with you." The two men looked enormously pleased.

A woman appeared next, sophisticated and lovely in a white linen pantsuit; she held a small white dog. She introduced herself and said smoothly, "Good afternoon, Miss Susan. Welcome you to Peace Apartments."

I was uneasy with the fact that she knew my name. Who was she? Still sweating profusely and feeling rather embarrassed, I said lamely, "Er, um, hello. I am sorry to have caused such a disturbance." I motioned vaguely to the ping pong table. "I thought I could just play a little ping pong."

She was scrutinizing me from head to toe, patting her dog who was snarling at me. My eagerness to play ping pong was beginning to wane.

"Yes, I see. Well, we have located someone to play ping pong with you, Miss Susan. Please wait here one moment."

She turned to the security guards and spoke sharply in Mandarin over the growls of the fluffy white dog. Soon another man, someone I had not seen before, shuffled into the room. He had clearly just been awakened from a nap. He looked at me quizzically—the sweating Big Nose Ghostie—and didn't seem very impressed. He mumbled something that didn't sound nice at all to the three security guards now flanking one side of the room, watching. One of them—the one who spoke such good English—narrowed his eyes and waved impatiently. "Play, play."

The sleepy man was an outstanding player and I couldn't manage to return anything he smashed over the net. I began to seriously reconsider the security guard's earlier suggestion of going upstairs for a rest.

From then on, during the three years I lived in the Peace Apartments, a security guard was allowed to play with me.

My child, never forget that you are Mine and I am yours. My voice will speak amongst many others. You must be still and listen.

When I was a child, my mother and I often played pretend games together. My favorite was "The Back Door." I would knock loudly on the kitchen door, pretending to be a nosy neighbor or a colorful character from church. My mother would dutifully act her "part" while she prepared dinner—baked chicken and green beans or roast beef and mashed potatoes. Our "conversations" would have us laughing until tears rolled down our faces. And as a minister's daughter, I had heaps of material from which to draw, as there was a continual procession of interesting, even wacky, people who made their way into the life of our family.

Our home was a center for people as long as I can remember. Before I turned six years old, I would listen for the phone to ring every Monday morning at six o'clock on the dot. Like clockwork, one of the older saints in the congregation called to "check up" on her feisty young pastor. My father would run down the hallway from the back bedroom, clearing his throat to avoid sounding as if he had just been awakened from a sound sleep. The day before had been a marathon for him with morning worship, Sunday school, choir practice and evening evangelistic services.

Still in bed, I listened to his side of the conversation. "Oh, of course not, Sister Coons. You didn't wake me. I've been up for hours, in prayer and study. . . . Yes, Sister Coons, the services did go well yesterday. . . . Next Sunday? Well now, I haven't quite decided on the text, but will be happy to call you as soon as I do. . . . Yes, of course, I'd be delighted to send you a sermon outline . . . You have a wonderful day. Good-bye and God bless you."

Click. Then my father would stumble back down the hall and collapse into bed.

A lot of wonderful folks passed through our back door. Our mother was teaching school and our father was very busy with his church; many people helped raise us three children, who were close in age (and mischievousness). They picked us up from school, babysat us, and brought us platters of freshly-baked chocolate chip cookies. I remember Mrs. Movius, who made play dough and let us mix the colors.

In later years, the younger couples and teenagers were the ones who drifted in and out of our home—joining our family for meals at a moment's notice and becoming part of our family life.

In those days, the stereo rocked and the house was full of friends spending the night, joining in late night swim parties in the summer and going up to the mountains with us for ski trips in the winter. Life was packed with a chaotic, busy schedule of basketball games, horseback riding, church activities, and music.

This "open door policy" was a pattern that continued far into my adulthood; it was difficult for me to establish any sense of boundaries for myself. Even in adulthood the back door of my life was open and, sometimes, I should have locked it.

For a period of several months I allowed a very ill person to slip into my life. I was working at my church's Christian school. Roy simply showed up one evening, claiming that one of the church secretaries told him that I always worked late.

The distaste I felt whenever Roy shuffled into my room brought a pang of guilt. After all, he attended my church.

Roy would slink into a student chair and hunch over the desk, staring at me through thick lenses. He said he wanted to help grade papers and that by allowing him to do so, I'd be giving him a reason to live, so he wouldn't "cut himself."

He discovered one of my passions—books. He knew where to find good used children's books for my classroom library and would scurry around the Bay Area on buses looking for new additions to my collection. He paid attention to my curriculum and found books on specific teaching subjects.

But I remained uncomfortable. There was a stale, yeasty-sour odor about him. He came into my classroom more and more often, and stayed late into the night. He left daily messages on my home phone. He came in and out of my life without invitation, but I hadn't the skills to say, "No, thank you."

His interest in me slowly turned from pleasant discussions about books, school and theology to the point where he was literally stalking me. His "godliness" would all too quickly become a fit, a tirade of sorts, if I was too busy to spend time with him. Since he was considered legally blind and didn't have a driver's license, he frequently called for rides, demanding to be picked up at all hours of the night. He'd be waiting, shivering at a bus stop, and I'd drive him to his parents' house where he still lived.

Then came the day when he announced that God had recently informed him of our upcoming marriage. I was first shocked, then amused, and finally scared. As the months passed and the realization of my lack of interest and cooperation began to sink in, his behavior became violent. One night he threw rocks at my car after I dropped him off at his parents' house.

I finally began to wrestle free of Roy and his toxic clutch on my time and my life. I began ignoring the long, emotional phone messages. I changed my phone number and locked my classroom door at night. Slowly, my life became more spacious, peaceful and calm. I felt less cluttered, more clear. I actually enjoyed doing all those small tasks he had begged to do.

And later in China I could look back and see that it was as if I were still playing the Back Door game. From time to time people had stood there as the screen door flapped in the breeze, taking their chance to slip inside, to try to inhabit the place where I held my thoughts and dreams. And they'd ride along, enjoying the view out my window. How much easier it was for them to hitch a ride—someone else was doing all the work, all the planning. I had provided emotional transport to those I was not called or equipped to carry. On those journeys that took me away from my own path, I had let too much slip through the cracks. I had left the back door to my soul wide open, and it had invited intruders to come inside. I had neglected to erect boundaries, to guard my heart with care and wisdom; and like a poorly-adjusted underslip, it showed.

Let things of this world fall away, My child. You have an eternity with Me and your happiness can only come from Me, the Giver of all good things.

*O*ne sweltering August evening I was lost in Tianjin. The street signs all looked the same to me on streets that all looked the same. I found myself outside an appliance repair shop squeezed between crumbling brick hutongs.

The shop owner—a disabled man who pulled himself along without the assistance of a wheelchair—beckoned me to sit on one of the low stools scattered about the sidewalk. He then graciously offered me a Coke from a dusty roadside stand. I plopped down among the rusting washing machines, fans, tape players and rice cookers. I soon discovered that this was a hub of social interaction. People of every social status and position dropped by this little shop to pull up impossibly tiny wooden benches and sit with cups of tea. The men smoked one cigarette after another, sitting with their shirts rolled up high on their smooth, beige chests in an effort to cope with the late summer heat. A woman in her thirties came running to perform an impromptu and charming sidewalk concert of The Carpenters' hits: "Rainy Days and Mondays" and "I Won't Last a Day Without You." She had memorized the words to all the verses. I began harmonizing with her and she beamed with pleasure.

Around us, people were gathering to watch and listen— grandmothers, teenagers, middle-aged couples and babies. Then a voice rang out from the crowd on the street.

"Where are you from?"

The English words were poetry to my ears, instantly discernible through the cacophony of Chinese.

"I'm from America," I called out in reply, searching everywhere through the throng of curious people to find the speaker of the strident English words.

As they realized the Big Nosed Foreigner was talking with someone on the street beside them, the crowd craned their necks and all conversation gradually ceased.

A man stepped out from the twist of people and smiled. "Hello, my name is Ouyang and I have been to America."

The people stared at him open-mouthed, then turned back toward me to see if I could understand his words. I was astonished to meet an English-speaking person who'd been to America, right here on this little corner.

"Really? Where did you visit while you were there?"

The crowd let out a collective murmur. The Big Nosed Foreigner and one of their own were chatting! This was something that didn't happen every day in their crumbling little neighborhood.

"I went to Las Vegas and San Jose," he explained proudly.

"Las Vegas and San Jose? Where else did you go?"

His voice fell a bit. "That's all."

I sat up straighter. "That's it? You only went to those two cities?"

Ouyang cocked his head in a gesture I would learn to know well. "Yes. That's all. I was with my cousin and he had the car."

"Oh. Well, at least you were able to see two very interesting and yet . . . um, er . . . different places. Did your cousin take you to see the Winchester Mystery House?"

He looked annoyed. "No, he didn't. *Hiyaa*! It doesn't matter."

"I'm sorry you weren't able to visit Yosemite or see the redwoods. You should have gone to San Francisco for a day."

He winced and shrugged his shoulders. "It was a so-so trip. Only so-so."

I smiled. "I can imagine. What did you do in San Jose?"

"I had to sit in my cousin's apartment all day long. It was very hot and boring. There was nothing to do but watch the television. Such idiots in America on television!"

I laughed. "Yes, there are some very silly TV shows, aren't there? It's really a pity you didn't get to see more places. When you drove from Las Vegas to San Jose did you see anything?"

He shook his head. "Nothing but desert. And we lost all our money in Las Vegas. There was nothing left. So we drove to San Jose and stayed at home."

"Did you take the coastal route up through California so you could see the ocean?"

"No, we drove up through the middle of the state. It was very hot."

"And you were so close to San Francisco, the most beautiful city in the world."

The appliance repair shopkeeper offered Ouyang some tea and a bench. He joined us and we talked. The night grew longer and the air cooled slightly. As the now-enormous group of people listened to our every word and commented loudly at each turn in the conversation, Ouyang and I happily figured out that we were neighbors.

He offered me a ride home on the back of his bicycle. I gladly accepted. He flew through the narrow streets where young couples were stealing private moments together and others were out taking late-night strolls in their pajamas. Old men were gambling and smoking by lantern light. The breezes whipped my long hair around and dried the day's sweat from my body. I felt far from all my problems. I had nothing of the comparatively-extravagant life I once lived. Yet it was peaceful to be riding along on the back of a bicycle, gliding through these ancient streets.

When we pulled into the drive of the Peace Apartments, as Ouyang skillfully avoided the potholes, we were aware of the curious gaze of hundreds of peasant construction workers. To see me being delivered home on the back of a bicycle must have been unexpected.

*Someday you will pass through the troubled waters, looking to your
right and to your left for help. I will be there, eternally loving you.
You may not hear My voice then.
"I will always hear Your voice, Father."
Not then, you will not, for you may not be listening. Listen for Me.
I am speaking in your heart, on the wind, in every simple thing.*

My dad's personality defies description. He is the ultimate
extrovert—outgoing, loud, filled with laughter. He makes friends
wherever he goes. He was born the youngest of four sons in a
family of men who were tall, strong and handsome in that "All-
American" way. When my best friend's husband met my dad, he
commented, "Your father is a total jock." He was. He still is.

My dad was fourteen years of age when his father dropped
dead of a sudden heart attack. As his world collapsed in a matter
of moments, he watched his mother crying over the body, "What
will we do? What will we do?"

It was a loss from which my father never recovered; one that
was never adequately addressed. My grandmother sold the farm
and red-brick farmhouse, and bought a large, gracious home in
downtown Fresno, where the air is rich with the aroma of orange
blossoms and peaches, mixed with the scent of cattle and burning
field fires in the summer. Dad was blessed to be surrounded by
older males who were strong role models. His brother Harold
picked him up from school each day and took him to his
piano lessons. Another brother was a dynamic preacher in a
nearby town. At seventeen my father was saved in a campmeeting
service at Beulah Park—a church campground in the Santa Cruz
mountains that later became the setting for some of my own
happy childhood memories.

My dad headed off to Pasadena College, a small private

Christian college, on fire for the Lord and determined to become a minister of the Gospel. He was talented and soon in demand as a preacher and musician. My mother arrived in Pasadena from Colorado (where her father was pastoring) and joined him on evangelistic tours around California. They were soon married. After graduating from seminary in Kansas City, my parents returned to California to pastor congregations in Los Angeles and San Jose before moving to the east Bay Area.

Dad spent a lot of time playing sports with my brothers and me outside our home in the afternoons. He played as hard as we played. We kids spent most of our time, though, either sitting in church or preparing for church. All three of us loved it. Our parents made church fun for everyone. They played music that rocked. The services were spiced with dramatic enactments of biblical principles. Peoples' lives were being changed. During the summers, my parents directed a high school church camp at Beulah Park, and those were the best days of our lives. We children had the run of the campground. As small children, we'd play from breakfast until late at night when the last embers of the campfire died. Every day we played baseball and basketball, and hiked to the creek; and often someone drove us to the beach, where there was an old-fashioned boardwalk and a wooden roller coaster.

One of my earliest recollections is of going with my dad to minister to a frail woman in her nineties, Mother Martin. For five years he drove to her home on his way to church and literally picked her up, carrying her to the car and taking her to church with us. I was somewhat intimidated by her demeanor—she wore a severe black skirt and blouse, hat and lace-up boots, like a character out of the Victorian Age. But she loved the Lord, and my dad cheerfully accomodated her desire to be in church.

On Christ the Solid Rock I stand, all other ground is sinking sand.

*O*uyang became one of my Chinese language teachers. Our friendship, begun out of the happy discovery that we were neighbors in this huge metropolis, deepened with time. I thought of him as a brother; and he considered me to be his elder sister. It was a comfortable friendship based on truth and honesty.

One day there was a knock at the door and Ouyang marched in, all business, depositing a plastic bag onto the sofa. "The cold weather comes soon and my mother is worried you do not have proper clothes. She buys you some."

"Thank you! But she shouldn't have done that. It's far too expensive, Ouyang."

"Susan, I give her money. It's my money, don't forget. I am a businessman in China and I am rich."

"Okay, well, thank you. Both of you have become like family to me. But I should buy my own clothes, you know."

He looked perplexed. "Before you moved to the other side of the world, didn't you think that you should perhaps study the climate of your new environment? This is not San Francisco, you know. The weather changes dramatically in Tianjin. You cannot wear beach shoes now."

I looked down at my flip-flops and polished pink toenails. "I should have checked it out more thoroughly, yes."

He motioned toward the closet off the kitchen. "You come unprepared for the snow and yet you bring ridiculous things— toilet paper! Didn't you think that in a country of over a billion bottoms there might be toilet paper?"

I bit my lip. "Well, I brought it because in 1980 there wasn't much toilet paper here. I didn't want to be caught unprepared."

"China has changed, Susan. We've had private telephones for three years now, " he added proudly.

I was boiling water for tea. I had learned that drinking tea in China was not just a matter of meeting one's physical need for liquid; it was a way of calming and centering oneself.

"The first water you boil must be thrown out. It is not good enough. The second boil is okay," Ouyang instructed.

"Why?"

"Because this is China! China is an ancient land and there are many customs carried on for thousands of years." He paused momentarily, casting down his black eyes. "And I must tell you there are many customs which have been carelessly discarded, as well. This is to our shame."

"I understand." I poured the tea. "Will you tell me about the winter? I'm nervous about the cold. I'm not used to it."

He thought a moment. "The cold is fine. You will be warm enough here in your nice home. It's the hot weather the Chinese fear. They die in the summer heat. In winter, just add more layers, add more clothes and you can stay warm."

I brought my Chinese language books to the table. Ouyang's eyes brightened. "Okay, time to study. Let's begin."

Throughout the next two hours as we practiced Mandarin tones and phrases, the leaves on the trees outside continued to fall. Autumn was turning into winter and I was in Asia. I was usually too busy during the school week to think about it much, but on the weekends while sitting at home or in Ouyang's mother's home the realization would hit me and I would suddenly see myself as a tiny speck on a big, turning globe. The world was spinning slowly on its course, and I was on a different point than before, far away from everything I once knew. And, at the same time, nothing was far away.

Listen for My voice.

*O*ur family moved to Livermore when I was twelve years old. I loved the Livermore Valley—the rolling hills that were velvety green during winter and spring, and, as John Steinbeck phrased it, like the tawny backs of golden mountain lions in summer.

The church was thriving and filled with teenagers that my two brothers and I knew from school. The school system was good and the district of churches to which we belonged provided an endless stream of activities—basketball tournaments for my brothers, Bible quiz competitions, choir tours and mission trips. Our house was a hub of life and activity and we were a happy family—with so much health and vigor on every level.

Dad was always such a loving man. He had a fierce love for his family and church people. That never changed. But gradually he did come to love something else too much.

He discovered how to make money—a lot of it. He began investing in real estate. He began to buy homes, fix them up and sell them at a time when the market was starting to boom. Our lifestyle did not show it, nothing changed in our daily lives; but our dad was rapidly becoming a very wealthy man.

His neighborhood friends and real estate buddies began calling him "the Captain." He was falling in love with money. I can still see the gleam in his hazel eyes when speaking about the stuff—the sideways shift of his gaze, the euphoric smile, even the way he rolled the word "money" in his mouth. It was a way he had of savoring the word, letting it linger much the way wine connoisseurs allow a fine wine to fill the mouth and senses.

Somehow, the passion of my dad's life shifted. My dad, the pastor, was all about people—leading, loving, and helping people. But my dad, "the Captain," was quickly becoming all about money. It was a divided existence and it was leading to disaster.

He had a church phone line installed in our house so that he wouldn't have to actually go to his office. Not that he was lazy—quite the opposite. He was busy searching for new property to acquire and, with his outgoing nature, was able to find all sorts of deals. He befriended and convinced an old man who owned an apartment building in town to sell the building at a fraction of its worth. From that apartment building, he went on to buy more homes and commercial buildings.

I went away to college in San Diego and was happy in

the routine of dorm life. But on visits back to Livermore, it was hard to ignore the changes taking place in my dad. During these years he began taking us to the Sierras. Money, we were surprised to learn, was of no concern. My parents took us to Tahoe for ski vacations as often as possible. After an exhilarating day on the slopes, we'd dress up and hit the casinos, often taking in a dinner show featuring stars like Diana Ross and Johnny Cash. Dad would approach the reservations desk and study the list of names, choosing one that was similar to ours. When the hostess turned to ask his name, he'd smoothly tell her that we were the Jensen or Johnson party—some name he had spotted on her list. We'd be escorted into the theater and my dad would give a tip to make sure we were sitting in the very front.

There were also shows with partial nudity. My college-age brothers were taken to topless shows. The first time this happened I was so upset about it, I spoke up, saying, "Dad, all our life you've told us we shouldn't do any of these things. The drinking, the partying, seeing things like this. Why have you changed so much?" But confronting my parents only seemed to make things worse. Then I wondered if there was something wrong with me. Perhaps I lacked the sophistication to handle the world's pleasures; maybe I was too immature. Whatever it was, I felt that I must be the one with the problem. Those evenings left me irritable, angry and confused.

As we trailed after Dad in the smoky air of the casinos, I wondered if he realized what kind of effect this was having upon my brothers. Little by little they were being introduced to a world they had been taught from childhood was wrong.

I remembered driving through Nevada on a family trip years before and Dad stopping to show us the casinos. We stood outside the window and stared at the people playing the slot machines, and Dad told us, "Kids, this is the devil's playground. These people are addicted to gambling. They spend their entire pensions and social security checks to take a bus and come up here, where they lose everything they have. Do you see the hopelessness on their faces?"

We nodded, sobered by the sadness being pointed out by our minister-father. He taught us that drinking alcohol was evil and would give Satan a foothold on our lives if we were to ever indulge in it. I remember feeling very secure in the structured framework in which I was raised. There were rules, yes, but I accepted that they were put in place for our spiritual good.

Only a decade later, everything in our lives had made a 180-degree turn. The reversal caused turmoil and heartache. After the Sunday evening service, Dad stood at the sanctuary door, shaking hands with the parishioners before catching the last flight to Reno where he studied statistics and made weekly bets. He had a group of friends—a realtor, a teacher and an insurance broker—that he met with each Monday. They became good friends of our family. But the messages that Dad was sending were conflicting with everything we had been taught. Suddenly it was perfectly fine to walk over the boundaries that had always been in place. It was a paradox: some of these new friends of my father's were kind and caring folks, pillars in the community, who set up fundraising events for needy people. But these best friends of my preacher-dad were also rowdy and wild. Something was wrong with our picture-perfect family.

Things were happening that made me worry and sometimes made me mad! We took a family vacation to Hawaii. During a dinner show featuring Don Ho, someone on Mr. Ho's staff came to our table with a message: "Don Ho wants to meet your daughter." I was terrified, but my parents were thrilled. I followed the messenger backstage and was shown to his dressing room. He greeted me, stood up and took my hand and pulled me close. He said, "Come here, Angel." And then, audaciously and inconceivably, Mr. Ho began to kiss me, thrusting his tongue into my mouth. I pulled away, disgusted, and left immediately. One of his assistants ushered me back to my table. I was furious at the situation and at my parents, thinking, "Someday I will have a daughter. And she will never have to do anything like that."

Other strange things happened. After college graduation, I took a teaching job back in my hometown. I was living in an apartment at one of my dad's apartment buildings. One day when I returned home from school, I was surprised to find my apartment empty. Everything had been moved out. I called my dad and he explained, "I needed that apartment, Susan, for a family in the church. You can move back to our house."

Secretly worried, I finished out the year living with my parents. Dad began gambling with the next-door neighbors and other friends. He started going to the horse races at the state and county fairs. He contined to play craps in the casinos of Lake Tahoe and Reno, only now it was more than just occasional ski vacations—he was going up at least once a week.

Out of love and loyalty, Mom accompanied Dad on his gambling jaunts to Reno and Tahoe, but after a few years, her interest waned. She began staying home. Dad continued his weekly trips to Reno, sometimes catching the red-eye flight after preaching on Sunday evening, to meet his gambling buddies, place his football bets, then return home by Wednesday evening.

My heart saddened each time I had to answer the church phone and say, "I'm sorry, my father is out of town right now. May I take a message?"

I tried confronting him. "Dad, I am worried about how your behavior is going to affect Steve and Paul (my brothers). Have you thought about that at all?"

He scoffed, "They're grown now. What I do is none of their business and won't have any negative effect upon their lives."

"Dad, they're still in college! Paul says he has sensed a call to the pastoral ministry. Give him a chance to thrive in school without crushing his spirit by this crazy behavior."

My dad was convinced that my brothers didn't need him to be a role model any longer. And there was nothing I could say or do to change his thinking.

I didn't realize it but I was slowly becoming depressed. I was taking on the burden of worrying for my dad. I had to pretend that everything was perfect and normal while at church, but I also had to accommodate the changes in our family's lifestyle. I was moving back and forth between two different worlds and it caused my soul to feel divided.

I found a therapist in the phone book and made an appointment. In the therapy session I tried to convey the panic I was feeling at the night-and-day differences to which my parents had expected me to adapt. His advice after listening for fifty minutes was: "You're twenty-three years old. That's old enough to find your own lifestyle. Your parents' choices shouldn't be affecting you so much." I paid the bill and drove home, more lonely and confused than ever.

I was swimming laps in the backyard pool one night, and I looked up to see Dad standing beside the pool, visibly shaking. He had just returned home from a church board meeting where he resigned from our church. I had mixed feelings, of course, but was too young and too loyal to look at the situation objectively. My mother seemed teary and exhausted for several days.

Without the church to think about, Dad's gambling endeavors took on noticeable intensity. He spent every day, all day at the horse races with our next-door neighbor, a foul-mouthed racing addict with a beer belly that jiggled with each step.

As he pulled up to the house each evening, Dad headed not to our home, but to the neighbor's, where he drank beer and told an endless string of mediocre jokes, apparently quite funny to his new, distorted congregation, his appreciative crowd of listeners.

I couldn't help but notice that even the way my dad pronounced his words was changing: his words were slurred, slowly beginning to sound like the speech of his new friends, of a different "class" altogether. There were times I couldn't help but point it out to him. But he just scoffed at my concern.

I was worried. I saw my mom become immersed in a solitary world that none of us understood and from which she would not fully emerge for almost twenty-five years.

One night the neighbor's oldest son, an unemployed high school drop-out, shot himself in the head, the brain matter splattering all over the master bedroom. My dad owned the house and thoughtlessly sent my two brothers over to clean up the mess.

One of my cousins called one day, inviting me to attend a singles' conference on the Queen Mary in Long Beach. The church in which I had grown up was hosting the event, and he wanted me to sing at it. I wanted to go, but I was afraid that, since people in that denomination knew about my family situation, I would be unwelcome. I had managed to save enough money for a trip around the world that summer—the trip that would take me to China for the first time. I told my cousin I'd be unable to make the conference. My world had been shaken by the battle of good versus evil that was destroying my family. I would seek solace alone with God and try to make sense of it.

My life—those things that meant the most to my heart, those things that measured my days—had become very different from the life my parents were choosing. When I walked into their home after my trip and took in the discarded bottle or two and the dazed look in their eyes as they halfheartedly watched TV sitcoms, I felt I was sinking into something I had to avoid. I could sense the tentacles of addiction grabbing at my parents. And I felt that, if it destroyed them, I would be the one responsible, as if the burden was resting on my shoulders.

The pressure was building for me. I moved to an apartment in Danville—desperately needing some distance from the situation—and as I did, I was surprised by the joy I experienced in setting up house, cooking and preparing meals for my friends. I nestled into each place I lived. I was working at a private elementary school that offered a solid, conservative education, and I was playing the piano in a dinner house at night.

I am Your Heavenly Father. I know all about you, from the

number of hairs on your head to the little-girl dreams living inside your heart, My child. You are always being loved and protected.

*E*ventually I caught on: Nobody but large hotel kitchen staff uses hot water to wash dishes in Tianjin.

After serving dinner to several of my Chinese friends, I retired to the kitchen to start washing dishes. As I began pulling on pink rubber gloves, Ouyang cried out, "No, let me wash them! I can wash with no gloves!"

I looked at him. "Why wouldn't you wear gloves?"

"The cold water doesn't bother my hands," he explained.

As I boiled water to fill the bowl in the sink, I gently explained that I needed the gloves not because the water was too cold, but because I intended to use very hot water.

His eyes widened with interest. "My father, a doctor, always tried to get my mother to wash dishes in hot water, too. He said it was healthier that way, but she refused. She thought it was another strange Canadian habit he picked up while lecturing in Toronto."

"But your mother's a doctor! Surely she knows that hot water is better than cold."

Ouyang looked down sadly at the floor. "Susan, water has been a problem here in China. We are not like Americans. We do not have a hot shower any time we wish, or at least we didn't. My family never had water in the house at all until just before my father died. Believe me, water is a problem."

"I see. I'm so sorry, I should have thought."

Then there is the curious habit of putting dishes away while still soaking wet after a quick rinse in cold or tepid water. When one reaches for a dish, there is most always a gray puddle at the bottom of each bowl or glass. The kitchen cupboards are lined with newspaper (a good idea, I discovered) and water literally dribbles from the dishes, dripping over everything—all the time one hears, *drip, drip, drip.* When I eat in a restaurant, I've noticed it is customary to shake the water at the bottom of the glass, swishing and sloshing it about until it's flung—at last—onto the floor. Food is even served on dishes with water at the bottom with no thought to the bacteria and germs.

Once I asked one of my Chinese friends why people don't dry dishes in China. She thought a moment, then cheerfully answered, "Because there are no dish towels."

Everything that happens can be used for My glory, for My purpose.

*D*r. John Travis was the pastor of my uncle and aunt's Presbyterian church in the heart of California's fertile San Joaquin Valley. He, his stunning wife and their two beautiful children had been on the fringes of my family life for the five years that they lived there, just two blocks from my uncle and aunt's home.

I first met Dr. Travis at a backyard barbeque. I barely remember the introduction, for I had brought Kyle, my fiancé. I was in love and barely aware of anything or anyone else. Mrs. Travis had graciously opened her home to my entire family and a host of assorted friends and distant relatives. I remember the men sat in the family room discussing theology, sports, and politics while the women prepared dinner.

The next time I met Dr. Travis was a year later, after the morning worship service at my uncle and aunt's church. My entire family on my father's side had once again gathered for a weekend together and as each of us was introduced again to Dr. Travis, he shook our hands with warmth and had a personal, winsome word for each of us. Dressed in his black ministerial robe in the sweltering August heat, he demonstrated remarkable focus and social skills, I thought. He kissed my cheek and said, "I hope we can get to know one another someday, Susan."

I remember thinking how suntanned his smooth face was, and feeling embarrassed and flattered by the intensity of his eyes.

His affectionate manner was unusual and indiscriminate. However, everyone around me seemed quite comfortable with it. My Uncle Jack proudly told us, "Now that boy is a preacher!"

One of my mischievous brothers hooted with laughter. "Did you see how he came on to Mom? Mom, you're such a hot babe."

We all laughed. Uncle Jack said, "He kisses everyone—even dogs and cats. Don't worry about that boy." He loved John.

There was something about Dr. Travis, some mixture of charisma and tenderness that drew people in. Impressive, emotional, barely thirty years old, he had a slight shyness and vulnerability about him that won people's loyalty. He exuded boyish charm. He had a practice of "telling on himself" that disarmed even the most skeptical of listeners. Stories about running out of gas time and time again, the health problems that plagued him, the heartbreak of losing his beloved brother to cancer, his nervousness in the pulpit—these all cemented the impression of his being the absent-minded professor, quite above the mundane concerns of ordinary people. There were many, including my uncle and aunt, who wanted to take care of him, reassure and comfort him. His loyal congregation made excuses for his bouts of forgetfulness and disorganization. They ignored the extremes in his behavior, especially the occasional aloofness and distant sadness that some couldn't help but notice. Most people assumed he was just over-scheduled. After all, he was the shepherd of a large congregation. He was also writing the first of many books and was in demand as an engaging speaker at conferences and churches across the country. And five years later he became our pastor in Danville.

Someday I'll have a husband, a house and a baby. Someday.

I once had the life of which young people in China dream. The peaceful town of Danville had slowly grown up in a narrow valley near San Francisco, under the watchful presence of Mount Diablo, a sentinel that compels with a silent beauty, whether draped with pewter clouds on wet days or painted ice blue against lavender skies. It stands over the steady stream of commuter traffic and boasts many namesakes, including a magazine, a school district and even appetizers or desserts served at buffets.

Danville was and is the best of two worlds. A thirty-minute drive from the sophistication of San Francisco, it spreads its rural charm where children can breathe fresh, country air, climb trees and play in their own backyards.

The lawns are small parks. The streets are quiet and immaculate. The Iron Horse Trail weaves in and out of mottled sunlight, bathed in the aroma of eucalyptus. There are trendy boutiques, sidewalk cafés and tiny gift shops tucked between fine restaurants and quaint shopping malls. If one can afford it, it's a perfect community to call home.

For the second half of our six-year marriage, I lived here with my architect husband Kyle, in an old Colonial-style white house just two minutes from the heart of the downtown area—so close we could stroll to our favorite restaurant on special occasions. Friends parked on our street for the annual tree-lighting ceremony held the day after Thanksgiving, when the entire town was given over to the spirit of Christmas. A few rounds of traditional carols sung by the local high school chorus serenaded the arrival of Father Christmas; and as he waved merrily from a horse-drawn carriage, the magical moment would come when the live-oak tree in the center of town was lit up with thousands of miniature white lights. Children were lifted to their parents' shoulders to see the spectacular display. With a collective crescendo of gasps, the glorious holiday season would officially begin.

Not that every day was a holiday. Those are just the times I find easiest to remember, the times that don't slam hard into my heart as I remember those years with Kyle. We felt more like a couple at those times and I felt more married, somehow, when occupied with the time-consuming task of celebrating Christmas. Kyle even called me "Mrs. Christmas" and we laughed as we cut down our own tree in the country, added ornaments to our collection and entertained large groups of family and friends. The highlight of the holiday was the succession of Christmas Eve services at our church, and I wondered when we would have our own children to delight with the gifts of a Christ-filled Christmas. I would gaze at the adorable little girls of my friends, their white-stockinged feet tucked into tiny black patent leather shoes, their eyes filled with anticipation, and I would pray for a daughter of our own. I daydreamed about the baby we might have someday, writing long lists and musing on the combinations we might produce. Soft brown eyes like my mother's or the light blue of his Germanic father's. I wondered if our daughter would be an artist like Kyle's mother. Would our son be an athlete like my brothers? I bought tiny, soft things like baby T-shirts and smocked dresses and bath toys, sweet sweaters and tiny tights. I started a holiday scrapbook with labels for the coming years—Christmas 1998, Christmas 1999—planning to raise a household of happy children. Slamming doors, tricycles strewn about the driveway, pancakes on Saturday mornings, bubble baths—I wanted it all—the noise, the clutter, the laughter and the heartbreak.

One year, after all the Christmas decorating had been done with as much flair as we could muster (we were pretty good at that sort of thing), I was sitting in the firelight near the Christmas tree, writing Christmas cards and listening to soft music.

Kyle came over, put an arm around me and smiled. "Honey, what do you want for Christmas this year?"

The answer came easily, but was not what he expected. I always loved Kyle's taste in gifts—the clothes he chose were lovely, the perfumes exquisite. He was particularly wonderful at finding just the right books—especially rare and first-edition volumes which he sometimes hand-covered in marbleized paper.

Even more special were the romantic cards that accompanied

each gift, always inscribed with words of love in his poetic style
and penned in artistic calligraphy. But now I looked at him,
wanting something far different, something I had asked for many
times but which now seemed crucial to the life and health of
our marriage.

Burying my face in his sweater, I cried, "Kyle, I want to feel
wanted by you. I want to know that what you want most in
the world is me." I was more than slightly embarrassed by this
request and feeling shy as I traced the fullness of his mouth with
my finger. "I want to make love on Christmas Eve and do it again
if we want to in the morning."

I almost had everything I wanted. We lived in my dream
house, with a beautiful yard that furnished me with plenty of
fresh flowers. I loved taking care of it and making it pretty.

And Kyle loved the way I made an effort to carry on traditions my southern-bred grandmother had taught me—starched
and ironed sheets, warm cakes waiting in the glass-domed pedes-
tal, gourmet meals served by the fireplace on wintry evenings.

My friends thought he was the perfect husband when he
surprised me at work with mugs of fresh coffee on cold mornings, delivered with beautifully-written love notes. One colleague
sighed and confided, "Susan, I want a clone of your husband."

He was a bright conversationalist. I thought (and still do
think) he was the best-looking man I had ever seen—gentle,
expressive eyes that twinkled with energy, well-proportioned
compact body, curly brown hair. No one guessed that once we
bid friends good-bye for the evening and the doors were closed,
the curtains drawn, we went our separate ways in a strange dance
of inexplicable irony.

*I want, I want, I want. Flipping through the pages, the shining
silver and the pristine garden. The home and the husband, the baby
I want. Someday.*

*Y*ing, our school secretary, told me one day, "Susan, you need an ayi."

"What? What do I need?"

"An ayi. Someone to do the washing and cleaning. And even cooking!" Her eyes shone with enthusiasm.

"Do I have to have an ayi?" I did these things for myself and wasn't keen on the idea of someone else taking over.

"Oh, yes. You don't know the language and you have to order water and gas and pay the bills. She will help you."

"Okay, then. That sounds great. Thank you, Ying."

Ying's best friend, Mrs. Zhang, became my ayi. Now middle-aged, Mrs. Zhang had been a Red Guard during the Cultural Revolution. She was part of that generation who missed their education and did their best to follow Chairman Mao's orders to "be violent." In the societal mayhem, schools had been closed and teachers banished. Absurdly, many were sent to the remote countryside to be "re-educated" by farmers, leaving the teenagers to reign over the streets of the big cities, roaming and raiding homes and businesses in search of anything that smacked of bourgeois. Their mission was to rid the land of the "Four Olds"—old customs, old ideas, old habits, and old cultures. And they went about their task with the sadism of zealots—beating up teachers, wealthy businessmen, and landowners. They smashed antiques, burned books and music, and destroyed the dreams of an entire nation. When Chairman Mao complained, "Peking is not violent enough," the Red Guards boarded trains and stormed the capital city, killing over 2,000 people in one month's time.

Eventually, the rage of the Red Guards dissipated in an invisible cloud of disappointment, lost dreams, and unfulfilled promises. Mrs. Zhang had married another Red Guard and had a son. She worked in one factory after another, joining the masses of former Red Guards who were left with only tormented and haunting memories of their days spent in unrestricted violence

and cruelty. They had been instructed to think of Chairman
Mao as their father, and his fourth wife—Madame Mao—as their
mother. They were compelled to turn in even their own mothers
and fathers for "re-education and relocation" for comments made
within the privacy of their own homes, "crimes" such as daring to
question Chairman Mao's outrageous cultural destruction, forgetting to carry the Little Red Book, or reading a book of poetry.

Now in her forties, Mrs. Zhang sought ways to forget those
days. I asked her about what happened when she was a Red
Guard, and she grew quiet. "I cannot think of that time. I never
want to remember the things I did." Scandal begs the memory
to be forgotten.

"But, Mrs. Zhang, you were young and impressionable. You
simply trusted the instructions that were given you."

"Yes, I did. But many things happened—unspeakable things.
I will not think about them."

She had permed hair, red lipstick, and jeans tucked into
boots. She rode a small motorcycle. She began working for me
immediately, first arranging for the delivery of huge plastic bottles
of drinking water. Next she managed to get rid of the construction residue piled in the kitchen sink. She washed floors, scoured
the shower, and sang as she worked. She prepared meals of rice,
vegetables and beef or chicken, and she sewed for me. Noticing
one day that I had forgotten to bring a summer nightgown, she
came the next day with a cool, cotton gown she had sewn, along
with a hair scrunchy to match. Later she sewed costumes for my
school productions, copying magazine photos.

She started an Amway business and informed me that she
would be buying only Amway cleaning products. I smiled and
said, "Okay." She blissfully sprayed dusting solution around the
rooms, humming Chinese melodies, leaving bits of phlegm on
the leaves of my green plants.

During one of the many expatriate gatherings in Tianjin, I
met Douglas, a businessman from Chicago. Soon we happily
discovered that we shared the same ayi. We also unhappily

discovered that we shared the same less than wonderful experiences with Mrs. Zhang. We had both found our CD collections missing several pieces or misplaced in different containers. I found there were several of his CDs sitting in my CD case and vice-versa. We also realized that our homes were being used as "love nests" on holidays when we were gone. We couldn't help but wonder exactly how many people had keys to our flats. But we liked Mrs. Zhang and knew she needed her jobs. We were committed to keeping her on, no matter what.

One day, Mrs. Zhang graciously invited both Douglas and me to her home—an event we looked forward to with anticipation. We took a taxi to the edge of town. After much searching through neighborhoods that all looked alike, we managed to spot Mrs. Zhang's longsuffering, toupee-wearing husband standing on a corner, waiting for us. We were hard to miss—Douglas was about 6'5", black and enormous among the Chinese men milling around staring at us.

After a long, dark climb up a dank stairwell, we reached Mrs. Zhang's home. We entered and found a one-room flat. The living room was also the dining room and bedroom and was filled with a large queen-sized bed, covered in an oversized floral print of yellow and purple. Matching drapes graced the windows that looked out onto identical, gray apartment buildings.

A foldout cardboard table had been meticulously set for lunch and the smell of food was delicious. On the wall a huge photograph of Mrs. Zhang herself smiled down upon us. In the picture, she wore only a red feather boa, draped seductively around her sloping shoulders. Heavy eye makeup and thick powder had been applied for the photo shoot, and I couldn't help but cringe at the thought of what it must have cost her.

Mrs. Zhang served the meal. As soon as the last tasty morsel was devoured, she dashed across the room to hook up a microphone and began singing in a startlingly high, shrill voice. I thought about the neighbors, all living in such close proximity. I shuddered, feeling embarrassed for her and for her shrinking husband whose toupee now appeared lopsided. He quietly did the dishes in the aisle kitchen. She stood directly under the eerily magnificent photograph of herself and sang song after song in an ear-splitting register as we gave her our undivided attention.

When she had completed her repertoire, Mrs. Zhang thrust the microphone into my hand. I looked at Douglas and he smiled, knowing I would refuse to sing into a microphone in this tiny apartment at the top of an eight-story apartment building. I declined and passed the microphone to poor Mr. Zhang, who had finished washing the dishes and might as well have simply removed the shiny toupee entirely at this point. It had slipped and was now hanging on the back of his head. Douglas and I eyed him in suspense, waiting for the precariously perched fur ball to fall off. His quick jerk of refusal sent the hanging hair piece somersaulting onto Mrs. Zhang's lap. She screamed in embarrassment. Then she reached out and hit him, suddenly incensed and chiding him in rapid and irate phrases. He soon disappeared, clutching both his toupee and a pack of cigarettes. Douglas and I took the opportunity to make our exits, as well.

As we hugged Mrs. Zhang good-bye, my heart ached for her. I thought about the incongruence of her singing performance underneath the glamorous photograph in this shabby building. This was one middle-aged woman who had probably stayed up all night sewing the floral drapes and bedspread to impress us, in an effort to make her tiny home beautiful. An expert seamstress and cook extraordinaire, she had shared her world with us; undereducated, marginally talented, yet attempting to impress her new friends with what little she had. She was racing to experience something new, and to get away from the past. I recognized what she was trying to do.

As the taxi driver, a cigarette hanging from his mouth, sped back from the fringes of the city, the realization hit me: Mrs. Zhang and I probably had more in common than I would ever dare to admit to anyone. Both of us were running away from memories as fast as we could.

Flipping through pages of magazines, books . . . waiting.

Most evenings Kyle and I went our separate ways after dinner—he to his home study or to the den to watch television; me to exercising or to bed where I wrote, read and tried to stay awake for him. Sometimes I would stop in his office, dressed in something I hoped he'd like, smile and drop a little hint like, "Honey . . . do you have any special plans tonight? Do you think we could, uh . . . "

He would smile, his eyes twinkling as he kissed me. "Of course, honey. Just go on to bed—I'll be right there. I'm almost finished with this. Just one quick last thing, okay?"

Sometimes he'd hold me and whisper into my ear, "You know, I love it that you want me, honey." And I'd feel relieved and affirmed. Then I'd light candles and wait in the bedroom—reading, journal writing, grading papers—but with very few exceptions, mornings would come and I'd wake to find the lights turned off, a book moved off the bed, and my glasses placed on the bedside table.

He was polite and caring, always ready for a hug and a cuddle. Just being in bed with him was wonderful to me, and early in our marriage, I reasoned maybe that was enough somehow. I loved easing into dreams beside him. He would laugh when he'd get up in the morning and I'd move over into the warm place where he had been sleeping. "Are you smelling me again?" he'd tease. He knew I loved even the scent of his body. We'd lie next to each other and as I'd touch his arm and move my hands along his body, kissing his shoulder and neck and face, I'd think, "Touching Kyle is like touching my own body. We are the same person sharing the same breath and soul."

This was all okay with him, even enjoyable—the kissing and

gentle intimacy, the sense of companionship. What wasn't okay was taking it further into the realm of sexual satisfaction. We never talked about it; admitting my desire for him felt humiliating to me. Nights turned into weeks and even months, and it didn't happen. Promises were somehow forgotten and our life went on this way for six years. Indeed, we had a great friendship; but starting with the honeymoon, months and years passed without sexual encounters. And that was my dark secret masked by the easy smiles, beautiful clothes, elegant car, and a charming circle of friends.

Do you like China, My child? You don't know yet about their suffering, their pain. But I do. I know them, and I love them.

*I*n spite of the abandoned structures looming over the neighborhood, my school stood in an area that exuded the charm of a bygone era. It sat in a maze of Asian history—the old, English concession, which was near the French, Russian and German concessions. Under the shade of mature red ash trees, these large, gracious homes once housed expatriate families. Each house was now filled to capacity with several families sharing cooking and bathroom facilities. Tucked in around each of the stately homes were the old brick hutong neighborhoods, where I found it magical to stroll along the lanes. On long afternoons when the September heat shimmered and the deafening chorus of the cicadas offered a surprising comfort, people often asked me to stop a while, sharing tepid tea and a smile.

For the first time in years, I had time to simply "be." What a marvelous experience to sit and chat, or just to listen. Time passes at a gentler pace in those old neighborhoods under the leafy trees. My new friends wanted to smell my skin, touch my hair, and learn how much money I made. I found that a hearty laugh often sufficed for an answer to the more penetrating questions. Smiles and laughter were nice defense mechanisms. I held their babies; I listened to the creaking of rusty bicycles, the calling of men collecting cardboard or the sound of the knife sharpener making his rounds; I soaked in the feel of old China. Many times I was invited to come further into the hutongs, to sit for meals at folding tables pushed up against beds, and to share in the life of the family. They enjoyed showing me their dusty possessions, which usually included a photograph, often of them standing near a famous place, such as The Great Wall or The Forbidden City in Beijing. The plastic frames had snappy motivational sayings printed on them in English, such as "Live a forever dream."

Most of those homes had one or two beds where whole families slept inches from one another. There was no indoor plumbing. In the mornings the "ladies of the house" dutifully trotted out to the street drains to dump the contents of the chamber pots, some of which didn't make it through the grating. Some women shoved the lot into a pile of ashes from neighborhood cooking fires.

I never knew what sitting out on the brick sidewalk would lead to. One night a young girl on a bicycle rode up and asked something of the old woman by whom I was sitting. She looked at me and nodded happily, gesturing for me to get on the back of her bicycle. I climbed on and we traveled a few blocks away where we disembarked. She introduced me to a woman who had a son. The boy, about fifteen years old, was sitting in the shade of the Chinese scholar tree. When I arrived he jumped up and greeted me: "Pleasure to meet you, Madam," then added, "My mother would like you to read English story to me. Please?"

We entered his mother's one-room home where a very nice dinner awaited us: hot peanuts sizzling in garlic-ginger sauce, sautéed celery with fried tofu slices, and rice in the rice cooker on the floor. The boy handed me a paperback book of English stories. "Please, eat and then read."

The mother shyly smiled and dug into the celery dish, placing a large serving on a plate for me.

"Do you live here with your mother only? Where is your father?"

"My father lives in Shangdong Province. He is a worker in a lamp factory. He comes to visit us twice each year."

I snagged a shiny peanut with my chopsticks and brought it to my mouth. "Where does your mother work?"

"She is worker in a garment factory. She works very hard to give me good life. It is her greatest wish I should speak English."

When we had finished the food, the mother took our rice bowls and filled them with soup, which is the custom in China. The Chinese believe that hot soup aids digestion. The teenager's mother had made a simple water-based soup with a few vegetables and a fresh egg cracked into the hot broth. It was bland but comforting.

After dinner, his mother rinsed the dishes, holding the chopsticks all together and turning them rapidly under the stream of cold water—*clack, clack, clack.* Then, as she straightened up the room, I read stories from paperbacks held together with rubber bands. Some of the stories were favorite fairy tales of children in Western countries. At nine o'clock I stopped.

"That was beautiful!" the boy exclaimed, his eyes glistening with tears.

His mother had tears in her eyes, as well. Soon the same girl from the afternoon rode up on her bicycle and motioned me to get on the back. Without a word, she pedalled me back to the Peace Apartments. I had no idea who she was. It was an experience wrapped in mystery, unspoken need, and joyful giving.

Even a stop at the bank was an experience. One afternoon I breezed into my tiny bank and could not find one teller awake. All eight were peacefully snoozing, their heads resting on the counter. I tiptoed out.

I had a similar experience one Saturday when several of my friends and I traveled up into the mountains. We wanted to explore some small villages and see Chinese life away from the big city. I wandered into a village store that sold everything from books to toothpaste. Sitting squarely in the center of the shop was a large queen-sized bed, in which several people were sleeping soundly. We saw no available clerks, so we tiptoed quietly out again, being careful not to wake the large dog snoozing next to the glass doors.

We stopped for lunch at a restaurant that seemed large, on the outskirts of a village that was less than two blocks in length. Surprised to have a vanload of foreigners pull up, the owner showed us to the largest round table squeezed into the small square room. We ordered several dishes. Near the end of our repast, we tried to find a toilet. I was still not quite skilled at using the holes in the ground behind some of these places. So the waitress offered the use of the pot kept on the floor, next to the table. I had thought it was for cigarette ashes, but she explained it was a "vomit receptacle" for customers who drink too much.

In many places there are Western-style toilets, but the Chinese don't necessarily use them the way we do. I often go to one of the big hotels to meet friends for dinner or to listen to music, write and think. I once entered a toilet stall, and noticed distinct black footprints on the toilet seat.

I turned around and asked the cleaner, "Were you standing on the toilet seat?"

She stopped scrubbing the already-shining sink and smiled shyly, nodding. For a Chinese, sitting on a toilet seat is simply another strange Western habit—like using a tissue for blowing one's nose. The Chinese blow their noses into the street or the air, with some flourish, leaving the globs of phlegm wherever they happen to land—be it a shiny department store floor or a cracked and broken sidewalk. They are appalled at the way Westerners use tissues and then carry the used tissue around with us, stuffed into our pocket or handbags.

China is a different place with different air and different

customs. But it was a place where I could seek the peace that my wandering and tormented heart craved.

You want so much, My child. All that you desire can be found in knowing Me.

There were times in my marriage when the emptiness could be almost forgotten. Activities and goals provided a focus for my energy, a place to look that wasn't painful. I was asked to be a guest speaker for an adult group at one point, however, and found that my depth as a person had diminished. I had very little to say, very little to offer. What could I talk about? I certainly couldn't share the fact that I was searching frantically for something to sustain me in a lonely marriage, that I felt like I was failing as a wife and that running underneath every breath I took was an increasing sense of hopelessness.

I couldn't explain that I was trying to be more of a perfect wife, in the hopes that my husband would finally find me attractive. I spent myself in trying better recipes, buying more expensive clothes, losing more and more weight in an effort to please him. The infrastructure of my life was too creaky, too wobbly, and I had nothing to say to these good people waiting expectantly for me to deliver a message that was meaningful and sincere. The emptiness of that hour rose in fidgets and all I could do was tell stories I hoped would entertain them.

With every annual marriage conference and family camp sponsored by our church, my hopes would lift. "Maybe this time we'll get it straightened out."

And off we'd go, notebooks and Bibles in hand, ready to listen, learn and have heart-to-heart dialogue. And each conference was good. We did what we were supposed to do and drove home in silence. I'd cook dinner with renewed creativity—a rack of lamb or pork tenderloin with baby vegetables and salad served on our creamy set of Lenox wedding china. I'd set the table with starched white linens and as tapers glowed from twin silver candlesticks, he'd say, "Honey, this is delicious."

"I love cooking for you."

"I know. And you are a marvelous cook, Sweetheart."

"Thanks, Honey. . . ." And nothing changed.

I'd cruise the Christian bookstores all over the Bay Area, scanning the shelves for anything even remotely connected to our situation. "Divorce? No, not that. I want something, something about marriage. No, not raising children, handling finances, or home management. I need to go all the way back, back to the beginning. Oh, hasn't anyone written a book for me?"

I could not find one book that fit my needs and I was too embarrassed to ask the women at the cash registers. What does one do, I wondered, when their husband seems to love God and is a lovely person, but doesn't seem to desire intimacy with his wife? It was bewildering and I was beginning to feel that sex might be something very bad. Or maybe that I was bad. I wondered if other married couples were going through this. I finally reached the conclusion that perhaps marriage was mostly about building a home together—painting walls and putting in tile and weeding the garden. Maybe if people were really open about it all, passion wasn't something normally a part of most marriages. Then the night would come and we were finally making love—after long months of waiting—and I realized that all the nights and weeks alone had begun to affect me.

"Oh, this is so nice, but I'm worried that it will be another eight months before we do this again. I need to make this really good. Oh, why is my mind wandering? Why now, when I finally have what I've been hoping for?"

I'd worry that Kyle was forcing himself to participate because he felt sorry for me, pitied me. And I found my mind backfiring on me. Of all the times to make a mental grocery list, think of great bulletin board ideas, or recall the way another man had made me laugh the day before.

One summer, Kyle and I were given a weekend at a Napa bed and breakfast by the parents in my fourth grade class. We made love and, surprisingly, I became pregnant. I was thrilled. My dreams of a family would come true!

Four months later, I lost the baby. I stayed home from work for five days, lying in bed and watching the tree just beyond our bedroom window. I could see the pain in Kyle's eyes. My mother took a day off from work to wash dishes and cook a roast chicken dinner. She hugged me and cried. It was one of the few times she had ever hugged me that way, the last time being when I was about nine years old. She was loving to me in her own way—but not physically or verbally affectionate. To be hugged that day only reminded me of some deep pain and sadness that I couldn't put into words, something that came up from some closed door of childhood. I was afraid of the emotion and terrified of the grief I had unwittingly caused her. I was afraid I had lost the chance to raise my own child in a nurturing, physically affection-ate environment. Inwardly I screamed, "No, it hurts too much, Mom. Don't you see? I loved my baby, and I will never get to hold her."

As I turned my face into the pillows, tears streamed out and the ragged crack inside my heart tore a little more.

My dad showed his sympathy by raking the autumn leaves from the lawn and hauling away yard debris. Late at night, when I was certain Kyle was sleeping, I'd get out of bed and take out the baby things and touch them. I kissed them, imagining the soft skin of our baby and folded them, again and again. Then I'd carefully place all the cotton T-shirts and blankets and overalls in the bottom of my cedar chest. I'd read the pages of a baby book I had begun, the love letters I had been writing to this child I had carried for four months. And, finally I'd turn off the lights and slip back into bed, back beside my sleeping husband, afraid I had disappointed him beyond repair.

The days became cooler. The golden leaves turned brown, red and orange and fell over and around our white house. I looked out the window and wondered when and whether I'd ever be able to get pregnant again.

Someday I will have what I want, all I want. I know what I want. A baby, two babies. Or more.

Tianjin is as flat as a pancake and ideal for bicycling. Everyone rides a bike in Tianjin. On hot summer days, the women ride deftly through the streets in their summery sleeveless dresses, sometimes using a plastic clothes pin or two to clip the ends for modesty; other times letting the skirts billow, enjoying the cool breezes. Newborn babies ride peacefully along in the arms of their mothers, who sit on the bar in front of their husbands. Mothers use red plastic string to fasten huge bundles on their bicycle—pink birthday cake boxes and new mops and duffel bags stuffed like sausages. In the summer months, old men ride in their underwear, lit cigarettes balanced on their lower lips. People spend hours each day on bicycles, riding to and from work through stifling humidity, or rain, or snow.

I finally felt brave enough to buy a bicycle and a friend took me to the Flying Pigeon bicycle store, where I found the one I wanted. The clerk carefully placed it in the trunk of the taxi and I returned to the Peace Apartments with my brand new green bike. I couldn't wait to try it out.

Instead of flying through the streets of Tianjin, however, I had to learn my first lesson: When you buy a bicycle in China , it is automatically assumed that it doesn't work.

I ran into the lobby, lamenting to the English-speaking blue-uniformed security guard, who was getting very well acquainted with me, "My bicycle doesn't work. And it's brand new!"

He laughed. "Of course it doesn't work. It's too new. Before you can ride it, you must have it fixed, Miss Susan."

I was frustrated. "Fix it already? You're kidding!"

He looked puzzled at my outrage. "Of course. This is the way in China, Miss Susan."

I turned around and walked the Flying Pigeon back out to the heat of the street. There I discovered several bicycle repair "shops." A small man would be squatting on the street surrounded by all sorts of tires and tools.

Then I got my second lesson in owning a bicycle in China: Getting a major overhaul is ludicrously inexpensive in China and as easy as pie to procure. It costs approximately forty cents to have one's bicycle fixed. After an hour or so, I was sure my Flying Pigeon was ready for a spin around the neighborhood. And that's when I learned my third lesson about riding a bicycle in China: There is a complicated pecking order on the massively crowded streets of Chinese cities, based on a hierarchy of importance, size and speed. Bicyclists are at the bottom of the list.

Topping the list are the nice cars. They get the right of way—so all drivers are continually checking to see how "expensive" the car is that is attempting to cut them off. When they see a Mercedes-Benz or a BMW, the drivers of the smaller cars scurry out of the way fast.

The second group down are the huge busses or the newer, larger taxi cabs which show up in greater numbers every day. The nicer the taxi, the more rights it receives on the road. And the same goes for the busses. Those that are old, those that shoot out clouds of black fumes are always choked off the streets. Their interiors are packed to capacity with people who have become accustomed to "sitting in traffic." In these busses, people fight for window seats like children squirming for candy. The unlucky passengers are the ones who stand in the middle of the bus, crammed up against someone's hair or if you're really unlucky, someone's armpits. I wonder how they endure the tedious bus rides, day after day, traveling hours at a stretch to and from work.

Motorbikes are the third level in the road rights hierarchy. They are quick and small and zip through traffic where seemingly no way can be found. They are a cheap, adventurous ride.

Fourth on the list are the vulnerable bicyclists. There is a fine art to biking on the city streets, with no other way to learn than to simply hop on and head out. Questionable moves involve crossing big streets (Where do you cross, and when do you cross?) and being literally squeezed off the road by busses or shiny new cars. Many times I've found it a good strategy to stop and think a while. Take time to have a cup of restorative tea and a nice, long chat with friendly people squatting on the sidewalk. Walk away from the bicycle and enjoy a long lunch at a tiny café and when you've become fortified in body and spirit, be brave and get out there to give it another go.

The last category on the list is the lowly pedestrian, who has no rights at all. My friend Ouyang puts it this way: "If people are so poor they cannot afford a bicycle, then they are too poor to worry about. At least, that is what everyone here believes."

I was riding to school one winter morning and found I was caught in yet another herd of bicyclists—all waiting for a traffic light to turn. People pressed in all around me, so close I caught whiffs of cigarette smoke from the older man beside me, sophisticated and elegant in his black overcoat. On the other side was a toddler sitting in a little bicycle seat and gazing in wonder at this foreigner with white skin and a "big nose." I ventured a finger out and touched his chubby pink cheek and he let out a belly laugh that was delightfully uninhibited and joyful. He kept laughing as I touched his hand through the layer of warm wool and then, again, his rosy cheeks. Parents in China are honored when their children are noticed and touched, physically, even by strangers on the street. His mother sleepily turned around and smiled proudly and all the bicyclists—the older gentleman and all the others—smiled and laughed, too. The baby's early morning joy was contagious, a trigger of happiness in commute traffic on a cold day.

One day, peddling along, I crashed into a big tricycle loaded with hot sweet potatoes and ended up on the ground surrounded by a crowd of curious onlookers. In China, any little accident will immediately draw a large crowd.

Fortunately, the man selling the hot sweet potatoes was fine; he wasn't too concerned about his roadside operation, as it had already been hit so many times it was covered with dents. My limbs were picked up and vigorously shaken, my pulse was taken, and someone finally announced that "the foreigner is okay." Someone put my Flying Pigeon into the back of a taxi and I was taken home to the Peace Apartments. There I discovered that the front wheel of the bicycle was bent and after three cups of tea and a chat with my neighbor's mother, I took my Flying Pigeon out to one of the repair shops. The man removed the broken wheel. I decided it had a modern, artistic bent to it and I hung it on the wall of my guest bedroom as a reminder of my Flying Pigeon adventure. I never bought another bicycle, deciding to stick with more reliable busses and taxi cabs.

Not one day passes that I don't see your pain, My child.

$\mathcal{K}$yle was outwardly even tempered. There were times, however, during the last two years of our marriage, when he would lose his patience, most often after a discussion about sex. I was stunned to watch him break furniture, throw dishes or split tables into pieces. He always apologized profusely and spent hours in the garage repairing or replacing whatever had been smashed or broken. Those infrequent times were crushing to my spirit, though, and something inside me was breaking.

I tried hard to be what I thought I should be—pretty, confident and assured, but beneath the surface I was a festering, bleeding mass of pain. It wasn't so far under the surface, either. It was right there—on top of everything and anyone who was even slightly sensitive could see the sadness. I'd try to work it out in prayer, Bible reading, church activities and writing in my journals. Propped against a stack of pillows, I'd sip tea or coffee and write for hours. I'd make lists of friends I admired and wanted to emulate. There was Georgeann, with her spiritual depth and culinary skills and Ginger, with her terrific figure and innate ability to mother. Then, there was Pattie's breathtaking home and genuinely kind heart. *If I could be more like others,* I thought, *perhaps Kyle would fully love me.*

One anniversary night, we were sitting in one of our favorite restaurants in the Opera Plaza in San Francisco, all dressed up. I looked across the table and wondered aloud, "Did we make love at all this past year, honey? I can't remember."

His hand reached out to finger the edge of my wedding band. "I can't either, honey."

He thought a while in silence as we ate our salads, then he said, "No we probably didn't."

The waiter refilled our water glasses. Then he said, "No, I guess we didn't."

I looked at couples around the room and wondered if their private lives were as lonely as ours. "Kyle, we're only thirty-three. That's young to be, for the most part, celibate, don't you think?"

Kyle said, "Well, it's hard to generalize those things, Susan. Look at Jay and Maggie. Didn't Maggie tell you that they don't have sex very often?"

"Well, yes, that's what she told me years ago. But, Kyle, she's pregnant with their second baby. Obviously, something had to happen at some point. Besides, does it really matter to us what happens in their bedroom? I mean, that's not our business, is it?"

Kyle thought a moment. "Yes, you're right. But remember what Derek told me? For men, sex after thirty is never the same."

"Kyle, you didn't even have sex until you were in your late twenties. You haven't given yourself much of a chance to get used to it . . . and something is really wrong here."

His green-gray eyes filled with tears and he whispered, "I am so sorry, Susan. I wouldn't blame you if you . . . had an affair or something."

I sighed and shook my head, holding his gaze. "Kyle, you know that will never happen."

He nodded as he stared into the candle's bright flame, tears slipping down his face.

"I love you so much, Kyle. I have no desire to go outside our relationship. I love you."

He smiled. "I know. And I love you, too. I will try, okay?"

I squeezed his hand. "We can make changes, I know we can."

He looked away and visually scanned the room, as he often did. "Honey, I want you to know that you please me enormously. You're a wonderful wife."

"And you are my dream husband, except just in that one area we need to work on a little bit," I teased.

He smiled. "We can make it; I think we can." It was a promise of change and that was encouraging.

My child, although you are very young now and don't see the future, there will be times of great heartache ahead. I know that these things will happen to you but I want you to know that My grace will be sufficient for you in the darkest hours. You will fall but you will not be destroyed. For I am with you and I am mighty. Listen for My voice.

After a few weeks in Tianjin, I decided the hard wooden chairs that were so popular in China were not conducive to relaxing. I wanted a couch and, after a little exploration, I was in luck. It was 1997, the year when cushioned Western-style sofas became popular in China, for those who could afford them. While I was at it, I decided to also buy a set of luggage with wheels. I couldn't continue carting cardboard boxes around the world.

I ventured out one Saturday morning to a large store in a dim warehouse three blocks from the Peace Apartments. First I stopped in the luggage area. I began opening up several suitcases to check out the interiors with the usual fifteen or so sales clerks standing around, watching my every move. I usually didn't mind the attention given to a Westerner, but it was cumbersome.

I discovered that more than a few of the suitcases for sale were being used as convenient storage containers. Bags of rice, popcorn, plastic containers of main dishes such as cooked chicken with vegetables would roll around inside as I lifted the luggage up to have a closer look.

I found one that was big enough and looked sturdy. I asked where I could find a "new" suitcase just like the one I was pointing to and the sales clerk simply frowned, took out all the food, shook off the crumbs and—looking satisfied—handed it back to me. Problem solved.

When I reached the furniture area I figured it must be lunch time, because the crowds of sales associates were sitting at the beautiful rosewood tables on display, eating their enormous and complicated lunches. Putting their thermoses of hot tea directly on the wood, they didn't bother to use coasters or even put down a paper towel. I could hear a vendor trawling the aisles shouting, "Mutton on a stick!" or "Chopped pigs' ears!"—providing fast food to clerks who were still hungry. One could hear a good deal of satisfied slurping, smacking of lips, spitting out of shells and bones heard from each lovely table for sale.

With discarded peanut shells crunching underfoot, I found "the couch" and thus began a few moments of lively bargaining. No sticker price in China was considered final, and even in nicer stores such as this one, extended periods of negotiating were expected before the final price was agreed upon. I ended up agreeing to a price of $75.00 for an attractive navy blue upholstered couch and the clerk kept the growing crowd of onlookers well informed as to the details of the transaction, written up on tissue-thin forms in triplicate. In the process,

I then had to laboriously take the receipt to three different locations.

A growing group of spectators followed me with interest, and we traveled en masse to three corners of the large warehouse, where I at last delivered the fluttering slips of paper amid verbal comments and opinions of the entourage. A host of comments then were shared in rapid fire Chinese. These ranged from "She paid too much, but that's okay, she's a rich foreigner" to "Doesn't she want some lunch?" "She's too fat already, why should she eat?" to "Why does she want that one? It's not comfortable and only two people can sit down on it."

The clerk took the receipt and with a beaming smile, showed me back to the couch.

We found a shopper lying on my brand new sofa, sleeping peacefully and snoring softly. Clad in very short yellow shorts, she had apparently just polished off a large bag of peanuts, for the broken shells were scattered all over her body, the couch and the floor. I looked at the sales clerks in dismay and asked if another similar couch was available. The answer was a firm "No" accompanied by a persistent wave of her hand. I soon came to conclusion that with or without discarded peanut shells, this was the couch I had purchased.

The sleeping beauty was awakened with some difficulty and the matter of delivery was then loudly discussed amongst all of us—me, the sales team and the group of curious onlookers, whose opinions were exuberantly voiced: "She's rich enough— let her hire someone to deliver the furniture." "She's an American. Let's see if she can carry it home herself!" I looked around at the crowd pressing in behind me and saw a variety of facial expressions—belligerent, resentful, amused, and a few were kind.

Finally, I agreed to pay an extra $10.00 to have the store deliver the couch, already slightly stained from the oily residue of the peanut shells. I rushed home, rearranged my living room and sure enough—about thirty minutes later, one very small man with a face like a deeply carved walnut came carrying my couch to my apartment on his tiny, strong back. It had been strapped securely to his tricycle and when I handed him a tip his narrow eyes disappeared in the wrinkles of a grateful smile.

I poured a Diet Coke, put up my feet and watched a re-run of *Hollywood Squares*. It had been a good day.

'Susan, a woman can never be too thin or have too many clothes,'
said my mother.

After six years of trying to make our marriage better, four of those years in therapy, I began to realize nothing would ever make a difference. I was about as thin as I could get. I couldn't walk much more than nine to twelve miles a day. I was doing four hundred abdominal crunches every night. I kept the house looking great. I studied clothes and the way women wore them—and soon Kyle was commenting, "You're wearing the exact style I've always wanted to see on you, Susan."

But still nothing changed. It wasn't working and I was frustrated. My marriage wasn't coming together. The seams refused to fit, the stitching was ragged, the framework bent. My emotions were raw and trembling beneath the cool façade. One day on a long afternoon walk, I reached the point where I could finally identify the feeling. "This is just pain. It isn't a huge mystery. It's pain. I can get through the pain, bit by bit." I wasn't considering divorce or even separation, for those possibilities weren't options to me. I didn't allow myself to contemplate such a dark thought. I was just getting in touch with my feelings, and as I contemplated the incongruent mystery of our marriage, a huge sense of grief began to well up within me.

Kyle was gradually beginning to turn on me during his times of intense frustration. He was out of work, I reasoned, so he had a perfect right to feel frustrated. One day, in a fit of rage, he became violent and he reached out and hit my face with his fist. I was shocked and appalled. It totally caught me off guard. I didn't know how to respond. I had never been treated like that by him, or by anyone in my life. I was just numb after that. I could sense my inner feelings shutting down towards him, which confused me even more because I had tried so long and hard to make everything perfect in our marriage. The strange dilemma that I was living was bordering on scandal. Another time he hurled a heavy architectural book across the room at me. I was really frightened by it, though, and afraid to tell anyone. Somehow, I reasoned, it had to be my fault. I was the only one around to blame. I was confused and disillusioned.

Kyle was highly esteemed in our Danville church congregation. He was a leader and considered to be a most amiable person. I reasoned secretly that I must be unknowingly provoking him to do these things. In my turmoil I tried harder to please him. I dropped a few more pounds and stopped asking him for intimacy. I didn't mention anything about a job, either. I had shifted into survival mode and I was shutting down emotionally—distancing myself from the man that I loved. It was inexplicably awful. Why and how was this happening to me?

One afternoon I walked into his home office to ask for the car keys and without any warning found his hands wrapped around my neck, clenching at my throat. I couldn't believe it was happening. Here was my husband, squeezing my neck so hard I could not breathe, his face inches from mine, muttering, "I am going to kill you."

We fell to the carpet and I froze in terror thinking I might be dead soon. I decided not to struggle and as I looked into his eyes, begging and pleading with my eyes, he seemed so strong, so filled with rage and frustration. He must have sensed that I stopped struggling against his force and he began to slowly relax his grip while I began choking in gulps of air. He turned from me, weeping in agony, crying, "I'm sorry, Susan. I'm sorry."

I cautiously crawled backwards out of the room, assuring him, "No, no. It's all right. I'm okay, see? Don't cry, please, Kyle. I'm okay now."

As I left the house, I could hear his anguished sobs of grief and yet I still feared for my own safety. I was terrified of him, and that realization in itself was horrific beyond words. I cautiously vanished in the car, not knowing where to go or what to do. The man that I loved had just attempted to take my life. I was totally desperate for help. "God, where are you?" My tortured soul and heart cried out in anguish, struggling for answers just as moments before I had been struggling for a breath of air. "Breathe, just breathe, Susan."

The next day it was impossible to cover the bruises and marks his hands had made on my neck. The weather was warm, and Kyle and I dragged ourselves to our weekly counseling appointment. The horrible events of the day before were all too apparent. Our wise and gentle counselor had been working for almost four years to help us achieve a satisfying marriage and most of the sessions from the past were blurred in my mind at this point. That day, as she looked at Kyle, sitting elegantly as he always did on one of the upholstered blue chairs, she asked, "Kyle, when you, uh, strike Susan, what goes through your mind?"

He thought for a moment then answered in his low, beautiful voice. "It feels like a movie to me, like it's not really happening. Sort of like I'm Rhett Butler and Susan's Scarlett O'Hara . . ."

I gazed out the window, feeling sure the beating of my heart could be heard across the room.

"It doesn't feel real to me."

"Do you think it feels real to Susan?"

"Probably. I think it hurts her."

Our counselor glanced at me briefly, jotted something on her yellow legal pad, then looked back at Kyle, and their voices drifted off. I felt that a deep mystery was being solved, that the silent, immoveable obstacles that had been keeping us apart were finally being uncovered from their hidden places in our marriage.

I looked out the window again and heard his voice still talking. "And then I kind of wake up, you know? And I see Susan and I see she's really scared and I think, *My God, what am I doing to her?*"

The room was quiet. The counselor's voice broke the stillness. "Kyle, what are you thinking right now?"

Their voices continued in a sad, soft dance as I sat looking out the window, and for the first time the idea of divorce entered my mind.

For a few more months we stayed together in the same house, existing in two separate worlds and never really intersecting other than addressing what had to be discussed. I was experiencing a cosmic loneliness, like when you are with someone, but in the reality of your perceptions you are really all alone. As much as I tried, I couldn't feel Kyle, I couldn't feel God; and strangely, I couldn't even feel myself. Throughout that summer he occasion-ally threw inanimate objects but never physically hurt me again.

Everything that will happen to you will be part of a tapestry, My child . . . a tapestry in which all things will be woven together for good . . . for your good and for My glory.

Mrs. Edith Hua was an extraordinary woman. Sophisti-cated, charming and gracious, she invited me sight-unseen to her home for dinner along with my friend, Ouyang, and his mother, Dr. Liu. She was living in a one-room, walk-up flat, waiting for her new, three-bedroom apartment to be completed—on the outskirts of town and away from where most of the gray-yellow haze of pollution hovered over the industrial city of Tianjin. Her cook was away visiting family in a far-off province, and the meal, made by Mrs. Hua herself, was a culinary delight. She had learned English from Russian nurses while working in Japan, so she spoke English with a unique Russian-Japanese accent.

Her first marriage had been unhappy; she had been poorly treated by her mother-in-law. She had rebelled against society and sought a divorce. I smile now as I write these words, thinking of how she must have been in those days—outspoken but beautiful. She had recently become a devoted Christian through the influence of her friends who gathered each week at the YWCA and she was living life with a bold, radiant faith. "I am Christian. I accept Jesus into my heart," she explained solemnly.

Elegant and refined, Mrs. Hua was lovely. Her eyes were large and round, and she used make-up tastefully to accent their expressiveness. She enjoyed looking her best all the time, and had extraordinary social skills. Within a few short years, she met another man—the wealthiest businessman in Tianjin. She was finally happily married for many years, with stepchildren that she genuinely loved and cared for.

I walked into her tiny temporary abode on that freezing January night, wearing a loose-fitting gray wool sweater over black leggings. She clapped her hands and cried, "Oh, you look just like a movie star!" Of course I didn't—but later I discovered that she had quite a preoccupation with Hollywood movies. As a beautiful, glamorous young woman she had probably had many unfulfilled dreams.

We ate the thick walnut soup. In her Russian-Japanese-English accent she said, "This is very delicious."

I asked her that night about what happened to her husband during the Cultural Revolution, being the wealthy intellectual her husband was with several businesses. Mrs. Hua didn't bother to sugar coat her words or look around furtively as so many did when asked that question. She explained, "So sad. So terrible. My poor husband. Once the owner of the companies, now forced to scrub toilets with his bare hands in his very own company."

She went on, "They took us both to the countryside, to be reeducated by the peasants. At least we were together."

I asked softly, "What did you do there?"

"I fed the pigs—a disgusting job."

"Did you have enough to eat?"

She nodded. "Yes, I made sure we both had enough to eat. I gave the cooks small gifts and asked for slivers of meat to be added to the broth. And . . ." Her eyes brightened. "Sometimes they even added some vegetables."

"But what happened to your beautiful home?" I had been told earlier that her home was one of those I saw often along the street where my school was situated. In fact, it was now being used as the most popular restaurant for the thriving expatriate community, a place where they gather for elegant meals in a charming old mansion.

"So sad. So terrible. We lost everything. The Red Guards— you know, the teenagers who didn't have to go to school any-more—came in and took everything. They stole all of our valuables—our books, our piano, our silver, our porcelain, all our antiques. Everything was gone."

I looked into her eyes as we all silently sipped the thick, walnut dessert soup. "That must have been unspeakably terrible, Mrs. Hua. I am so sorry this happened to you."

Then she said something that amazed me. She wiped a tear from one beautiful black eye and looked around at the tiny apartment. "But, Miss Susan, look around you! See all that I have! I have everything that I need!"

I looked around, my eyes sweeping the room quickly and see-ing—well, not much. There was a mint-green washing machine and a tiny folding table on which a puzzle was half finished. There was a single bed, a few photographs of her now-deceased husband, and other photographs of people I hadn't yet met. I smiled back at my hostess and glanced down at the still-brimming bowl of walnut soup, wondering how I would be able to finish it all.

Ouyang's mother had been listening and now softly offered her own story of the Cultural Revolution. "I remember hearing something very strange one night and I looked out the window and saw the Red Guards cutting off the long, black hair of a young woman. They cut it completely with sharp knives and left her sobbing on the street. So I ran out and helped her to arrange her chopped hair in a way that made her feel better. I tried to fashion some sort of wig for her, but couldn't manage a way. It was a terrible time in Tianjin."

Mrs. Hua explained, "Most people stayed inside during those days. It was too dangerous to be out on the streets. So we stayed in our homes, waiting for the Red Guards to come and find us, to ruin our homes and take us away to the countryside."

Another dinner guest, named Vivian, a little younger than the other two women, had been staring down at her bowl of walnut soup. She suddenly looked up and said, "I also suffered greatly during those years. I had been a teacher and was punished and sent home by my own students. They made me kneel on a platform wearing a clumsily-made sign. They fastened my arms behind me with ropes, tying me up and threw tomatoes and rotten eggs at me. My very own students did these things to me!"

"Then what happened?" I knew I'd never be able to finish the dessert soup.

"Well, after many hours of kneeling in an uncomfortable position, they sent me home. I stayed inside, hiding under the kitchen table with my tiny daughter. I held my hand over her mouth so that she would not cry out. I was terrified the students would find me there and hurt my daughter and kill me. We had nothing to eat."

Ouyang prompted his mother, "Mama, tell them about the time we existed on one bowl of rice."

Dr. Liu, a soft, gentle and pretty woman who looked years younger than her actual age, smiled poignantly at the memory. "Yes, my husband was the chief surgeon at the hospital and I was a cardiologist. The Red Guards sent us both home without jobs. It was their way of trying to punish us for our intellectualism. As you can imagine, food was very difficult to find. I once made one small bowl of rice last three days. We gave the most to Ouyang of course, and the two of us had very little to eat."

During my carefree, blissful, well-fed years of eating as a child in California, these new friends I now shared a tiny cardboard table with had been barely surviving. Other than the occasional reminders to "Eat all the food on your plate; children in China are starving," I had no idea until now what was really happening.

That was the beginning of a warm relationship with Mrs. Edith Hua. From that night forward, she issued a standing invitation to dinner on Sunday evenings. When she moved to a new house ten miles away from the city center, there was plenty of room for all her guests. Professors, doctors, teachers and students anxious to practice their English shared the large table, always laden with delicacies cooked by Shouxing, her housekeeper/cook, who was one of the tiniest women I've ever met. I became acquainted with Mrs. Hua's long list of contacts and heard their stories of survival during the Cultural Revolution. And I came to regard her stepchildren and their children as my own family.

These Sunday evenings always began with a time of watching sports on TV. There were enthusiastic, loud cheers for the Chinese volleyball and soccer teams, followed by quieter moments of peacefully cracking walnuts and working on jigsaw puzzles. I always felt a sense of "being home" in Mrs. Hua's house, squeezed among her interesting guests, conversation floating half in Chinese and half in English. I marveled at the contentment I could feel so far away from my home in California. It was as if this place—this Middle Kingdom—was as much the "center of the world" as it thought itself to be.

Though I felt at home, there was always some little culture shock—like the fat fish swimming around happily in the toilet, waiting for the moment when Shouxing would capture it and prepare it for the huge dinner to come. And I never knew who would be there nor what they would want to talk about. Sometimes neighbors dropped by to show me photographs of their beloved child living in America. Other times we'd take a slow walk around the complex along with all the other people—

usually wearing cotton pajamas considered appropriate outdoor wear—who were out walking their tiny, fluffy dogs or pushing baby strollers.

Mrs. Hua would link her arm through mine and comment, "This is very beautiful place to live, yes?"

There were times I wanted to say, "No, Mrs. Hua, this isn't beautiful at all. It's dusty, there is no grass and there certainly aren't the gardens that were promised when you bought your house. It's polluted and all the buildings look exactly the same." But I didn't. She had become too special to me; too precious a person to hurt with the truth that she, herself, knew all too well.

Mrs. Hua loved to play her piano, which was excruciatingly out of tune. She was occasionally invited to participate in piano recitals, and I always attended, along with my brother, when he lived with me for a year in Tianjin. We were charmed anew by her endearing personality, as she bowed graciously to the applause, wearing her best clothes.

After I moved to southern China, my school mailbox was filled with frequent packages of spicey walnuts addressed to me in Mrs. Hua's wobbly, rounded handwriting. To return the favor, I lovingly packed up boxes filled with things I knew she'd appreciate—vitamins, Spirulina, which she took for health, and other treats I had purchased in America: a pink T-shirt with a gold cross appliqué, a few pairs of comfortable pajamas, and a hostess gown she could wear for her weekly dinner parties.

One spring, Ouyang sent an email: "Susan, come quickly. Mrs. Hua is in the hospital dying of liver cancer and is requesting your presence."

It only took an hour to consult with my administrative staff, secure a substitute, send for an emergency air ticket, and pack a small bag. Mrs. Hua was in the best hospital available in Tianjin, but it was almost unbearably stinky. I found her wearing the pink T-shirt with the dangling gold cross worn over her hospital-issued, blue-striped pajamas. Ouyang's mother whispered, "She won't let them take off the Christ shirt from America."

Ouyang added, "And she made her housekeeper dye her hair so that she would look the way you remembered her."

Just as he had warned, she was very ill. She reached for my hand. "Susan, my daughter. You came to see me. Please pray for me. I want to go to heaven and be with God."

And so in a hospital that reeked of urine and other unspecified odors, surrounded by people pressing in to listen to every word, I knelt beside her bed on the hard linoleum floor, and prayed for the peace of God to be with her then and forevermore. Ouyang was translating and soon I could hear sniffles coming from all directions. I prayed she would be somehow released from the pain she was in. Then I sang the old hymns of the church, those from my early childhood. They were simple songs of faith and hope, with deeply significant words that struck deep chords in my memory, and apparently in those of my hearers as well. Perhaps these songs had been sung in their own childhood, too. Doctors and nurses kept coming in to listen, with unabashed tears streaming down their faces. And in a few moments, Mrs. Edith Hua, an elegant woman living in a broken world, wearing her pink "Christ shirt," passed on to another world—one that is whole and perfect—to be with her Lord and Savior.

I want you to hear My words and never forget them, for they are words of life.

*O*ur church had a new pastor. My husband had written one of the letters of recommendation and we were elated that Dr. John Travis had been called to our congregation. His sermons were marvelous, blending scriptural truths with real-life examples and illustrations carved from ordinary people living ordinary lives. The people responded with great warmth and enthusiasm to his ministerial style, which emphasized the unconditional, extravagant love of God. These busy executives and professionals were hungry for John's message of divine acceptance and grace.

Kyle was invited to join a small, weekly men's group of which Dr. Travis was a part. They seemed to enjoy a genuine friendship and it was because of this that I chose not to seek John's counsel at any time during the painful years of our marriage. I was assuming Kyle had met with him privately, speaking man-to-man, friend-to-friend.

It was not until Kyle and I separated that John Travis asked me to meet him in his study one Saturday morning to discuss the details of the impending divorce and all that had led up to it.

He gently expressed his sympathy and with care and pastoral concern encouraged me to give the marriage "another chance." I asked him what I should do about the violence. He dismissed that question, saying that nothing should be allowed to end my marriage. His words only further reinforced the spiritual impact he had already made upon my life as my pastor. I believed I could indeed trust him. So I told Kyle that I would be willing to stay married if we could compromise on the issue of sexual intimacy and if he would agree to refrain from any physical violence. I suggested this reluctantly; it seemed demeaning to have to "schedule" something like romance and affection. Still, even if we had intimate relations once per month, that would be a huge improvement on what had been our pattern.

However, my trust and respect for Kyle had been greatly diminished. I wondered secretly to myself, how long things would last. The alternative was to end our marriage, which was at best tenuous. Still, I believed divorce was wrong. I had meant my wedding vows. I thought of myself as a woman of high character. I believed profoundly in marriage and in the power of God to heal broken lives.

Kyle listened carefully to my words of consolation and need. Then he took a short trip to the Napa Valley, saying he'd "let me know" what his decision was after talking it over with his college friend, Jeremy.

The weekend passed in a slow crawl and I called him twice. "How are you doing with your decision?" I asked.

He was distracted. "Huh? What decision?"

"You know, the decision about our future?"

"Oh, we're playing this really cool computer game right now." He laughed. "I know it sounds like a waste of time, but it's fun. We just ordered in pizza and beer. This is the most fun I've had since college, Susan."

"Oh."

"So what are you doing this weekend?"

"Oh, I am doing what I always do. Walking and cleaning and working at school. We had worship team rehearsal this morning. So, Kyle, do you have any direction about this? When do you think you'll decide about us, about our marriage?"

"I dunno. We'll talk about that tomorrow, I suppose. See you then."

"Okay, well, have fun. Say hi to Jeremy." *Click.*

When he walked in the door after ten o'clock the next evening, I was nervous and he seemed to be avoiding the topic. We chatted about his old friends and computer games, then I finally asked, "So, Kyle, what did you decide?"

He looked at me. "Susan, Jeremy and I talked about it right before I left. He really understands how I feel. He said, 'There comes a time when you just don't want to try anymore. You know?' When Sharon and Jeremy split up, he felt ready to let her go. And I guess that's how I feel, too."

I locked eyes with him. "So, you're saying you want a divorce?"

His eyes followed the lines of the ceiling. "No, I'm just saying that I don't want to put any effort into this marriage. I can't guarantee that I'll be able to change in any way and if you're frustrated now, you'll remain frustrated for years. Maybe we should get the divorce."

Gradually we made the mutual decision to dissolve the marriage. Throughout the pain and fear of those days, we were friends—sometimes having a meal together and ironically, sometimes we were able to share what was inside our hearts more than we ever had before.

During this time, he said he felt "freer" to confide in me. He explained his deep respect for me as a person, but also his desire for a different sort of woman as his wife. Gently, he described his "ideal" woman—someone who made more money than a teacher—maybe a lawyer or a doctor. Someone with blonde hair and blue eyes, like the Germanic side of his family. Someone very lean. But not too small. He wanted someone who was—perfect.

One afternoon we were in San Francisco having lunch. We realized too late the shopping trip planned for the morning was poorly-timed. Would we buy something for his home or my home? Things were just awkward. So we abandoned the shopping expedition and found a cozy café, where we ordered coffee and sandwiches. Kyle began telling me more about his hopes for finding the "right wife" someday. He wanted his heart to pound when she walked into a room. I listened and understood, for he was describing exactly the way I felt about him. I looked across the table at my elegant husband in his tweed blazer and stiffly starched blue button-down shirt, his gray-green eyes scanning the room, and I knew I would love him always. I knew what it was like to have a pounding heart when one's love entered the room—for that is what mine did for him.

The next day we took a long drive in the country and he told me about his fascination with pornography—the stacks of magazines hidden in his office. I had never found them—indeed, I had never thought to "search" his office—and I was shocked to hear this confession.

He told me about his addiction to x-rated movies, his fantasizing about the perfect women pictured on the glossy, airbrushed pages. He tried to explain to me the way his private world would not allow him to make love to a real person. He shared the irritation he felt when he sensed me moving into his private world of fantasy life. I had been fighting a battle I never knew existed.

When he typed out the divorce papers two months later, he called out casually from his office, "Susan, I put your name down as the one who wants the divorce, okay?"

You must guard your ways so that you don't sin, my child.

I was relieved when the heat of September quickly turned into a pleasant October autumn. The red ash trees were shedding their leaves sending them in a turning, twisting dance to the ground. I could go on long walks without feeling like I was in a sauna. I was enjoying my afternoon walk one Saturday and heard a glorious baritone voice singing "Edelweiss" from *The Sound of Music*. Amazed, I looked around, trying to find the source of the voice resonating along the Asian street, now decorated for fall in mottled amber and chocolate. There was a soccer game in the stadium close to the neighborhood and traffic had been closed off to cars. A smiling man in his forties rode toward me, peacefully pedaling his Flying Pigeon.

"What a lovely singing voice you have!"

He stopped. "Thank you. Are you from America?"

"Yes, I am and I love that song you were singing."

His eyes lit up. "*The Sound of Music!* Yes, I also like it."

The next day as I walked, he found me again, this time belting out, "The hills are alive with the sound of music . . ."

I joined in, harmonizing, "My heart loves to sing every sound it hears."

"Come to my restaurant. Here, get on the back." He patted his bicycle.

"I can't come right now. Perhaps I can come tonight instead. What is the name of your restaurant?"

He pulled out a business card from his pocket and carefully handed it to me with both hands. I smiled. "Thank you! I'm so sorry I do not have my card with me today."

He rode away like the wind and I later called Ouyang to see if he would accompany me to the restaurant. Ouyang was happy to do so and we took a taxi there that evening. It was a restaurant that specialized in jiao-ze or dumplings, the delicious steamed morsels of flavor so beloved in China. Ouyang, as usual, did the ordering: three varieties of dumplings—chicken, pork and shrimp. He taught me the proper way to eat them—a bite of dumpling first, after dipping into the aromatic sauce filled with fresh ginger, then a bite from a raw clove of peppery garlic, finally the enjoyable process would culminate in the enjoyment of chewing and swallowing. It took me a while to catch on, but I soon got the hang of it. We ate our fill of fragrant, plump dumplings. Then we sipped tea and chatted with Mr. Tan, the talented singer/restaurant owner.

As we prepared to make our exit two hours later, Mr. Tan opened a narrow door adjacent to the restaurant entrance. I saw a small bed, a chest, and sink. "What is this?" I asked "A little apartment for someone?"

Our host's eyes clouded over slightly. "No, this is where I sleep. In fact, this is where I live."

Ouyang spoke up. "This is very common in China, Susan. People often live where they work, in simple rooms and go home to visit their families when they can."

Mr. Tan nodded. "Would you like to visit my family with me, my friends?"

I looked at Ouyang, then said, "Yes, we'd love to!"

As we took the taxi back to the Peace Apartments, Ouyang groaned. "I do not like the way you do that, Susan. We do not need to visit the man's family. But, since you are an American and very curious . . . I will go with you."

He was resigned to the fact that I wanted to see as much as I could. We met Mr. Tan the following weekend and all three of us hopped into a taxi to drive to his family's home. The day turned into night during our journey, and by the time we

arrived, we could barely see to find our way through the yard
that surrounded the old building, one of many identical buildings
that shared a common courtyard. Mr. Tan whistled out a melodic
greeting and one of the upper windows flew open.

"I'm home. I've brought the American!" he called out.

As we started up the stairs I couldn't help but cover my nose
in response to the strong stench of urine.

"Breathe through your nose," Ouyang ordered.

We climbed six flights of stairs then came to his floor. I asked,
"Is your wife waiting for us?"

"No, she lives in another place."

"Why?" I was slightly breathless from the climb.

"Because . . . because we do not have money enough for
her to live here."

I was indeed the curious American. "So who lives here?"

"My daughter lives here."

"Oh," I said, slightly confused.

Mr. Tan stopped at one of the doors and knocked forcefully,
calling out a cheery greeting.

Ouyang hissed under his breath, "Susan, you ask many questions. . . . I suppose it is all right to ask, since you are a foreigner."

A very round middle-aged woman opened the door with a
toddler on her hip. The toddler immediately burst out into a
smile, holding her arms out. Mr. Tan murmured something and
grabbed her, kissing her face all over while she laughed and kicked
her legs in happiness.

"This is my daughter," he said.

"Oh, she's a baby! How beautiful! You have a baby. . ."

Ouyang smiled lovingly at the little girl, his voice suddenly
softer. "Yes, she is very lovely."

We were invited to sit down on the only two chairs in the
room. I soon learned that the woman was a full-time caregiver.
She wasn't related even distantly to Mr. Tan, but she had—out
of the goodness of her heart—opened her home to care for
the little girl. Mr. Tan's wife didn't know about the baby, in

fact. She lived with her own ten year old daughter in another neighborhood. I didn't ask where the baby's mother was, but later Ouyang explained that many men had more than one wife, secretly. Strands of the ancient system of having a concubine or two still existed in today's Chinese society and it was not considered shameful to have more than one wife, although it was against the law. The baby's mother might have been a casual girlfriend or someone Mr. Tan wouldn't be seeing again.

"And, the problem is, the baby may never be able to have an ID number. It's possible that she may never have medical care."

"Maybe she can immigrate to another country when she's older," I suggested.

"Chances are she won't be able to. She can't obtain a passport without being a recognized Chinese citizen. She might not be able to secure permission to be married, either." He gazed sadly out the window. "I'm sorry to tell you this, but that little girl may have to live here forever as if she does not exist at all. Why didn't he have the mother abort the child? Such senselessness, such selfishness . . . bringing a child into the world that way."

"Ouyang, they wanted their baby, or at least he did," I retorted. "She's a child, a human being! He loves her—"

"Susan, you are being an unrealistic, silly American again. One cannot live by feelings in China. This is a country where people live with logic. We think: What is practical to do? What makes the most sense? We do not allow ourselves to think about our feelings. Such waste, such rubbish! It's better not to think about love. Just live your life and don't worry about the things that don't matter. This is what we must do in China."

I turned from his anger and stared at the darkness of the road and at the people on the streets. My emotions welled up within me in a stew of culture shock at the lack of respect for human life, the heartlessness of a repressive regime, mixed with the ragged emotions of my past. The darkness was so thick, I could feel it.

My love enters you and remains with you through My own Spirit.
No outside force can come between you and My love.

When I first joined the Danville church, I met a couple with an adorable baby girl. Within five years, three other children were added to their family. My husband and I grew quite fond of the entire family, especially the children, and we'd be invited for small celebratory dinners or informal backyard barbeques. It was easy to remember the children's birthdays and their mother, an incredibly intelligent and focused woman, would often send handwritten thank-you notes that said, "The kids love the presents."

One evening after my divorce, I returned from my aerobics class to my desk at school to find a brown paper grocery bag, crumpled and filled with all the most recent gifts I had given the children—the cards removed from the still-attached envelopes, the presents unwrapped, the ribbons bent and askew. Accompanying them was a 3x5 index card that read,

Dear Susan,
   While it is very kind of you, [we] feel it is beyond the bounds of our friendship for you to be giving presents to our children. Please don't send any gifts or cards to our children. Thank you for honoring our request.

I was numb. What was wrong? What had I done? Tears stung my eyes as I thought with humiliation of my excitement whenever I had stumbled onto each little gift—a book, a tiny purse for one of the girls, a can of Silly String® for their son. I was embarrassed, suddenly, at the significance I had assumed I had in their lives.

At a graduation brunch two days later, I greeted the

mother—my friend—warmly, as usual, but did acknowledge her request by apologizing, "I am sorry I overstepped my bounds. Thank you for letting me know."

Her eyes were darting around the room as she sighed. "The kids just have so much junk. I'm so tired of all their stuff."

I nodded, wanting to understand, but changed the subject to something more neutral. Later, it was awkward as two of the children hovered around my chair, expecting their usual dose of hugs, just as their son, playing on the lawn, called out, "Watch me, Susan!" as children do.

I decided to accept my friend's explanation at face value, tried not to read too much between the lines. But it hurt. I tried to tell myself that what seemed to be a strange, unexpected request might have been only exactly what she said it was—frustration at dealing with all the "junk" four children could easily accumulate. I reminded myself of my own difficulty I had in keeping my own things in order, let alone the belongings accrued by four children under the age of ten.

I feared the real reason that my friend didn't want those special gifts was because of my divorce from Kyle, and that now they wanted to distance themselves and their children from me. I felt spurned and devalued, even if it was in my imagination.

So I learned to be content with watching them grow from afar, holding the memories I treasured in my heart of their baby days. One of them would dash by to get punch on a Sunday morning between worship services or breeze up the stairs, taking two at a time with long, lean legs on their way to Sunday school classes. I'd stop and remember their fat, pudgy baby days with great fondness.

Eight years later, while living in Asia, one of my Mandarin teachers expressed surprise at the way her daughter loved me. "I have never seen my daughter love anyone like she loves you!" she remarked as we sipped tea.

When I heard these words, I looked down at the index cards labeled with my Chinese vocabulary and all the pain of that

long-ago rainy Thursday night came rushing back, fresh as ever.
I could feel the pain once again, the night I discovered the bag
of unwanted birthday gifts waiting for me on my desk. The sting
of that evening was surprisingly sharp—even after all the years
and I suddenly felt so foolish—why did I have to be so weak,
so vulnerable to allow such a minor thing to affect me so? The
scandals of my life could sneak up on me unexpectedly, like an
Asian monsoon.

I looked up and quickly assured my teacher, "Oh, please don't
feel that way. I'm sorry."

She laughed. "Oh, Susan, I don't mind. I love it. I am thrilled
my daughter loves you so much. You are her Auntie Susan."

I looked into her eyes glistening in the candlelight and
saw her sincerity, felt her trust, but resolved to pull away—just
slightly—from her little girl.

A teacher friend and I were in Beijing one snowy Saturday
and a small boy walked up to us, holding out his hands for
money. I tugged at my friend's arm. "Barbara, look at his hands."

We were horrified. The little hands were black with dirt and
cracked, broken and bleeding with the cold. Without thinking
twice, I pulled off my own wool gloves, fitting them over his
fingers. He smiled broadly and walked away gazing at his new
gloves from every angle, smelling their perfume, turning his
hands first one way, then the other.

I jumped into the taxi which Barbara had, in the meantime,
hailed, and she said, "You were an angel to him, Susan."

I smiled. "He sure needs one. What I want to do is take him
home with me and put him into a hot bubble bath."

"I know, I had the same thought. You really love children,
don't you? I mean, teaching isn't just a job to you."

I thought back, as I often did, to my young friends of long
ago. "Yes I do. I love children. But, sometimes…"

I looked at Barbara, pausing, remembering the sting of the
past. "Sometimes it hurts to love so much, you know?"

A wise and gracious person, Barb didn't say anything more

and neither did I. The silence between us was golden as we drove back to Tianjin in the gathering darkness.

Wherever you go, you will never be far from My gaze.

*I*n the months following our decision to divorce, the church—which had been a major influence in both our lives—became even more important to me. Kyle moved to Los Angeles; but I stayed in the community. Church provided a focal point for my energies and talents, and it became a substitute family of sorts, as my own parents' lives were deteriorating. Unwise decisions that they had made had come home to roost and they were going through their own painful separation.

My mother tried counseling with some of the best counselors available, who advised her to divorce my dad in order to try to salvage what was left of their finances. But she loved him; divorce had not even been a possibility in her mind. So she ignored the advice at first. She assumed, I believe, that by hanging in and supporting him, he would somehow be changed by the power of her love. They moved into a home just across the bay from San Francisco and it wasn't until then that she tearfully realized that every asset my dad had once enjoyed had been totally and irreversibly lost in his nonstop gambling frenzy.

What had at first been harmless and fun—possibly part of a midlife crisis—had turned into a powerful addiction that had gradually eroded their marriage. What at first glance was simply a step into an attractive new world of fun and glamour had become a somber death march of a marriage and home life—marked with a deceit that was shrouded in secrecy and so subtle that it revealed itself only in layers, lifting themselves one off the other until all that was left was the skeleton of a former family life.

It was a dark time. Mom spent a few months slowly collecting boxes from behind grocery stores, and we often found her sitting sadly in the midst of half-filled boxes, an empty wine glass sitting beside her. She would be tearfully packing, almost collapsed on the floor.

Dad pretended nothing was wrong. He was in total denial as to the imminent collapse of our family and his marriage. He cheerfully and robustly walked around the stacks of boxes, playing the host and pouring beverages for anyone who happened to be there, claiming confidently that there was nothing whatsoever to be worried about.

I asked him, "So, um, Dad. Don't you see that Mom is moving out?"

"She won't move out—that's ridiculous."

But she did. She had to or she would have lost the little she had remaining.

Three weeks later, I took a day off school and with a friend, drove up to help Dad vacate their home, the last of the many houses he had owned. The divorce papers my mom had finally filed, as a last resort to avoid being responsible for Dad's years and years of owed taxes, had arrived. He seemed to be accepting the inevitable, although he had not begun to recover emotionally. Dad piled his few belongings into a borrowed truck and moved into one of his former properties, out in Livermore—not much more than a wooden shack.

I wanted to help my parents, but I had very little to offer emotionally or spiritually. I was empty, fearful, hiding.

I assumed that burying myself in church work was safe. It never occurred to me that it would be within these sacred walls that I would fall so hard and be badly wounded. Sometimes we fall because we aren't paying attention and we become distracted. Other times we fall because someone is purposefully laying a trap for us and we are caught spiritually unaware and unprepared. As I was painfully discovering, Satan is always up to no good, and sometimes he uses the most unlikely people.

I stumbled because of all these things—not only was someone carefully and methodically laying a snare for me, particularly calculated to fit my exact weaknesses and vulnerabilities, but I was appallingly unprepared.

No other voice but Mine . . .

*T*he newness of being in China was beginning to wear off. One day I got into an argument with someone. It was not normal behavior for me, and I found myself perplexed as I lay in bed, trying to sleep that night. At my insistence Ouyang had reluctantly taught me a few of the terms the Chinese use in reference to Americans. These names weren't glowing. I often heard phrases such as, Long-Nosed Ghostie, White Ghost, and Foreign Devil.

As I waited in a hotel lobby to meet friends for dinner, I listened to the usual comments being shouted back and forth across the cold and cavernous lobby. My anger rising, I approached the front desk and asked, "Why are you calling me such ugly names?"

The sweet-faced girl with the foul mouth looked shocked then smiled brightly. "Call you names? What do you mean? You want to make a call?"

"No, I want to know why workers at this nice hotel would call foreigners such rude names."

"Which name you want to call?"

"I don't want to call any name. I want to talk about the names some people here were calling me." I was clearly losing ground and sinking fast. I knew this, but the anger building up within provided impetus to continue. "Why do so many Chinese people call foreigners such bad names?" I wanted some answers from this woman with the frozen smile.

She thought for a moment. "Ah, you want to call a foreigner?"

"No, I don't want to make a telephone call at all. Why can't you understand that? I am asking you why you were talking about me a moment ago to your comrade and why you were saying such unkind things about me. You don't even know me." I was homesick, cold and lonely. I had had enough of listening to the conversations of Chinese when in the presence of foreigners.

She was perplexed but undaunted. "You want to call a name? You want to make telephone call?"

"No, I do not want to make a telephone call. I want to ask you why you say such bad things." Someone handed me a glass of warm tap water and I knew that drinking even one drop would give me instant diarrhea.

She pointed to her name tag. "My name is Lele."

I tried softening my tone. "It's nice to meet you, Lele. My name is Susan. I would like to talk with someone about some of these workers using such bad language when they talk about someone like me, an American, a foreigner."

She raised her hand to stop me from going any further. "I know. You want to talk about name."

I nodded hopefully. Maybe we were making some progress towards world peace.

She continued, "You want to use telephone?"

"No, I do *not* want to use the telephone. I think it may be impossible to explain my problem to you."

A small woman in an official-looking blazer suddenly stepped out of a back room, walking briskly, her heels clicking out a pattern that meant business.

"Hello, my name is Miss Wong. I am the manager. How may I help you, Madam?"

I considered explaining that it was not appropriate to call me "Madam," but I decided to stick with the subject at hand. I was in a bad mood and knew I would lose this argument but I kept at it.

Pretending to be as cool as she was, I spit out, "Thank you,

Miss Wong. Lele and I were just talking about something. Er, it's a misunderstanding."

She said, "I can help you. I speak English very well."

Twenty black eyes were now watching me. Miss Wong reached up and pushed her smudged glasses up on her oily nose.

I said weakly, "Well, Miss Wong, when I first arrived here, these workers were saying I was an ugly American pig. I asked them why they would say such rude things. This is a nice hotel and why would workers in such a nice hotel say rude things about a foreigner?"

Miss Wong cocked her head slightly. "I don't know rude." She thought for a moment, then brightened up, "I know! You want to use the telephone! Right this way, Madam. Please follow me."

I said, "No, thank you, I do *not* want to use the telephone. My friends will be here soon. Rude means not nice. It means to be unkind. Not kind."

She stared at me. The twenty black eyes also stared.

I continued, "I feel upset. I feel unhappy. I feel unhappy that these lovely girls were saying such unkind words about me. They were shouting to each other across the room and I could hear them. They said many rude things about foreigners, many rude things about me. And that just doesn't make sense to me."

Miss Wong's black eyes widened. She raised one tiny but strong hand again and waved it across her chest. "No, they never say that. I promise no worker here say such thing. No Chinese say such thing. This I know because," she pounded her chest, "I AM CHINESE. I don't cheat you."

I looked at her. I looked at the workers staring at me. I felt utter defeat and self-contempt for allowing myself to behave like this, like an ugly American.

One of the workers piped up in a shrill voice. "She's a foreign ghost and she's a cow."

The girls giggled. Miss Wong ignored them.

I decided the situation called for a different approach. I used Mandarin this time, even though I knew I would make many mistakes. "I heard what she just said. I understand those words."

Miss Wong was surprised. Her eyes flashed in anger and embarrassment as she said in a brittle voice, "Oh, you know Chinese."

"Not very well, but I am learning."

She took a deep breath, closed her eyes, pushed up her glasses again and smiled. 'You like China? Welcome."

I sighed. "Thank you, Miss Wong." She gave me one last smile and I knew that the conversation was over.

She turned abruptly and returned to her office. The twenty eyes disappeared, leaving Lele staring in contempt, her cheeks flushed. I met my friend for dinner and, as I reflected on the exchange, I realized I had something new rising within me—a seething anger. But with whom was I angry? My parents? My former husband? Or my former pastor? Maybe I was mostly angry with myself, I decided.

I could still hear the voice of my parents: "Don't be angry, Susan, be kind. Never be angry. You are the minister's daughter, never forget. You are an example to all the other girls."

How did I let myself lose control that way? What is wrong with me? Those poor girls were only acting the way they have been taught. It's not their fault, I scolded myself as I turned in my bed, trying to find a comfortable place, turning, twisting.

An apology in China was rare in those days. A decade later, in the south, the phrase, "I'm sorry but . . ." is abundantly used along with, "Excuse me."

And in the south the same rude words may be used to describe foreigners, but they are uttered with a bit more savvy, under a person's breath or in private, behind closed doors.

Paradoxically, behind some of the hurtful words lie some of the kindest hearts I've ever known. One of my Chinese friends and I were having a hot pot dinner at a small corner restaurant one night. The people at the table beside us were making unkind comments, laughing at my "big" nose and white skin.

I looked at my friend and asked through tears, "Why do they say things like that?"

She thought a moment. "They say cruel things with their mouth. But in their heart is very good."

My child, only I can give you all that you desire. All hope begins and ends in Me, for I created it. I am Life.

Angel was a teacher's assistant at my school. Thirty years old, she lived with her parents and younger brother, a high school student. They all slept in one room divided in the middle by a sheet hanging from a sagging wire. Angel and her mother slept in one bed; her brother and father in the other. They only had enough room to keep what was absolutely essential, and everything else was kept in a closet they rented from a friend. Angel's family shared a toilet and gas cooking area with four other families. There was no hot water, so Angel usually tried to get to school early to wash out her underwear in a sink. Work environments are required to provide a shower for the employees in Tianjin, and Angel was one of many who took a shower at school during her lunch hour, emerging with a smile from the dark shower room in the basement with wet and dripping hair.

Angel's parents had worked in factories all her life. Her recollections of the Cultural Revolution were of long days waiting in lines while both her parents were at work. She took home the meager food rations—mostly rice—knowing she was doing something significant for the survival of her family.

Angel was smart, spoke English beautifully, and rode her bicycle to and from school—a two hour round trip each day. She was an obedient daughter, but had never cooked a meal on her own. Her mother, retired, did all of that. Angel's main responsibility was to study English, under the dimmest-possible light bulb in their one-room apartment. She dutifully gave her parents every bit of money earned as a teaching assistant, which they tucked underneath their mattress.

Angel felt she had failed at her most important job in life—to marry and produce a grandson for her parents.

One Monday morning I noticed she was wearing sunglasses. Behind the dark lenses were bruises—horrible red and purple swellings. I was concerned. "Angel, it looks like you've had an allergic reaction to something."

She was evasive and changed the subject, continuing to wear the sunglasses for two weeks. When she removed them at last, I was stunned to see that her eyes had been surgically altered to appear rounder, more Western. Her single-lidded eyes now had double-lids. In fact, she didn't look like Angel anymore.

"Angel, why did you do this to your beautiful eyes?"

She smiled proudly. "You like them?"

I wanted to be truthful. "Well, you really do look like a different person, that's for sure. Is this what you wanted?"

She knew me fairly well and wasn't convinced of my appreciation for her new look. "Susan, you see, my mother saved her money for the surgery. We have a friend, a doctor, who does this kind of medical practice. And she gave us—what do you say in America—a good deal."

"Yes, I understand; but is this what you wanted, Angel?"

She lowered her now-round eyes groundward. "Well, my mother is—how shall I say—disappointed that I am not married. She says I must look more like an American to get married."

She looked up, her eyes sad. "I am old, Susan. For Chinese girl this is very bad, not to be married. I must get married. I have never had a boyfriend, never had—you know, that feeling."

Her pain was searing. I reached for her hand and the tears began to flow.

"And my mother and I have planned for me to go to America to the university where I will be happy and meet a foreigner, an American, and get married."

I asked, "Then what, Angel? What will happen then?"

The question surprised her. "Well, of course, I will meet an American and have a son. We will live in America, and I will bring my family to America to live with us."

"And then what?"

"Well, of course, we will all be rich then. And happy. Very happy. Right?"

I sighed. I explained to her, as gently as possible, how the American universities would be happy to take her life savings and her parents' life savings, only to send her back to China at the end of four years.

"But what will you study in school? You've already completed five years of college here."

"I will go to University of Nebraska and become a psychologist," she announced proudly.

"You mean, you plan to begin an entirely new major? You are going to go as an undergraduate?"

"Yes."

"Angel, that is so much work, to do it all over again."

"Yes, but I will be happy and successful and rich someday. It is okay, Susan. . . . I want a house and a beautiful yard. I have seen them in the magazines from America, in the teacher's room, you know. The houses are so big and so nice, with big windows. And when I am rich I will bring my family to America."

"But it may not happen the way you expect it to, Angel. In fact . . ." I sighed heavily. "Angel, my own mother just moved out of a converted chicken coop last summer."

"What? A coop, what is that?"

"A place for the chickens. Well, it started as a chicken coop. It is now a quaint one-room cabin, but very simple."

She was shocked. "People live in places that have been used for chickens—coops?—in America?"

"Probably not often, no. But my mother did for a few years, sadly enough."

"Why didn't she live with you?"

"Good question, Angel. I don't exactly know the reason.

Anyway, the point is there are many rich people in America, but there are also many who struggle to survive financially. Things happen there just like they happen here in China and life can be very good but sometimes it can be hard, too. America is a free and beautiful land, but there are many challenges for most of the people there."

I told Angel how my own family went from abundant wealth to absolutely nothing. About the bleak January day when my mother moved out of her lovely home with a view of the San Francisco Bay—a day when heartbreak hung over our souls like the stubborn Pacific fog clinging to the trees, a day that tore huge rips in our hearts. The scars would take decades to heal.

Mom's sister and brother-in-law arrived with a truck and two U-Haul trailers, which they quietly filled with her beautiful antiques and packed boxes.

Dad was sitting in his favorite chair in the family room, mindlessly flipping through channels with the remote, fighting back tears. Mom left him their bed and most of the bedroom furniture, his beloved ratty chair and a few pots and pans.

My mother's youngest sister and her husband had a shed on their property that used to house chickens. They converted it to a guest room, with carpet, a tiny stove and sink. Being an expert seamstress, my aunt had hung cute curtains at the windows. Still lacking a bathroom at that point, it now became my mother's new home, a temporary respite where she could rest and think about what she needed to do next. She had to use the shower and toilet in the main house, and she was constantly moving and restacking her things in search of a solution to the challenge of living in a small space; but she was grateful for her sister's help. She had decided she couldn't accept my offer of a room in the three bedroom townhouse I lived in. She didn't want to be that geographically near my father; she knew if she were he'd come every day to see her until she moved back in with him. She wanted to listen to her heart. It was something she was just learning to do. She knew that she needed space in order to accomplish that. It was not an easy task for a woman who had followed her husband in total trust, followed him without thinking or questioning his judgment.

My mom could do anything, it seemed to me. I had watched her all my life playing the piano for gospel services. She got up early on Sunday mornings to drive around the neighborhoods that were close to the church, picking up children for Sunday school. She went to their homes earlier in the week to invite them to church and arrange the plans with their parents. She did this out of a heart genuinely concerned for these children who were being raised outside of the positive influence of a church. She entertained dinner guests most Sunday afternoons and later served cake and coffee to newcomers on Sunday evenings. She taught in a school for the mentally challenged. She wrote plays and sang solos and arranged flowers. She cooked great meals for her family and took us to concerts and ballgames. And now she was going to go back to graduate school. Mom had been a public school teacher for many years and could rely on that now—as a substitute in the surrounding school districts. But she knew it wasn't enough for her and she felt as if she was floundering, both emotionally and financially. She decided to return to graduate school to begin work on a special education credential. As soon as this decision had been made—the moment she had a focus, a goal—her spirits began to lift.

Going back to school at the age of sixty was no easy task. Day after day brought new challenges, as she sought to regain some of her lost self dignity. She applied to several graduate programs, but she was rejected over and over again—her undergraduate grades had been too low.

What a shock! That had been forty years earlier, when she was balancing being a full-time student and the wife of a seminary student, a young mother, and a waitress at night. She felt now that it was almost the cruelest joke, after all she had been through. What a travesty after making it to this point in her life. She was to be "punished" for her lack of foresight forty years ago! She asked, "Don't they realize I'm a completely different person now?"

Finally, after months of fighting red tape and writing numerous letters, an acceptance notice quietly arrived in the mail, and she began the next phase of her life as a returning student. She was the oldest student in every class she took.

My friend, Daniel, and I drove up to visit her and she proudly took us on a tour of her campus. I was proud of her, too, and both of us chuckled at her enthusiasm.

"This is where I park—if I'm lucky enough to find a space. Otherwise, I have to use the lot at the far end of the block, and it is dark by the time I get out of class. I finally bought a backpack, though, so now it's easier getting around with all my books. You know, we never used backpacks in the old days."

I worried about her substitute teaching all day in different schools, then driving on icy mountain roads to get to classes that stretched on for four long hours, pulling into her driveway about eleven o'clock, staying up to type that day's class notes, then finally going to bed—in a room with little heat.

The alarm would ring at five in the morning and she would do it all over again, a rough schedule for a young person, but especially for a woman in her sixties.

Guard your heart, which I have made My own home.

I looked at Angel, sipping tea thoughtfully, and asked, "Do you have relatives or any friends in Nebraska?"

"No, I have none in America."

I asked her if she realized how far away she would be from her parents. She shook her head sadly and admitted she hadn't thought much about that part. I reminded her that she had never slept one night in a bed without her mother beside her and that she would need some basic laundry and cooking skills.

"I don't even know how to buy vegetables!" she wailed. "I can't tell how fresh things are. My mother has to do that."

Last summer I asked Angel if she would like to live in my apartment while I was in America for six weeks. The idea of spending even one night on her own was intriguing to her. I suggested that this might be a chance to learn how to prepare her own tea, cook simple things, and wash her own clothes. I showed her how to operate the CD player, the DVD player and the washing machine. I encouraged her to invite friends over to chat or watch movies. She seemed delighted.

When I returned from America, I found that Angel's mother had made the two-hour bicycle journey every day to bring her meals. In fact, she had spent the entire day in the house with Angel, bringing her tea while she studied for yet another English test. And while she was at it, the middle-aged woman had even provided meals for my teacher friend who decided to stay in China that summer.

Angel had not had one friend over the entire summer. She had spent all six weeks studying—day and night—and being waited on by her mother.

Today Angel's eyes are resisting their new shape and are returning to their original Asian shape. She wasn't able to get into the University of Nebraska, having trouble obtaining a visa. Most of her money is gone, wasted on a surgery that didn't quite "take." Years have passed and she still does not have a boyfriend. For Angel, hope has been elusive. I know how that is. Hope seemed to elude my tattered journey also, and I was left with an empty soul and empty arms.

Someday it may be hard for you to trust Me the way you trust Me now with your child heart. I will be there, though, walking beside you, even when you fail to see Me.

$\mathcal{M}$y friend, Daniel, drove me out to see Dad on a Sunday afternoon. At first, Daniel waited in his black cherry Lexus, watching me pick my way in high heels through the junkyard that led to the wooden shanty. Then he came running to help me navigate my way through the abandoned engines, nail-studded wood, and strewn garbage. As he caught my arm to prevent me from falling on the dirt, he had tears in his startlingly blue eyes, "No daughter should have to come to a place like this to see her father. This is outrageous, not to mention dangerous."

Soon after that, Dad moved into a one-room basement in Vallejo, just two doors down from his closest gambling buddy. I visited him there, as well, with Daniel once again standing guard outside, uneasy about the drug addicts and shady characters loitering in the neighborhood. In the dank and dingy basement rats often crawled up and down the stinky walls. My heart broke as I thought of my little grandmother, my dad's good mother, and the pristine home she had carefully maintained.

After living behind her sister's house for several years, going back to school and earning an advanced degree, my mom moved to Los Angeles and took a job in the LA Country Schools as a special education teacher.

Did she look back later and say, "Aw, it wasn't that bad." No, she didn't. It really was "that bad" and it really was "that hard." There's just no getting around that fact. She had been completely contented as the wife of a pastor, living in a parsonage. She was totally fulfilled in loving her family and serving others. She never thought of accumulating property and wealth. She loved the church work and put her entire self into it.

When her husband led her by the hand into a foreign world that was the opposite of all she had known, she had tried to understand him. At first she had accompanied him, standing by him, as she had always done, even though she detested casinos and loud crowds. But after a few years, realizing that going with her husband on his gambling excursions wasn't going to convince him to stop gambling, she stopped going entirely. She was hurt and felt betrayed by life. She struggled to live with the consequences the gambling had dumped upon her.

Her mind had been confused, her body exhausted, and her spirit crushed. There were times when after a full week of teaching troubled junior high students with special needs, she would spend an entire Saturday in bed, recuperating. She never had summers off, teaching summer school for twelve years.

But she also learned that she was indeed bright and capable and could do anything she set out to do. At first she was so worried about grades and papers and tests, she could barely sleep. Then, while she would rather read a book, walk the dog, sew a quilt, construct a dollhouse for her granddaughter or bake cookies for her grandson, she had to buckle down to write papers, memorize facts, and study for tests. She had learned to use the lurking fear of failure to accomplish what she needed to do. Of course she missed being comfortably married, missed her house, her dogs, her former life. And, on the down side, her sadness and loss brought on a whole new unsavory group of compensatory behaviors, it seems. It was not an entirely rosy picture, but my mother learned to survive. . . . And so did I.

Only I can rescue you from the pit, the deep despair of sin and sadness.

Being from California, I was surprised by the early winter in China. But I loved the snow.

Each morning I walked two miles to school, watching women empty chamber pots and street sweepers wield long bamboo brooms. A man missing both legs sold cigarettes. I always stopped at one corner for a vigorous handshake with elderly man in wool gloves and a Mongolian fur hat who waited for me, shouting "Good morning!" over and over again as I approached. And then there was a food stall where I would stop for a breakfast omelet/pancake. The vendor broke the eggs onto his portable wok as he saw me turn the corner a block away; then he sent me off to school carrying a steaming breakfast, cheered by his warm smile.

A lady sold noodles on the street across from the Peace Apartments. She had been standing in the same spot all autumn and most of the winter, selling bundles of soft homemade noodles for less than a nickel. I would add fresh garlic, sliced tomatoes, green onions and olive oil for a fabulous dinner.

One night as she handed me the brown paper-wrapped parcel, she grabbed my arm. Having just finished a twelve-hour work day, I was tired and felt a quick flash of resentment at being grabbed. I whirled round to face her. Bundled in the cold, only her eyes were exposed, illuminated by the lights of passing taxi cabs. She reached up to pull down the bit of wool covering her mouth, exposing her smile and broken, gray teeth. She pointed at me and then back at herself. "You—me—friend?"

I smiled in return, and feeling guilty for misjudging her assertiveness, slowly nodded. "Yes, I am your friend."

Her eyebrows lifted and she reached around and produced a small wooden bench. "Sit down."

My toes felt numb from the cold and I couldn't wait to take a steamy hot shower, but I sat. How could I resist? For the next thirty minutes, as people stopped to buy her fresh bread or noodles, she announced, "American—me—friend." Some looked mildly impressed, but most studied me doubtfully. When I finally reached the warmth of my twelfth-story flat, I chuckled to myself, humbled by yet another strange experience that made living in China such a chaotic adventure.

The next night I slowed as I passed her stand, but didn't intend to buy noodles. The lady's eyes lit up like stars on a black night, and a man stepped into the light from the shadows on the street. He was an interpreter and had been waiting next to her for my arrival. He invited me to come to her home for dinner the next evening. I accepted the invitation. The following night, a translator friend and I found her tiny, dark apartment. The flat was larger than some: two bedrooms, an eating room, and the ubiquitous dark, mysterious hole of a kitchen. I wondered why, in a country that loves its food more than anything, the kitchens are tacked on to homes as if merely an afterthought.

My friend and I removed our bulky jackets and took off our boots with the help of the noodle lady's seventeen-year old daughter—a tall girl with smooth skin the color of creamed coffee, light brown eyes and high cheekbones. Her dazzling smile showed straight, white teeth—unusual in Tianjin.

Before we even sat down, the girl's parents began chattering in Chinese to my friend.

"Susan, this woman wants to know if you would like to have her daughter."

Busy trying to crack open a peanut shell between my teeth, I laughed. "What did you say?"

"Um, Susan, I think she's quite serious. They would like to give their daughter to you. They say she is clever and loving."

The girl, Ling Jiao, smiled and said, "Yes, they speak true. I would like to be your daughter."

I laughed again. Then, as we ate boiled beef and shrimp under a bare light bulb, we talked. My friend explained, "In China, we do this sometimes, in special situations. If parents find another person or family that can better afford to raise their child, to give them the things that they cannot give them, and if the child agrees, they will give the child to those people."

We talked, throwing peanut shells and shrimp skins on the floor. After dinner, we sipped tea and continued to talk. The daughter wanted to go to America. I asked her, "What would your parents do if you were so far away? They would miss you."

She grinned. "They would come too! First me, then them; there, we could be rich and happy."

I turned to her parents, who were beaming with joy. "How do you know I am a trustworthy person?"

They smiled. "We have watched you closely."

By the end of the evening, I managed to convince the family that I was not in a position to assume such a responsibility. They accepted it graciously; but the woman was cold toward me after that—preoccupied and distracted whenever I stopped at her noodle stand.

I felt I was living inside a surreal kind of puzzle, which was complicated, scandalous China.

Never forget that I created you and know you.

*O*ne Saturday morning. I was sitting in Dr. Travis's study, wearing a teal-green shirt and blue jeans. It was late June and the sun burned hot in the blue sky, alternately hiding behind white, cottony clouds. I had stopped for a cup of coffee and was holding it tightly in my hand as pastor John talked to me.

"Divorce, like any sin, is forgivable, Susan. God does not smile upon it; but neither does He approve of any other sin— gossiping, overeating, lying . . ."

I felt understood by John. He guided me in a fatherly manner through the post-divorce period, suggesting that I not sing any solos in church for a while. He assured me that my divorce would in no way affect my employment at the church school, where I taught fourth grade. He did say that I could continue to play the piano for worship services, since it was less visible. He constantly emphasized Christ's love and forgiveness.

Our quiet talks, in the privacy of his study, surrounded by the warmth of polished wood, brass lamps and shelves of books, were nothing but pastoral in nature. The direction of the counseling sessions indicated nothing but the purest of motives and intent.

There had been times, though, during the years of John's ministry in our church, when something he said or did—a word, a line of teasing—had caused both Kyle and me to squirm.

At a dinner party in a lovely home, hosted by one of the church elders, John had been seated beside me. Out of the blue, he began teasing me. "Susan, tell us about your honeymoon."

My face slowly grew hot as I looked around at the other dinner guests, most of them elegant and refined people.

Nancy, John's lovely wife, playfully hit him on the leg. She whispered, "John! Stop that."

I stumbled my way through a poem I had given my husband on our wedding night, and the topic turned elsewhere. As Kyle and I drove home that evening, I commented on the general tendency of our pastor's jokes to be off color in nature and leaning toward the sexual in content. Kyle agreed, then concluded that pastors were men, too, and there had to be times when even ministers needed to let off steam. We let the matter go.

On another occasion the church school hosted a roller skating party. John had taken me by the arm, wrapped his other arm around my waist, and we skated around the rink. I was aware that all eyes were upon us, but thought that since he was the pastor, there could be nothing wrong in what we were doing. I dismissed my doubts as to the wisdom of the activity and began enjoying myself. John was a strong athlete and it was exhilarating to skate beside him. There was something both forbidden and acceptable about skating arm in arm with the pastor.

Years later, a woman would remind me of this skating party, accusing me of "chasing after the pastor, skating with him in broad daylight and all."

"I wasn't chasing him or even interested in him. He was only my pastor," I said truthfully. But she didn't believe me.

I should have given heed to clues along the way. I should have trusted my instincts. But my years as a minister's daughter had taught me that the man in the pulpit was always right. And even, under God's great heaven, if he wasn't right, it was my implied responsibility to hide that fact or, at least, to smooth it over.

Watch and listen for My leading. It won't always be easy to hear Me after you're grown, but I will make a way for you.

*O*ne morning a young mother stopped me on my way to my classroom. She was trembling and fighting back tears. I paused, balancing my cup of morning coffee on my pile of notebooks, intrigued because I knew of her reputation as a prayer warrior.

"Susan, I know you don't really know me, but—"

"I know who you are." I smiled as students streamed sleepily around us.

"I had the strangest dream about you and I feel God wants me to tell you about it."

I shifted the things in my arms, trying not to spill my coffee, and said, "Go ahead, I'm listening."

"Maybe we should find a more private place to talk," she suggested.

We ducked into an empty Sunday school room and she spoke rapidly, with tears in her eyes. "Okay, here it is. You're sitting on the front row in church. You're trying to take notes and listen to the sermon, but other people keep moving in and blocking your view. You get up and move to a row or two behind, sit down again, and listen to the sermon. It's not long before people crowd in front of you again, blocking your vision, and you keep getting up, moving further and further back, until finally there's no place to go. You're hurt, frustrated, and you can't see or hear anything. So you end up leaving."

Her story gave me chills. Every fiber in my being recognized her dream as being true, something from God. I fought back tears and said, "Well, it's about time for class to start. Thank you, Kelly. I have to go now." It was a short conversation, but I would never be able to forget her mysterious, penetrating words.

I want, I want so much.

A nice aspect of living in China is the fact that one can learn almost anything inexpensively. I've had teachers come to my home to teach me calligraphy, traditional Chinese watercolor, and pottery. I've studied flute, clarinet, and violin.

My violin teacher traveled quite a distance to give me private lessons and was thrilled that I took that into consideration when paying her. She was entirely no-nonsense, wearing shapeless skirts and shirts and no makeup. She did not want to have a cup of tea when she arrived—of course not. She was there to give me a violin lesson and that is precisely what she did.

After several lessons, she looked at me in despair and said, "Miss Susan. You don't look like a teacher at all."

"Huh?" I was concentrating on practicing a vibrato technique.

She adjusted her glasses and studied me carefully. "Miss Susan, really. Pardon me, but you don't look like a teacher."

Realizing she meant business as usual, I reluctantly put my bow on the table and gave her my undivided attention. "Okay, Flora, tell me. Why don't I look like a teacher?"

"Well, the way you dress. How can you dress that way and be a teacher?"

I looked down at my carefully chosen outfit for the day: navy pencil skirt and a matching silk/wool sweater, navy tights and what I considered "sensible" two inch heels.

"Um, er . . . well, Flora, I sort of look like most of the teachers at my school."

She sighed heavily, looking annoyed and irritated. "But a teacher in China would not wear such things, things that show the shape of the body. It is distracting to the students."

Beginning to understand, I nodded slowly. "Yes, I see. Tell me more, Flora."

I offered her a cup of tea then, which after months of refusing to indulge, she gratefully received. *Maybe we're becoming friends,* I thought.

"And it's not just your clothes," she continued. "It's your makeup. No Chinese teacher would imagine such a thing. Such waste, such indulgence. Very extravagant."

"Oh, I see." I sipped my tea.

"The colors you put on your eyelids, what you put on your eyelashes? The lipstick—this is the way a prostitute dresses in China, not a teacher."

I looked at myself in the mirror and tried to see her point of view, but—truthfully, all I could see was an exhausted teacher in her forties who appeared particularly pale and colorless after a long day in the classroom. And the shape she mentioned? My squarish shape was hardly anything to be noticed.

"Flora, this is the first time you have told me your opinions. Thank you. I don't agree with you, but I thank you because I am getting to know you better."

She ruffled slightly. "These are not just my opinions, Miss Susan. This is China. This is the way teachers must be."

We moved on to another topic and she—for the first time— invited me to visit her home, where she lived with her parents. The next Sunday afternoon I traveled over an hour on a succession of busses to spend time with her elderly parents, who made me feel delightfully at home. Flora was far more relaxed and even let out a laugh once in a while. From then on, whenever she came for my violin lesson, she brought a little gift from her parents: a bag of oranges, a box of treasured tea, or red bean cake wrapped in brown paper and tied with strings of red plastic.

My joy will be your strength. All joy is birthed in Me and found in Me. Apart from Me, you will have no joy.

One Sunday morning, after a particularly hope-filled worship service, I was walking from the sanctuary to the gymnasium where people enjoyed fellowship over coffee. A saintly older woman—known for her prayer life that opened up heaven—stopped me. She held my arm, looked at me thoughtfully and said, "Susan, you know, I have to tell you: I see Jesus in you. He's shining through you."

I smiled at her words—I could sense Jesus within me, too. I knew what she was saying and loved her for it. I was feeling a sense of getting stronger spiritually and drawing closer to the Lord—even after the heartache of my divorce.

My family used to tease me: "Susan, you're always so excited about everything!"

I was. Life for me was a plump, round peach—delicious with flavor: tangy, saucy, and refreshing. Even through my divorce, even through the roller coaster ride with my parents—there was still in me an underlying sense of joy and an undeniable presence of the living God. In spite of the pain, my faith in God was a daily presence that kept me buoyant and hopeful.

There will be a time when you will doubt. You will look for Me and not find Me. But I will be with you in the middle of your doubts, My child.

When my parents' divorce was final, Daniel, who was a significant part of my life at that time, began arranging to have my dad join us for weekends in Pebble Beach, inviting him to his home near Spanish Bay. Dad loved it—being treated royally, going to the finest restaurants at night and watching the waves from the fireside picture window by day. And one hot September evening, Daniel surprised us by organizing a birthday party in Dad's honor—at an exclusive East Bay restaurant.

These special occasions were bright spots in what threatened to become a lonely existence for Dad. He fought depression by reading self-help books, rekindling his passion for playing the piano, and making new friends. It seemed obvious to me that God was taking care of his needs—the people who lived in the apartment above him gave him a set of keys and invited him to practice on their piano while they were at work. He began to play piano in a small Napa Valley restaurant where he quickly drew a following. Even during those difficult days, my extroverted father was surrounded by people.

One weekend, Daniel and I decided to go up to Reno to have dinner with Dad and his gambling buddies. The six men were regular weekend guests of Harrah's, where complimentary suites were always waiting for them. The hotel manager escorted us to an elegant restaurant above the casinos where Dad loved to play craps. We dined on steak Diane and lobster, cream of asparagus soup and cherries jubilee—all house specialties. During the meal, one of Dad's friends was telling a story and his voice was rising. "And then he said, 'Jesus Christ! What are you doing?'"

Dad stopped laughing and said, "Okay, Jim, my friend. You know I love ya', buddy, but that's where I draw the line. Please don't use the name of the Lord in vain. Jesus is my personal Lord and Savior."

His friends grew silent and Daniel looked at me, his eyes filling with tears. Later, he confided, "Susan, that was quite a moment. I was moved. I don't believe he stopped the language just because we were there. I think your dad still loves the Lord."

I thought about it during the long drive back down the mountain. Dad was still a believer, in spite of his habits and the company he kept. I had assumed that he had left behind his first love to chase after new adventures found in casinos and at horse races. I began to realize then that his passion for gambling was an uncontrollable disease. I wondered how many other people's lives had been destroyed by the addictive scandal of gambling.

Listen for My words. When all is clamoring to seize your heart and your attention, heed My voice.

I was adjusting to the life of a single woman. In most ways it was almost the same as being a married woman, but I missed Kyle's friendship. The loneliness seemed easier to bear than the marriage had been, though. It was a relief to now have nothing to hide. I loved my new baby niece, my aerobics class, weight-training routines, worship team rehearsals, and my teaching job. The lightness in my step reflected genuine peace and content-ment with life. I hoped I would be married again someday, but for now I was focusing on God.

As the days moved along, I rarely stopped in Dr. Travis's office. While he was someone I respected and trusted, the idea of John being more than my pastor and confidant never occurred to me.

One afternoon I was walking through the upstairs hallway at church, on my way from the school office to my classroom when John stopped me. "Susan, I've been looking for you everywhere. Why don't you stop in and see me anymore?"

His head was almost imperceptibly shaking from side to side, and his voice was slower and thicker. "Well, John, I've been very busy lately and feeling so good about everything. I assumed you'd be glad not to have to worry about me for a while!"

He leaned close. "Meet me in ten minutes in my office."

Surprised, I did as he requested but wondered what was going on. There must be something very important, an emer-gency perhaps that he wanted to discuss.

When I arrived, he patted the pale green sofa beside him and handed me a stack of letters. "I am under so much stress, Susan. Look at these letters. I get hundreds of these every week. Did you know that?"

"Wow, John, that's a lot of letters!" I stammered, setting the stack on the coffee table.

"Susan, I want you to read them. I want to share them with you. I want to share everything with you." He leaned back against the sofa, closing his eyes. "Read them, please. I trust you, Susan." Opening his eyes, he asked, "Do you believe that? Do you believe I trust you?"

"John, of course I believe you. Why wouldn't I?"

"Read them, Susan." He closed his eyes once more and waited for me to begin. I skimmed the first letter, feeling embarrassed to be reading something not intended for my eyes. I thought about the man who had written it, someone I saw often in roles of church leadership. "Please, John, I just can't read these letters. They are confidential letters."

He then sat up and began asking a series of calculated questions. Would I tell him again about the way my father had turned from the pastoral ministry to a career as a professional gambler? How was I feeling about that? How was I handling the pain, the sense of betrayal of watching my father turn from the church to such a different lifestyle?

I began answering his questions, and soon was crying into tissues and apologizing for my lack of emotional control.

He listened and seemed to be even gentler than usual, assuring me that pouring out my inner emotions was perfectly safe— but not with anyone else. He told me we would always be kindred spirits, he and I—and that he, and he alone, would keep my secrets.

I blew my nose and dried my tears.

He whispered, "Don't ever worry about burdening me with any problem you have. There is nothing we can't handle together, Susan, nothing we can't bring to the Lord together."

He held the heavy door of his study open for me, smiling tenderly. "Just keep coming to me, Susan. Everything will be okay, I promise. And more importantly, God promises."

As I left his study, I thought about how I had had a strong, happy day until I went to John's office. I shrugged my shoulders then and decided maybe that was what spiritual growth would require of me—times of releasing the private pain of my family's situation. John was my pastor; surely he knew best.

Everything else withers and dies. Only My Word remains.

"Chairman Mao had worms on his privates."

"What?" I almost choked on my braised pork. "What did you say?"

"Believe me, he did." Ouyang was chewing soft-shelled crab, working the shells off the meat with his mouth, then spitting them out before he swallowed the tender flesh. His mouth worked and worked, his face turning as pink as the crab shells that littered the restaurant floor.

I whispered, "How do you know?"

"Believe me, I know."

I rolled my eyes. "But how? You never actually saw his—privates—did you?"

He rolled his eyes, mocking me. "Of course I didn't. How disgusting. But I know he had white worms crawling all over it, in and out of it."

I was losing my appetite. "Oh, gross. That's totally awful. Why are you telling me this?"

"I know this because my father's best friend was Chairman Mao's personal doctor. He went everywhere with him and conducted private examinations of his body."

I stared at him in disgust. "And he told your father about

it? And then your father told you about it? That's not proper conduct for a doctor, you know. They never reveal private facts about their patients."

Ouyang shook his head, spiked with coarse black hairs. "Once again you forget you are in China, not America. Besides, doctors consult with other doctors anyway. You know that."

"Okay. So poor old Chairman Mao had worms on his—"

"Yes, he did. It was very ugly. Very disgusting. And let me tell you something else about Chairman Mao. He did not believe in washing himself. He never washed."

"Oooh, how gross. I'm getting sick."

"Really, I tell you the truth. Chairman Mao considered his intimate relations the most effective way to wash, particularly when the woman was a young maiden. Can you imagine such a man leading this great country . . . becoming a god in the minds of ordinary people?"

"I'm not sure I believe you, Ouyang. Surely this can't be true. It wasn't as if he lived in medieval times, you know. Yuck. Let's talk about something else."

A few years later, I read the memoir of the doctor who was Ouyang's father's best friend and it confirmed the story. Banned on the mainland, the book was for sale in Hong Kong. I bought it, removed the cover, then read the forbidden memoir on the train as I traveled back across the border.

I have learned a lot of strange things about China. Some of those things I don't like knowing.

Sometimes what seems right will not be the right way. Do not listen to the wisdom of men, which perishes.

I felt a certain vulnerability at this time, a sense of isolation as a newly-divorced woman in a megachurch filled with married couples and beautiful children. My friend's request that I distance myself from her family had hurt me more than I wanted to show. I admit the concept of setting healthy boundaries was not one with which I was familiar. Dr. Travis picked up on this.

"Sometimes when a woman is newly single," he said, "when she has just lost a husband through death or divorce, she can be very threatening to other women, especially married women."

"But I'm not interested in being with someone else's husband, John. I don't think I'll be interested in *anyone* for a long time."

He listened intently, then said, "Susan, you are a passionate woman who has been starved for physical affection. Maybe you aren't even aware of what you might be capable of doing."

Those were not exactly inspiring words for me to hear. I tried laughing them off. But Dr. Travis had always had an inside track on my laughter. He knew almost everything about me and I began to dread those counseling times because I always seemed to leave with a feeling of discouragement.

I began wondering about the single woman's place within a church. I wondered how other people viewed my new role as a divorcée. An ugly word, a descriptor I had not planned for myself. As I watched the single men and women in our church, I thought about how lonely life's road can be for them. Those nearest my age group seemed to suffer from some malady, from some degree of emotional impairment, in fact. Most of those beyond the age of thirty were still living with their parents and were trying to decide what to do with their lives.

One man talked about how he had once dated a witch who stole his virginity. He described how he could start a fire with his eyes and wrote dark poetry delivered in clumsy bundles on lined paper to the single women in the group. Scary.

One woman was always on the verge of losing her cool, fired by a resentment that smoldered dangerously close to the surface of every social interaction. I was attracted to her brilliant mind, but repelled and nervous to think that she could blow up at any moment. I could sense the brokenness and sometimes even strange behavior in many of my new, single friends. My own life was a paradox of grief, uncertainty and new-found freedom.

Frustrated, I wondered where one goes to find healthy friendships, to laugh and think and discuss ideas. Other than aerobics class, where we cheered each other on in the quest for physical strength and health, it became apparent that Dr. Travis was going to be—just as he had forewarned—my only confidant.

Twirling, turning, twisting . . . inside and out . . . upside down.

My friend Lynn and I were learning basic Chinese watercolor techniques from a famous artist who had advertised his services in the newspaper for expatriates. We loved this time. I played traditional Chinese music on the stereo and served soothing chrysanthemum tea. We probably talked more than we worked, but we had fun.

Our instructor, Mr. Wang, was a sculptor, known for being able to form busts of people in his pocket without looking. He was often asked to perform his amazing talents before visiting dignitaries and heads of state in Beijing. Over 6'3" tall, Mr. Wang was also a widower, his wife having died of cancer.

One evening Ouyang called me. "Your teacher, Mr. Wang, invites you to hear the symphony. Do you want to go? Yes or no?"

"Oh, tell him yes!" An evening listening to beautiful music sounded wonderful. I could hardly wait.

As Mr. Wang and I entered the lobby of the dilapidated hall not far from my school, we were startled by camera flashes. The guest conductor for the evening was from Germany, a special occurrence in Tianjin, and television crews were out en masse. Then, the music was so wondrous that I barely noticed the people behind us chomping on pig trotters and caring for fussy babies. After the concert, we went to my home for tea and sat struggling to communicate, using English-Chinese dictionaries.

A few weeks later Mr. Wang invited Lynn and me to his home for tea. Lynn's daughter and Ouyang accompanied us as our translator and we hopped into the yellow taxi and clattered off to an area of town I had never seen. His home was in a building that reminded me of a warehouse portioned off into separate one room abodes with very high ceilings and a small, attached toilet room. He explained that this was a government-issued home, provided to those who offered unique services.

The space was tightly packed with sculptures that were sold on the Ancient Culture Street, a famous tourist attraction and a charming avenue where I often took leisurely walks.

Now, as Mr. Wang prepared the tea (the Chinese art of serving and drinking tea is a fine, acquired skill) we waited in almost-reverent silence. Then, in walked a very old gentleman, similar to many I had noticed around the city. He was in his eighties, bald, with a long white beard that tapered to a point. He wore a classic English blazer with a tie over an argyle sweater vest. He carried a pipe and he wore scuffed leather slippers. Mr. Wang introduced us. To our delight the old man spoke English with a sophisticated vocabulary and accent.

"I am very pleased to have the honor of meeting you," he said as we quietly enjoyed the Pur'er tea, an expensive brand from Yunnan Province.

The old man told us that long ago he had gone to school at Eric Liddell's parents' school for young boys. I was fascinated by Eric Liddell, who was the Olympian athlete featured in the movie, *Chariots of Fire.*

"Oh, please tell us about the school!" I begged.

"We had chapel each morning at precisely ten o'clock," he said. "Headmaster Liddell made a valiant effort to convert each student in his charge to Christianity."

"Did you convert? Did you become a Christian?"

"I was deeply touched by his endeavors," he diplomatically

answered. "The Liddells were deeply devoted. They cared about our souls and our characters. I have not forgotten their influence."

"Did you ever see Eric Liddell run?"

He thought back and chuckled. "Oh, yes. We thought his running suit was quite humorous. He was a famous runner, you know. Did you know he is buried here in Tianjin?"

I found it interesting that the famous missionary and former Olympic champion who "ran for God" gave his life to bring the gospel of Christ to some of the grandparents of the people that I rubbed shoulders with. I wondered where those converts or their children might be. Were they killed in the Communist Cultural Revolution? Were they currently leaders in the underground Christian church in China? It was intriguing that someone as world famous as Eric Liddell would come to such a difficult place and care about people that he didn't know, lay down his life and athletic career for a chance to win someone in China to Christ. I thought it heroic and sacrificial, and it warmed me from the inside out, just as the Yunnan tea did.

The man went on to tell about his son who lived in America, and we relaxed into a pleasurable experience of chatting, tea-drinking, and sharing of cultures with this interesting gentleman who appeared at Mr. Wang's doorway on a winter afternoon.

Through the seasons of life, I am with you

John continued to bring up painful memories during our frequent counseling sessions. As soon as I would turn a corner to begin a definite movement toward deeper healing and growth, he seemed to catch me and pull me back into an invisible web I wanted so desperately to move beyond. I was vaguely aware that my ability to erect firm boundaries was flimsy, at best, but I was struggling to establish some guiding perimeters. And at my very core was the message I had grown up with: The pastor, the man in the pulpit, has special needs and we always do what we have to do to protect him. The stage was set for painful consequences.

Swirling, twirling, falling into the gray mist.

*T*he topics of our discussions in the senior pastor's study were growing more personal as time went on. "Susan, why do you exercise so much?" he asked one day.

"John, you of all people know why I exercise so much!" I laughed.

He studied me seriously. "Well, sure, I understand, but to some people it might look as if you're trying to—well, to be more beautiful than other women, to get a husband. My own wife mentioned that just the other day."

I was stunned. "What exactly did she say?"

"That you were going to aerobics to be sexier."

I took a deep breath. "John, you know how much I love aerobics. I love the music and the people there. It's something completely different in my day—I don't have to think, you know? I can put my brain in neutral and push myself physically. And then I sleep better at night and am a better teacher during the day. It has nothing to do with men."

John nodded. "Susan, you know *I* understand. I'm an athlete. I know exactly what you're saying." Then his voice softened. "Susan, other people may never understand you, nor your intentions, but you always have me. I think you should keep on exercising to your heart's content, and I'm proud of you."

Years later, when I had stopped going to aerobics classes and started eating junk food, when my little car started to smell like French fries, when the floor was piled with empty cardboard carry-out trays and Styrofoam cups, there was actually some degree of "relief" in knowing that I was rapidly becoming unattractive. There was a sense of safety in my "disguise" and while concealed in new, ugly layers of flesh, dressed in cheap "fat clothes," I knew that there was still one thing I could control. No one would ever be able to accuse me of trying to be "sexy" or "trying to get a man." That was one thing I would no longer have to worry about and there was a degree of satisfaction in that.

As the days passed in a blur of teaching responsibilities, exercising, and daily conversations with John, he must have sensed a new vulnerability in me. "Susan," he said, "it will be hard for you to find women friends at this point in your life. Nobody will be able to understand what you're going through, what you're feeling . . . but I'm here for you. I will always be your safe friend. I believe in you. I alone know how much you love God."

His words had a paradoxical effect. He was saying the right things, but the things that he was saying were not right.

I will save you from all your uncleanness.

*B*efore I moved to China, a teacher friend living in Shanghai wrote me describing the day her husband decided it was time for a haircut. He left the apartment and returned two hours later, saying, "That was the best haircut I've ever had." My friend Amy smiled, nose still in her book, "That's nice, dear." The next day after lunch he said, "I think I'll go get another haircut."

This time Amy sat up and put down her book. He then explained that a haircut in China involved much more than a quick wash and blow dry. The girl who had cut his hair had also given him a one hour head massage, which as she explained, came along with the "package deal." Amy wisely decided to go along with him this time, and indeed the head massage that accompanied the cut was marvelous and did last at least an hour.

One Saturday I decided to dash across the street to one of the many salons that dotted each block. My hot water had gone out, yet again, and I wanted a shampoo. On Saturday morning, I had a difficult time finding a salon that was open, which was curious. When I found one, everything inside seemed normal: two hair-washing sinks, a rolling plastic tray with compartments for brushes, combs, scissors, and a few hair products.

"Nihao!" I called out enthusiastically.

I waited a long time, but I decided it was worth the wait. Eventually, a lovely young lady emerged from a dark room in the back and when she opened the door, I could see beds, all separated by very flimsy curtains. Things were getting a bit confusing, but I forged ahead and smiled at her. "May I please have my hair washed and conditioned, with a blow dry?"

She stared at my feet, then her eyes traveled slowly all the way up to my eyes, where they settled at last into a sullen gaze. "No, we don't do that here."

I was new to China and tried to remember that it was my job to try to enter into the culture. I wondered if my Mandarin accent was hard for her to understand, lacking the Tianjin slang she most likely used. I concentrated and tried again to explain what I wanted, pointing to the hair styling tools resting on the portable cubby hole filled with products. I sat in the chair and leaned my head back over the sink. "Please, could you wash my hair? Forget the blow dry . . . all I want is a good wash."

She stood silent and immovable as stone, grinning slightly at my impromptu game of charades. Again she said "No" and waved her hand in front of her chest in the distinctive Chinese way that meant, "Forget it. It's not going to happen. Not now, not ever."

When my brother, Steve, moved to Tianjin a year later, he explained this cultural mystery to me. As we walked through the streets, he pointed out the extreme number of these "beauty salons" and showed me the hours of business that were clearly marked, usually opening at ten o'clock at night, and closing at eight o'clock in the morning.

On our long walks through the city that had us under its magical, exotic spell, we noticed girls reporting to "work" very late at night, the lights clicking on and a fan or two being turned on to cool the hot rooms.

Living so near one another, Ouyang and I often ventured out to small restaurants for dinner, usually with his mother. One night, as we were enjoying a long walk after our meal, we stopped at one of these places and he convinced one of the girls to give me a foot massage, which was being advertised on the flashing neon lights outside. I was disappointed at first—the tiny cubicle where I was taken was filled with a narrow cot covered with a very dingy gray sheet. A clean white towel was draped over that. After much discussion, Ouyang convinced the manager that all I wanted was a foot massage.

The girl who finally peered around the corner was adorable. Ouyang insisted on staying for the long-awaited massage, just to make sure that things were going to be handled properly, I suppose. And he was simply curious. The girl was from the countryside—a peasant daughter of hardworking farmers. Her eyes were round and black as ink, fringed in long lashes. Her skin was translucent, the milky-white color that was highly desired in China. Her silky, black hair reached almost to her waist, and she seemed to appreciate being asked to give me a foot massage—which she did very well, although the plastic water bowl was dirty and the water gray.

She shyly opened up to us. "I just arrived here two months ago from Gansu Province. I work here to send money back to my family. I can make much money here."

I asked, "How old are you?"

She shrugged her narrow shoulders.

Ouyang pressed her. "Please tell the curious American lady how old you are."

"Sixteen, maybe. Or fifteen, or . . ." She hung her head. "Maybe fourteen."

I asked, "Are there some people who want . . . er, more than just a foot massage or a hair wash?"

She blushed and hung her head. "Of course. Of course."

I asked her, being an inquisitive American who liked this young child-woman, "Do your parents know about your job? About what you do here?"

She smoothed cream onto my foot, her lower lip quivering as she fought to keep back sudden tears. "No, no. Of course not."

I didn't know the Chinese word for "condom," so I enlisted help from Ouyang. He reluctantly agreed to ask her my very personal question, but let me know that it was clearly not the kind of thing one normally asks in China. I insisted and he finally asked her if she was careful to use a condom every time she was "with a customer."

The girl hung her head and looked into my eyes. "Most of the time I do. But—there are some customers who refuse."

I felt outrage, but also sympathy for this child. I said, "You really must insist on it if you're going to work here. Your health and the future of your entire life could be at great risk."

The fourteen year old then turned to Ouyang and explained with trembling confidence that there were no cases of AIDS in China—at all. And furthermore, there wasn't a problem with other sexually-transmitted diseases in this country—at all. So, happily, there was nothing to worry about.

Ouyang and I looked at each other. Just that afternoon we had been discussing the latest reports (that was 1997) that there were an estimated 400,000 carriers of the AIDS virus in China.

I said, "Young friend, I have something important to tell you. You have been misled. There is an epidemic of AIDS in China."

The girl, her long hair falling over her slim, beautiful shoulders, completed the foot massage. I took her narrow hand with the typically long Chinese fingers that so many men here find alluring, and said, "Please look for a different kind of job, my friend. Find something in an office or work as a housekeeper, but don't risk your life and your health in this way anymore. Your mother, your parents, they love you. They would not want you to be doing this sort of work. You can do much better. I'll hire you as a housekeeper and you can live in my guest bedroom. Anything to get you out of this business."

I had hit a nerve. Her tears flowed now, but she waved that beautiful hand across her chest and said, "No. No, I must."

I pressed my business card into her hand and encouraged her to go home early that night. As Ouyang and I left the tiny "beauty salon," I was quiet and sad, ready to burst into tears. He reminded me again to "try to think logically, like the Chinese."

"Ouyang, tell me. Are condoms readily available here?"

He shrugged his shoulders. "I do not know. A Chinese man does not prefer to use a condom."

I stopped underneath a streetlight's amber glow. "Ouyang, why not? There are many sexually transmitted diseases these days. With all these "hair salons" around, there must be a lot of unprotected relations going on—and it's just deadly! Think about the beautiful young girl. What chance does she have in life?"

Ouyang looked at me in genuine bewilderment, as I cried out, "I know AIDS is a problem, yes, but there are many other diseases, as well."

"You mean hepatitis?" he asked.

"Well, hepatitis is one disease. There are many more."

He began walking slowly. "This must be a big problem in my country. Men do not think about using a condom."

I reached for his arm. "Ouyang, tell me. Do you have unprotected relations with women?"

He looked irritated. "Of course I do, but I am not a dog."

I was confused. "But your girlfriend, Spring Rain, is in Singapore, yes?"

"Yes. But I am a normal man, Susan. Chinese men have

freedom to . . . enjoy different women if they choose."

"How many different women, Ouyang?"

"Many!"

I was dumbfounded. "Where do you meet them?"

"Everywhere, Susan. This is China. Business agreements are concluded in karaoke bars and women are usually a part of the deal. Sometimes I have to reserve hotel rooms for this purpose."

"Oh, I hate knowing so much about this place. It was easier when I knew less."

Ouyang shot back, "Then don't ask so many questions!"

"Ouyang, if this behavior is protocol for business etiquette, then using a condom is important, don't you think?"

Ouyang was annoyed. "I am a responsible Chinese man. If any woman gets pregnant, I will do the right thing and arrange an abortion immediately."

"Ouyang, it's not just about dealing with an unwanted pregnancy. What about the morality of the situation? Having so many sexual partners can't be healthy for your mind, either. Christians believe in abstinence, you know. Waiting until you are married. And physically, it is just dangerous. Your life or the life of that young girl could be destroyed so easily."

Now he was furious. "Susan, I am a Chinese man, not a Christ man. We have very little freedom in China. One's personal sexual life is the one area of freedom we have. Many men enjoy pleasure and there is no police for this in China."

"Ouyang—"

His voice was getting shrill and many heads turned our direction. "Chinese men are not dogs, as you seem to think."

I sighed. "I am not thinking that. I am just worried about possible risks for you. Okay. We'll talk about this another time."

We stopped at a small restaurant to have a pot of black tea and as we continued to chat, my mind was filled with the realization that I was living in a different land with different air and a very different culture. A few of Ouyang's middle-school (equivalent to our high school) classmates happened to be there and the conversation grew livelier. I thought about America, which now seemed impossibly far away.

Look to Me for your strength, My child, not to those around you.
Fix your gaze on Me alone.

Late one summer, on a very warm August evening in Danville, I had prepared a salad for my supper and was eating out on my little patio facing the golf course. I felt contented. It was a perfect Saturday night. I had put on one of my favorite CDs and felt the calm of being spent, having walked close to ten miles that day. I had a clean conscience, and was looking forward to an extended time of prayer after eating a nutritious meal.

The phone rang and it was Dr. Travis, speaking once again in that thick, slow voice I was noticing on a more regular basis. "Susan, whatcha doin'? Nancy's out of town and I was wondering if you could come over and watch a movie with me? We could make some popcorn—?"

"No, I can't, John," I said, feeling uneasy. "I'm really exhausted. I walked miles and miles today and had planned to read, pray and turn in early."

He was quiet, then said in measured tones, "Okay, Susan, no problem . . . hey, you know that dress you have with all those little dots?"

I was curious. "Yeah, I think so. The navy blue dress?"

"I don't know what color it is. I'm color-blind, remember? But it's short and looks good. You know the one I'm talking about?"

"Yes, I think so—"

"Could you do me a big favor?" He waited for an answer.

"I guess so, John."

"Would you wear that dress tomorrow for me?"

"Well, it's a little short for church. I have other dresses—"

"No, that's the one I'd like you to wear."

As I hung up the phone, I felt even more uneasy. It is hard to explain the feelings one has when their pastor begins to express anything but the purest of motives. The bigger part of me chose not to look at what I could not accept. I refused to see the truth. To look at it head-on would have been too painful at an already painful time in life. With my parents in a tumultuous divorce I felt I had no one to turn to, other than Dr. Travis. The other men in my life had either betrayed me straight out or made an exit that left no room for conversation. I was grasping at the smallest bit of human consistency that I knew. In spite of the inappropriateness of his comments and his mysterious aloofness, I tried to push down the sense of uneasiness to a place so deep within me I wouldn't be able to touch it.

I kept reasoning that the senior pastor of an enormous church has incredible stresses and tensions. He was probably simply letting off steam in a harmless way. And anyway, I reminded myself, he was my friend. My uneasiness in the relationship was countered by the feeling that I was starting to need him in a way that I could not explain.

I am always speaking to you. Listen for My voice of love, no matter where you are and no matter where you go.

*T*raffic snarls in Chinese cities. What incredible transport knots one faces—with the cab drivers honking and cutting each other off. They swerve from lane to lane without signaling or looking or seeming to care about the consequences.

One day I was sitting in a taxi on the way home from work. The weather was particularly steamy that day and the air conditioning wasn't working in the car, so I had the window wide open. Pedestrians were brushing up against my elbow, which was extending precariously out the window. Beggars were standing in the middle of the enormous streets with their bowls out and ready, and motor bikes were making quick, impulsive dashes across the streams of traffic to get to their destinations.

It was so hot I could smell the people around me. My Ghostie Big Nose was having no problem ascertaining the odiferous scents of the afternoon traffic and its participants. I could smell unwashed hair, garlic, tobacco, a distinct lack of toothpaste and deodorant, known as "foxy odor," the term used for the stench of unwashed human bodies.

The driver suddenly decided to lean out of his window to fling an enormous bit of chunky snot onto the street, finishing the whole business with spectacular Chinese flair as he shook the stubborn remains from his nostrils.

As he wiped his fingers on his trousers, I noticed the one long fingernail on his little finger and wondered, yet again, why so many men had a single long nail. Some said it was for ear-digging, a task sometimes attended to by long metal utensils in corner massage salons. Others said it was to show the world that they were not common laborers. There was also the rumor that some men used their one long nail to dig out last bits of solid material from noses or other places, but that was only a rumor. I suddenly became almost nauseous with anger and stared at him meaningfully, but he laughed almost manically and shrugged his scrawny shoulders as if to say, "It doesn't matter."

I closed my eyes and tried to find a calmer place within myself, using mind over matter—something I was getting better at everyday. But in this situation it wasn't working.

I knew we would be stuck on this overpass for a long time trapped there by busses that were emitting clouds of foul-smelling fumes while the passengers inside stood silently, smashed like sardines. Those lucky enough to find window seats had their heads practically hanging out the open windows, some sound asleep and others staring absentmindedly or curiously down into the cars that passed below them.

I whispered in my heart, "Father God, these people! For heaven's sake, it's awful here sometimes. Look at them. They smell, they don't know how to behave, and they certainly don't know how to drive."

I sensed a still, small—but very distinct—voice within my heart saying, "Mmmm . . . that's true, isn't it?"

I was in the mood for a bit of an argument, so I continued, "Yes, it is true, as a matter of fact. And it's amazing to me that you love them all so much."

Again, that sense of the Almighty God spoke in a silent, yet definite way. "Yes, it is amazing. And it's amazing that I love you, too, isn't it?"

I smiled. "Yes, that is amazing, God. Most amazing."

He continued, "They're just like you, aren't they? Human, obnoxious, revolting sometimes, rude and selfish."

I hung my head and the stinky taxi cab was suddenly transformed into a holy place. "Yes," I responded, "I'm just like them. And yet, you love us all. I'm sorry, Father. Please forgive my arrogance and impatience."

As far as the East is from the West

I was stunned.

John and I were sitting in my car on a Saturday morning, having just gone to pick up yogurts for lunch. I was on my way to work in my classroom, he to an empty room to practice his sermon for the next day.

His hand moved over to rest on my thigh. "I feel so vulnerable to you, Susan."

I reminded myself that this was not only the senior pastor of my church, but this was technically my boss, the trusted confidant of my favorite uncle and aunt, and my safe friend.

John kept a roll of breath mints in his pocket at all times, being able to take one out to pop into his mouth in a matter of seconds. He did this now, sliding a mint into his mouth and swallowing hard. For a second, he looked like a lost little boy, then he grinned and playfully slugged me. "Hey, wanna wrestle?"

I smiled, responding to his boyish humor by trying to laugh it off, but I thought, *What's going on here? He's acting like a little kid, but this is my senior pastor, Dr. Travis. What should I do?*

I decided to bring up his wife, Nancy, thinking that it might bring him back to reality. "John, what about Nancy? Why don't you spend more time with her?"

He laughed. "Well, what about her?" He laughed again, reaching for another breath mint. "Susan, there's something you don't know about Nancy. I've never told you this, because I didn't want to burden you with my problems, but Nancy and I basically have no physical relationship at all. Not since Brendan was born. And he's eleven years old, you know." He winked at me.

I looked at him in dismay. What could I possibly say?

"Do you believe me?" I'd hear that question hundreds of times in the next few months. How could I not believe him? He was my pastor, the man with authority, the man in the pulpit!

I answered incredulously. "Of course I believe you."

With characteristic tenderness he continued. "Susan, I know I can trust you with this—this secret about me and Nancy. I wouldn't tell you about it if I wasn't sure I could completely trust you. There are so few people who know this secret about me and my marriage. He motioned with his finger, back and forth between us. "But we are kindred spirits, you and I."

I thought about all the things he had learned about my marriage, how he had held his own problems back while I had talked on and on about myself, being so self absorbed. I began to feel guilty, ashamed of myself, and suddenly I felt very sorry for him, suffering in silence the way he had for so long.

"John, I will never tell anyone about this. I promise."

He gazed at me, past me, right through me. "In twenty-five

years of pastoral ministry, Susan, I've never known a woman quite like you. I think God gave me a special gift when He gave me you—someone to finally talk with, to be myself with. And, as an extra bonus—" He winked. "Not only did He find such a wise, godly woman, He found someone beautiful for me. Gorgeous. Yeah, that's my word for you, Susan. Gorgeous."

I fidgeted. I knew I was not gorgeous and I was not comfortable with his words. His flattery scared me. I changed the subject. "John, why don't you and Nancy go to counseling?"

He laughed dryly. "Believe me, Susan, that was the first thing we tried. It didn't work. Nothing works."

There was a long pause and I reached for my purse. "I've got to go, John. I've got lots of work to do."

He looked thin and sad sitting there on his side of the car. "Susan, you know, I've spent a lot of time with you, time I could have spent studying or writing or being with my kids."

This was something new. "Um, thank you, John. I really appreciate all the time you've given me so generously."

He asked, "Can I give you a hug at least?"

I laughed nervously. "John, you hug me all the time!"

He laughed. "I hug everybody all the time, Susan. This is different. I really need a hug today. Do you mind?"

He held me tightly, right there in my car in full daylight on the church parking lot. I naively reasoned it had to be above board, with so many people coming and going. Certainly he wouldn't try anything audacious in such a public place. When I pulled away, he dropped his head onto my shoulder. "Susan, I think I love you."

I laughed. "John, like you've said so many times. I'm the sister you never had, right?" He nodded slightly, his hand still gripping my elbow. "Maybe that's it, Susan. Or maybe it's your black nylons."

I mumbled something about his silly sense of humor, grabbed my purse and school books from the back seat and shut the door. I looked toward his office. Everyone was gone.

Nobody was there—no secretary, none of the thirteen other staff members, nobody. I was feeling strangely panicked and confused—but nothing had actually happened, I assured myself.

When someone in a position of authority says something inappropriate, it is natural that the other person—the one in the subservient position—will absorb the guilt and the shame.

*E*very Saturday I had breakfast at the Tianjin International Building. At first I went there for the coffee and American basketball games, and then because the store on the third floor began selling imported cheeses, whipping cream, and New Zealand steaks. In the winter, I'd bundle up against the cold in winter or the heat in summer and catch a cab that dropped me off in front of the ultramodern tower—paradoxically situated in a bricked hutong neighborhood. This combination of the old and the new is the paradox of China.

It seemed as if I was always the lone diner in the large ground-floor restaurant. I would enter the deserted, dim restaurant on the first floor, turn on the big-screen television to watch Larry King or basketball on CNN, and pull out my journal to write, sketch, or make notes until someone noticed I was there.

The waiter prepared my coffee—a single cup of perfect espresso. Then every time (for about three years, once a week) he stood with his pencil poised, asking my order. I'd order two eggs over-easy or maybe poached. Sometimes I requested for them to be scrambled, fried or hard-boiled.

He'd listen carefully, nod seriously, and write it down. When the breakfast was ready, he brought it to me with a broad smile of satisfaction. He brought toast with jam, no butter, along with bacon or sausage. But the eggs? The eggs were always the same—sunnyside-up—no matter how I requested them to be cooked.

My brother Steve moved to Tianjin and also began enjoying the ritual of breakfasting at the TIB. When he realized he would never get scrambled eggs as he ordered, he offered to give the kitchen staff an impromptu cooking lesson. He disappeared into the back room for thirty minutes, and when he returned, he warned me, "Susan, never, ever go into that kitchen. You'll get sick, guaranteed." Then he added, "I don't think he appreciated my cooking lesson."

Our dad flew over for a month's visit and was excited to have a Western breakfast. At the waiter's encouragement, he ordered a bacon and cheese omelet. I just smiled. The waiter nodded promisingly. I warned, "Um, Dad, don't get your hopes up. I mean, he'll write anything you say on his piece of paper, but that doesn't mean much, unfortunately."

His plate of sunnyside-up eggs arrived shortly.

By my third year in Tianjin, the TIB had expanded their menu to offer a delicious, Western brunch and dinner menu. But their eggs still only came one way, no matter what. Somehow, in spite of the frustration, this weekly routine had its own calming, humorous effect and was something to which I looked forward.

Sin is forgiven, yes, by My divine grace. But there are consequences. The wages of sin is death.

As time went on, I had my good days and bad days. It was more than the normal ups and downs. Sometimes the stresses that a woman experiences in the daily grind of life sneak up on her and pull the rug out from under her emotional stability. I sometimes wondered about the possibility of depression in my life. Although I had many good days, even days that I felt like God was reaching deep into my soul and touching those hidden places of pain, the joy in my life was beginning to be pulled out, bit by bit. It was a slow and gradual process. But this joy stealing seemed to be coming from an ironically strange source.

A year had passed since Dr. Travis initiated this new phase in our pastor-parishioner relationship. I was no longer shocked at seeing my pastor in this needy state. It was a low-grade worry that lived underneath my days, poking its unpleasant head above the reality line in my life at the most inopportune times—breathing and beating out its persistent energy. It wore on me.

John's long stories were beginning to move into a place of their own within me, taking up space and life and beginning to flatten my natural exuberance.

This approach of profound neediness was particularly effective. Later, I learned that there were many other women he was pursuing in similar ways—there were certain triggers within each woman. With me, this desire to finally be needed was my particular button. He had found something that clicked with me and in doing so, had found a way to get into my heart. I was aware of what was happening, but my security and my job at the church school were tied to my relationship to John.

I listened to him now as he poured out his problems, reminding me that I and I alone was sent by God to help "carry his cross." He had new stories every day. . . . His wife wasn't feeding the children in the mornings. What sort of breakfast could I suggest that the kids would be able to make themselves? (I suggested toast with peanut butter and honey.) He suggested that his wife was beating his daughter. Would I give him a key to my townhouse for his daughter to use if she needed it when he was out of town at a speaking engagement? The stories continued, day after day. I can now see how he was wearing me down, getting inside my head and heart with his "kindred spirit" ways.

Later, I could see that his wife had been a most dedicated and loving mother, and I still wonder how I could have ever taken his stories seriously.

One afternoon he sent a message to the school office and

had me called out of a faculty meeting. The principal of the school took me aside, the meeting temporarily adjourned—my colleagues burning with curiosity and concern. I was apparently "needed" in the pastor's study.

With apprehension I rushed up the cement stairs, into the administration building, then down the hall to his secretary's office. Carol, his administrative assistant, was smooth and never missed a beat. I searched her face for some clue as to what the urgency might be, but she seemed unconcerned. "Go right in, Susan, he's expecting you."

Opening the door to the darkened study—so large and luxurious, more like a comfortable living room in a grand home—I was surprised to find a fire blazing in the stone fireplace, the lights so dim I could barely see John, who was slumped low on one of the two oversized sofas. As I looked at him, he lifted his hand, motioning me to come closer and sit beside him.

"Hi," he said. His head was doing that weird thing again—moving from side to side almost imperceptibly. His eyes were glazed and glassy. "How's your day going?"

Stunned by his relaxed state, I shifted my gaze to the fire. "It's going well. Busy, though. How are you?"

"My day is okay. Just okay, Susan."

"What's going on, John? It's not even cold outside."

"What?" He seemed perplexed. "Oh, the fire. Well, I couldn't very well tell Martin I needed one of his best teachers because I had a fire burning just for her, could I?"

Now I was perplexed. My teaching was something I took very seriously.

He was obviously pleased with his ingenuity, and patted the upholstered celadon-colored sofa, beckoning me to come closer to him. "I do want to ask you for a special favor, though, Susan. That's why I made the fire."

His words were slow and thick again and there was a heaviness in his voice. Or was I seeing exhaustion and stress? I wasn't sure and was unable to pinpoint my impressions. The picture was starting to blur, the lines fading slowly into a fuzzy situation that confused me.

His voice went on, barely audible. "Susan, if I die, and you know my brother died at a very early age . . ." He often told me this story of how his older brother had died of cancer in his late thirties. "Well, I want to ask you to sing at my funeral."

He took my hand, stained with felt tip markers and trails of hardened Elmer's glue, in his soft hand. "Would you, Susan? Sing at my funeral?"

I bolted up. "Are you sick, John? I mean, really sick?"

He seemed amused, even delighted, at my concern. "Well, no, not right now. But I could get sick at any time, of course. Things happen when we least expect them. And you know better than anyone how much stress I'm under."

"Why are you asking me this, John? Why now?"

"Well, I've been thinking a lot about this issue and of all the singers I know, out of all the people I know, you're the only one I want to sing at my funeral."

Many talented singers in our large church had much better voices. But I said, "Well, sure, I mean—of course, I'd be honored to sing at your funeral, John. But I think it's way too early to begin planning it right now, don't you?"

I edged to the other end of the sofa, and he suddenly burst out in a loud voice, "How do you like the fire?"

"I like it. I have never seen this fireplace used before."

His eyes were far away. "I made it just for you, Susan."

I answered very slowly. "Thank you, John."

Slumping down deeper into the sofa, he said, "I've had a stressful day."

"John, I'm sorry about that. Really. I've also had a stressful day." I laughed. "You wouldn't believe what the kids did today—" I stood up and flicked on one of the brass lamps. "Speaking of which, John, I need to get back to my meeting. Okay?"

He looked away, shaking his head. "Okay, but—" he looked

at me again. "Susan, are you promising me, then, that you will sing at my funeral?"

I sat down again. "John, please, this isn't making any sense. You're not . . . well, you're not thinking of taking your own life, are you? I mean, because of all the stress?"

He lowered his voice to a whisper. "No, not that. I'm just so . . . lonely, Susan."

He smiled weakly, as if he was trying to put on a brave front. "People think my life is so glamorous, you know. A good-looking pastor, best-selling author, traveling all over the world to speaking engagements, book signings and radio appearances. . . . But just between us—it's true what they say: it's lonely at the top."

"Yeah, I can just imagine. I'm sorry it's so hard right now, John. Are you going to be okay?"

"I'm going home to my family in a few moments. I'll be better then."

I reached for my purse. "That's good. That's really good, John." The faculty meeting was surely over by now and I had a five o'clock high-impact aerobics class.

His finger motioned back and forth, as he sat on the sofa, his shoulders hunched over, looking thin, his face unusually flushed. "You are my beloved, Susan. My friend—my only friend. We're kindred spirits, you and I."

As I slipped out the door, I passed Carol's office where she was typing, her back turned. I was overwhelmed—no person had ever needed me this much, relied on me to such an extent. I felt privileged and pursued—by an important man who really needed encouragement and solace from my friendship. But to sing at his funeral? I hoped that he was okay.

I whispered, "God, give me the wisdom I need to know what to say, how to be the friend John needs me to be."

At the deepest places within me, I knew that I wasn't nearly the friend John thought I was and I was aware of my divided heart. There was a deeper level that bothered me about John, his bizarre words and odd behavior. Were we really, as he said so often, kindred spirits? What did that actually mean? I was confused and seemed to be falling deeper into a numbed state.

Know Me as your Father, your loving Father. No man can take My place, no other power can save you.

At school I met Lily, a tall willowy young woman in her mid twenties. She was outspoken and glowed from within, exuding enthusiasm for life.

She often stopped by my flat in the evenings. She liked to drink the coffee I bought in Beijing and we'd munch on peanuts or orange slices, and talk. Sometimes I'd make dinner—a fish simmered in soy sauce, vinegar and scallions with fresh ginger slices. She enjoyed flipping through the magazines a friend sent me from America and we discussed fashion trends. Lily's mother was an expert tailor and could copy the clothing from pictures spread on the glossy pages.

Tonight Lily wanted to talk about something, I could tell. She was sitting on the gleaming hardwood floor, her long, lanky legs curled underneath her 6'1" frame. (Where did the stereotype of the short Chinese body get started?) Her velvet-black eyes traced the line of molding that followed the seam between the ceiling and the walls. "Susan? I am wondering about something."

I poured another cup of tea. "What's on your mind, Lily?"

"Well, I'm wondering what really happened on 6/4."

"6/4? You mean—in 1989?"

There was only one rule for us expats living in China: Never discuss the sad events of June 4, 1989—the Tiananmen Square Incident. That is one topic which is never up for discussion, all across this vast country. People only mention the subject in whispers behind closed doors, and only very rarely at that. Most Chinese citizens—under fear and duress—were required to sign statements declaring they supported the events of that tragic day. Teachers never mention it in classrooms; parents don't breathe a word of it in homes. It was a big scandal that rocked the world.

"What have you heard about it, Lily?"

She fingered her cup and saucer. "Well, I was so young then—when it happened—that I can't remember anything. And nobody would ever tell us what really happened."

I nodded, looking into those intelligent eyes.

"My parents tell me not to think so much and I know I should follow their advice, but then I start thinking again!" She laughed at her own words and there was a pause as she studied a photograph of Princess Diana on a yacht with her boyfriend, who had been killed three days after I arrived in Tianjin.

Lily looked up. "Can you tell me what happened, Susan? I know you will tell me the truth."

I could not tell her that Tianenmen Square had been filled with over 300,000 college students, engaged in a peaceful protest for democracy and that in a matter of forty minutes, just before dawn on June 4, a combination of tanks, armored cars, and troops with batons and guns "cleared the Square." I couldn't tell her that, in spite of official reports stating no protestors were killed, the Beijing Red Cross estimated 2,600 dead. I could not tell her of the reports that claimed a river of blood had flowed down Chang'an Boulevard that early morning, and that bullet holes in the concrete remain visible to this day. But I had a book on my shelf published just that year—a book that was banned in China, and one in which the actual story was graphically outlined: *Red China Blues: From Mao to Now* by Jan Wong. Ms. Wong, a reporter who has been banned from China, saw the events of that infamous day from her hotel room, and she watched the soldiers fire point-blank into crowds of idealistic and passionate college students.

I wrapped the book in a plain bag and handed it to Lily. "This might help to answer your questions, Lily."

She clutched the package close and promised she'd never tell anyone where she got it. After she left to bicycle home, I thought about the fact that Lily and I weren't all that different. Like most people, both of us were inching our way through the darkness in our paths and were, little by little, catching flashes of light, pieces of truth that were sometimes neon signs and sometimes whispers in our hearts.

Three weeks later she quit her job and moved to Beijing to begin work as a fashion model in runway shows.

A hand reaches for me surely and slowly, suffocating my breath and joy.

That Saturday morning I woke slowly, clasping my fingers with a special fragility, a fineness of some low emotion—almost as if I was straining to wake or yearning for the purity of sleep. It was a day of tall clouds, a gray November day.

I hurried off to a low-impact aerobics class, then showered and slipped into jeans and sweater before driving to church to catch up on paperwork. Surrounded by stacks of papers to grade, I looked up when the far door eased open. I expected to see Bruce, the maintenance man, who usually brought a news clipping or funny story to share, or perhaps Jim, who sometimes shuffled in wearing his black leather jacket and offering his curious philosophical views on life. But it was John—carrying his study Bible bulging with sermon notes. He usually rehearsed his sermons a few times before Sunday morning—to practice his vocal inflections and even plan physical gestures to specific detail.

"Hi," he breathed, sliding into one of the kid-sized chairs near my desk. "How are you?"

"I'm okay, John." I glanced at my desk. "My class was great this morning. We had Deborah."

He nodded, recognizing the name of one of his parishioners,

a favorite aerobics instructor in the valley. "Oh, that's great. She is amazing."

He was scanning the room, eyes moving from one bulletin board to the next, as if he was about to make a monumental decision. Finally he looked at me again. "Susan, can you come down to my office?"

There was an adolescent catch in his voice, something new in his eyes. I winced, thinking of my tendency to procrastinate. There was nothing I wanted more to do than spend this cloudy day getting caught up in my schoolwork. In fact, a darling little girl, one of my favorites, had asked me that week, with a tone of exasperation in her tiny voice, "Isn't your desk ever clean?"

"I'm so behind in my work. Can I see you next week?"

For an instant anger flashed across his smooth face. Then he sighed. "Well, okay. Go ahead and finish your work." Then in a teasing voice he added, "You're always behind, aren't you?"

I laughed. "Well as they say, a teacher's job is never done. I don't know, John. I love teaching; it's just the paperwork I don't like."

He laughed with me, then seemed to relax. "So, can't you take a half hour out of your day for me?"

There it was. The button, the click, the guilt.

He knew well this pattern of compulsion in my life. The inner tape in my brain played: "Never let the church down, never let your pastor down. He works so hard for God." Growing up as a minister's daughter, I had been taught to put the church first, no matter what, and John knew that. I exhaled slowly. "Okay, I'll come down, but just for thirty minutes, okay?"

He swallowed hard. "Great. I'll go first, okay?" This sounded odd, but when you trust a person, certain possibilities never enter your mind. He turned to face me, clutching his Bible, and spoke deliberately. "Can you come through the back door of my office this time?"

I paused, wondering what was different about him today. Accompanying his recent neediness was something that I didn't recognize. Use the back door? It was a strange request, but he was an eccentric person, I reasoned. Eccentric, but loving and godly. My safe friend. My only safe friend, I ruefully reminded myself.

As he turned to go, he said softly, "I love you, Susan." His voice cracked again and I smiled, thinking how dear and strange he was. So frail and vulnerable.

As I walked around the back of the church, through the educational annex and past the gymnasium, down the long corridor and in through the back door of his expansive study, a part of me did indeed have a sense that I needed to flee. I was being warned from deep within myself. I felt trepidation. Wisdom had been instilled in me when, as a young child, I accepted God and His divine wisdom into my life. But I was not ready for what I was to encounter—the power of darkness that can be found in the heart of a man who had lost his moral compass. That tragedy was about to become my scandal. I hadn't developed the boundaries I needed to protect myself from insidious manipulation. I had not yet learned to keep the back door of my life locked and safely closed to intruders who would steal my soul. I hadn't yet learned to listen to that inner voice, but I had most certainly learned to listen to Dr. John Travis.

Someday there will be those who will strive to catch you in their snares, in their plots.

𝒳u worked as one of the human resource specialists at my first school in China. One of the most amiable individuals I've ever met, Xu was serious yet always ready with a humorous twist on everyday life. He worked hard and he genuinely cared about each of the teachers on his staff.

When Xu was just starting middle school (equivalent to high school in America) the Red Guards were called by the

Great Helmsman himself to seek out all who showed "rightist" tendencies. Xu watched as his well-educated parents who were distinguished faculty members were tortured and humiliated by their university students, then sent off to separate remote labor camps to farm stones and rocks.

Xu remembers feeling as if he might never again see his humble, beloved parents who had done nothing wrong other than to provide a good education for their students. He stayed cowering alone in their ransacked home, hiding from the troops of angry Red Guards until he was finally discovered one cold night, crouching under the kitchen table. He, too, then was punished and sent off to work somewhere in the countryside. In fact, he had no clear idea of where he was. But there he stayed for three long years. He worked in the fields, under a blazing sun or in the freezing winters, subsisting on flavorless, clear soup and singing, around the campfire at night, songs written by the "Great Father and Mother," Chairman Mao and his wife.

He obediently memorized the Little Red Book, the only book allowed in China at that time, and wondered secretly where his parents had been taken and whether they were still alive. He passed sleepless nights, shivering on his wooden bunk and daydreaming of happy days in his childhood home. He longed to sit with his father, study English and science, or hear his sweet mother read to him.

When the nightmare and terror of the Cultural Revolution finally ended, Xu was reunited with his parents, now emotionally and physically broken by the years of "reeducation by the peasants." He was able to take a test, bypass middle school altogether, and enter university as a full-fledged student. Slowly, life improved.

He and his adorable wife own a nice, new apartment on the outskirts of town, near Mrs. Hua's. Their daughter is a typical middle-school student, wearing blue track suits and red neck scarf indicating that she is a Young Communist. They are appreciative of the fact that they have a shower with hot water in their home and don't need to use the public facilities, as most people do.

In times of unbearable pain, fear not; I am with you.

Once behind the locked and heavy doors of his office, John eased himself onto one of the two full-length couches, wiping the sweat from his face—even on this cool day with the sky filled with tall clouds, he was nervous.

He said, tremblingly, "Mind if I lie down, Susan? I've been under so much stress. . . . . Just look at my hands shaking."

They were indeed shaking. And they felt cold and clammy as he reached for mine. He pulled me into a kneeling position beside him on the floor, one I would become very accustomed to over the next three months. I remember thinking how strong he actually was—and how this physical strength, this sure and steady grasp was—in direct contradiction to his frequent references in and out of the pulpit to his weak health and susceptibility to illness.

He said, "I have a headache. I've been working too much again. This always happens when I don't take time for rest."

I suggested he close his eyes, then I clambered up to close the blinds.

He brightened at that idea. "Good thinking."

After darkening the room, I returned to his side, still unsuspecting of what would happen next. Opening his eyes, he looked at me intensely for a long time. It was almost as if he was trying to hypnotize me. I couldn't pull my eyes away from his gaze.

"Gorgeous Susan. That's my special word for you, you know. Do you remember that?"

I muttered something. I hated it when he called me gorgeous, a word I used to describe my beautiful mother. I knew I definitely was not the gorgeous one in my family.

"I remember. Yes, John. Now try to rest."

He suddenly raised his head close to mine. "Could I kiss you?" Without waiting for a response, he pressed his mouth hard against mine and I remember thinking, *This is not what I want. I don't like this. I don't want this.*

What happened next was what had happened with over fourteen women, later estimated at twenty-two women, I would discover. And it happened to me time and time again over the next few months, a few times each week. There was never a need for me to get undressed myself—it was all about John and his needs. I was coerced and manipulated into a darkened office, doing it for this needy man who was strong in all the ways he needed to be.

When it was over, he suddenly had more than enough energy and strength. He jumped up and reached for the telephone while I held a tissue to my mouth and waited awkwardly in front of his desk, wondering what to do.

He was talking to someone, but waved me aside, motioning to me that I should once again use the back door. I waited, though, until he was finished with his phone call.

There was a slight harshness in his tone. "Look, Susan, I'd love to chat for hours, but I have so much work to do."

"Er, uh . . . well, yeah, I understand. I don't have time to chat either. I wanted to stay and tell you that what happened just now was, uh, something I have never done before. I am not used to doing anything like that. I'm—"

"Oh, so it was real special to you, then, I see." He looked up briefly, a stack of letters in his hand.

I couldn't speak. I felt like I was falling off a high cliff. As he was looking through his sermon notes for the next day, he murmured, "May I call you 'Honey' now?"

"What?" I asked. This entire scene was the worst nightmare of my life! First so clinging and needy, now all business-like. I felt dizzy—falling and falling into a chasm, twisting, turning, spinning and tumbling, ever falling.

He set aside the papers, and turned to face me with a burst

of enthusiasm. "You are gonna love this, Susan. I want to do this for a long, long time. For years and years, even after you get remarried someday."

I started to cry. I hated to do it, but I couldn't help myself. I blurted out, "John, I've never done that before. I haven't even thought of doing that before. I don't know how it happened—"

"Susan, don't worry." He stood and reached to move a piece of my hair behind my ear. "There is nothing to be upset about. I love you, remember? I'm not using you and I promise I never will. This is about two people who love each other and know each other and are each other's safe, beloved friend. We're—"

"Yeah, I know. Kindred spirits."

His words gradually rang with more and more pastoral authority. He was seamlessly segueing into his ministerial role.

I felt humiliated, too numb to find words. I just stood there crying, watching him reach for the bottle of cologne he kept on the shelf behind his desk.

He laughed casually. "Now, Susan. I have to preach tomorrow. You need to get outta here."

I turned without a word and carefully left through his back door, feeling conspicuous. I trudged up the stairs to lock my classroom door, then in a dark mental haze, I drove home. The tall clouds had disappeared from the sky, perhaps snagged on a high ridge, snared by trees and shifted into shards. Scandal had stalked me, hunted me, and made me its victim. And a despoiled feeling overwhelmed my soul that would continue to pursue me half way around the world.

You will walk through a valley of death which will beckon you to its depths. Come to Me and repent. Only repentance will set you free.

I worked until sunset one night and as I walked home

to the Peace Apartments in the bitter cold, feeling sleepy and
worn out from the day, the lights along the street turned
on, one by one. Children, who had fallen asleep against their
mothers' backs while riding bicycles, were being awakened.
The knife sharpener, riding his tricycle, was calling out his
song. The teenager with Down's Syndrome stood behind the
screen door to his father's home, watching the gentle flow of
traffic. I always watched for him—tall and overweight—his
face swollen with pink pimples, nose pressed against the dusty
screen. He rarely ventured beyond the green door frame of his
father's one-room home.

I turned left onto a busier street, and was swallowed by
a crushing mob of people. I looked to see what the interest
was—expecting the usual quarrel or collision that always attracted
spectators. To my amazement, I saw a cage being hoisted from
a flatbed truck and carried into a popular restaurant. Literally
stuffed inside the cage was a beautiful baby panda bear.

I turned to an elderly couple beside me and asked, "They're
not going to cook the panda, are they?"

The woman smiled at me and shrugged. "Maybe."

Her husband, whose face resembled a crinkled paper bag,
muttered, "Of course not. It's against the law to eat panda bears."

I knew he was right, but after seeing the grilled bear paws at
the market, there was more than a slight doubt in my mind.

When the panda's cage disappeared inside the restaurant, the
crowd dispersed and I was surprised to see the owner of the
restaurant beckon to me in the upside-down gesture which in
China means "Come, come."

I responded by shaking my head. It was growing colder and
darker by the minute and I had to get some work done at
home. But the crowd kept pushing me—gently—through the
corridor that had been created and the restaurant owner smiled
and clapped, which in China signifies "Welcome!"

The very moment I stepped through the threshold, I was
blinded by a flash of cameras and a microphone was thrust into

my bewildered face. I squinted. A local television news reporter was asking me questions.

"Hello, what is your name? . . . Did you come to see the panda bear? . . . How long have you lived in Tianjin?"

I stumbled my way through the interview, but now I had a closer look at the poor panda bear quivering with fear, trying to hide itself from the noise, lights, and curious stares.

When I stopped at the corner again the following afternoon, the panda was no longer there. Nobody could tell me where it had been taken. When I asked, all I got was the Chinese shrug.

A few days later the restaurant owner motioned to me again, this time handing me a photograph—of the frightened baby panda bear, me, and the news reporter.

Sin brings death, My child.

I took two showers in an effort to remove the smell of John's cologne from my hair, then crawled between fresh, white sheets and tried to sleep. Something tender inside me had broken, something precious in my soul had split into pieces. There was a division of rightness and wrongness that had invaded my weeping heart. What had happened? How did it happen? I felt wretched to the core of my being. God seemed very far way. In fact, the hardest part of it all was that I couldn't find a way to approach the God whom I had known and loved. There seemed an urgent distance—as if my phone line to Him had been cut. It was like I could neither feel my own soul nor the One who made me.

That Saturday morning stamped itself upon my heart's memory. The damp autumn coolness of the fresh, clean air, the glazed hunger in John's eyes, waking up with a clear conscience but going to bed feeling scarred and broken beyond repair.

The next day was Thanksgiving Sunday. On most Sunday

mornings I was busy organizing and rehearsing music, participating in the worship team, and locking up the piano after three worship services. Today, however, was a special celebration involving elaborate costumes and a food contribution table. The Thanksgiving service, organized by John's creative wife, Nancy, had become a beloved tradition in our church.

Instead of sitting on the front pew as usual, I sat in the middle of the congregation, between friends, but feeling alone. As John confidently walked onto the platform, I worried that the events of the day before would somehow lessen the impact of his words and take away from the spiritual strength of his sermon.

I watched carefully and was relieved that nothing seemed out of the ordinary. John's mannerisms and charm were exactly the same. His eyes sought me out and finding me, his boyish grin broadened into a huge smile. I felt puzzled and confused. How could he hide his guilt so effectively? It didn't make sense.

I thought, *Perhaps he seems at ease because he knows the events of yesterday won't ever happen again. Yes, that's it. It won't ever happen again.* Surely that was why he could speak so eloquently and focus on spiritual things without any guilt. That was how he could look at me and wink—peaceful and in control of the situation. I began to breathe easier, realizing I could trust him after all. Or, at least I could trust part of him. John knew it was wrong and he was still a safe friend.

On that day I had no way of knowing that John had been through this scandal many times before. He had learned to wear his façade even to the point of making eye contact with a woman who felt guilt-ridden and isolated from the rest of the congregation. He was on comfortable, familiar ground.

His sermon was the same style as ever—a biblically-authentic message enthusiastically received. As the congregation filed through the glass doors at the rear of the sanctuary, most waited to shake John's hand or give him a quick hug. I waited in line. When I reached him and as he drew me in for a hug, I whispered through tears, "John. I'm so sorry."

He looked at me in surprise. "Why are you sorry? I loved it, Susan. And so will you, in time."

Appalled, I turned and followed the knots of people heading out to the parking lot.

I was aware that something serious had occurred within my spirit—something I barely understood, but which had life-and-death consequences. Gradually, an unseen but discernable gap opened a shuddering chasm between a holy God and my own soiled soul. I didn't know it then, but it was as if a storm window had been opened wide in my heart and the deep truths that I had known and loved were slipping into the wind. Like the autumn leaves, they were being blasted away, lost. A cold slumber began to take over my life that would freeze my spiritual character. It crept slowly in, almost unnoticed, and frosty enough to ice over the unspeakable secrets that would lurk in the darkest corners of my heart for years to come.

I am your Sustainer and Keeper. When you fall, I will be ready to pick you up again. My love for you will last forever.

This city was unbearably ugly and bitterly cold. There was no blue sky, no trees, no grass—only dirt and the incessant whistling of the workers. The yelling, hammering and yammering never stopped. Even in the darkness of the early hours I could hear them screaming shrill words up and down the walls and operating their noisy, antiquated lift. It ran all night, in screeching tones. *Do they ever sleep?* I wondered. The men lived in temporary sheds a few meters from my flimsy skyscraper apartment building. They didn't look as if they got any sleep. Neither did they look as if they ever took a bath or changed their clothes.

Sometimes a group of them were sent off for one reason or another and they rolled up their thin blankets, then stood waiting by a barrel fire. They rolled cheap cigarettes and waited for a dilapidated bus to rattle into the driveway to collect them. Then off they clattered back to their villages in the countryside.

Thin and gaunt they were, with stained, shapeless clothing and shaggy hair hanging on their chiseled brown faces. Sometimes I tried to look at them more closely in an effort to turn a blank stare into something resembling communication, but it was a struggle of wills—both theirs and mine. Looking into their hopeless eyes was painful.

I would rise before sunrise and shuffle into my little kitchen to brew coffee—a luxury from Beijing. I could feel their eyes watching me—the ubiquitous handful of workers from the roof just outside my window. And I mean just outside—inches away. I wondered to myself what sort of building codes they had here, if any?

I could feel their eyes watching me, wrapped as I was in my thick robe made by Mrs. Zhang from wonderful terry cloth sold in the fabric market. In a land where privacy is a foreign concept, within two short years I had almost given up my strong American sense of private space. I became so accustomed to the presence of the workers, it almost didn't bother me any longer.

So okay, I thought. *If they want to stand in the cold, watching me make coffee every morning, who cares?* I just turned away.

One particular morning, as I turned my back to the staring workers, the ugliness of the city angered me. I thought, *These people struggle to simply survive, to keep warm enough, to get to and from work. I love this country and I especially love this northern city, but it's a love / hate kind of thing. I despise the way the people cough out black globs of phlegm, especially in the winter when the coal is burning everywhere. I ache when I see students gathered around dim yellow streetlights, struggling to read their textbooks—and for what? To learn to say, 'How can I help you, Madam?' in English so they can work at dreary, cavernous train stations or jam-packed McDonalds taking orders from overweight foreigners? Perhaps they want to study their English in order to stand listlessly behind counters at one of the*

7-Eleven stores perched on every street corner in southern China? All things Western—things of the mind, things of the pocketbook, things of the heart—are all the rage here.

I took my coffee cup, filled to the brim with coffee (as strong as I could make it) back to the privacy of my bedroom and snuggled beneath my warmest quilt. I began jotting furiously in my journal, drafting a list (I love lists) entitled: Top Ten Things I Most Hate about China:

1. I hate the "nothing matters anyway" attitude that permeates everything around me . . . the falling bricks, the spittle in the streets, on restaurant floors, and even on gleaming new department store tiling. I hate having to pick my way around the spit, the annoying puddles of black or green or yellow piles of drying phlegm wherever I happen to be.

2. I hate having to organize my eating and elimination patterns to avoid the foul-smelling public toilets.

3. I hate having no access to medicine when I have a bladder infection or a sore throat.

4. And I *really hate* the donkey "private parts" stand *just* outside the front door of the Peace Apartments, where the cheerful worker is ready with her knife to slice off juicy pieces of the cooked delicacy, anxious to send me on my way with some fresh Private-Part-on-a-Stick to chew on.

5. I hate it that I can't see anything out my windows today. The cold has turned the world into a white land, and it's definitely not a winter wonderland.

6. I hate it that my Chinese tutor is so frail, that she lives in the tiniest apartment I've ever seen, that she has to climb eight flights of smelly stairs with mushrooms growing up along the sides of the stairwell, resembling some third-grade paper maché project gone awry. I hate that she has to dodge rats as large as cats and crunch on cockroaches on the way up to her tiny home where she lives with her well-educated, dignified husband—the president of the Foreign Language Institute—and her eight-year-old daughter, Hope. I hate it

that she arrives for my Mandarin lessons shivering in spite of her four layers of clothing, uncomplaining but determinedly proclaiming in her small voice, "I am thin but strong."

7. I hate it that Hope has no toys other than a collection of objects in a tattered shoebox under the bed she shares with both her parents—the same bed which serves as a place to sit while they eat dinner. The other night Hope showed me her beloved treasures, carefully reaching for her shoebox and lifting off the lid. There was a Barbie doll with scraggly blonde hair, wearing a ball gown of frayed pink polyester. Along with her Barbie, which she had named "Mary," she had several 3-D pastel paper stars. That was her entire toy collection.

8. I hate hearing the metal bars clatter against each other all night—metal clanking on metal—and the strident, piercing sounds that must be signals of something important, but which now simply exhaust me as I listen, night after long night, year after cold year.

9. I hate the river across from the driveway, just minutes from the Peace Apartments. I've watched it change through the seasons, from a stagnant polluted mess, brown and stinking, to a frozen "catch all" for garbage, including tires, plastic bags, and human waste.

10. I hate the smell in the elevator after the garbage is carted down.

Trust Me. I alone can heal and deliver.

No matter which door I used to exit John's office, I encountered people. The church facilities were enormous and bustling with a thriving senior center, a full academy, preschool, and women's groups meeting every day of the week. As I walked down the staircase leading from the pastoral staff complex, I noticed questioning looks from curious people.

One day a parishioner named Pattie stopped me on my exit from John's office. "Susan, why is it that I always see you coming from John's study? Why does he have so much time for you, yet I have been waiting to see him for two months?" I couldn't say anything, but my heart burned within me. I felt I had no escape out of the emotional trap destroying me inside.

I was experienced at protecting the man in the pulpit. A familiar black sorrow perched on my shoulder as once again I had to hide in corners, running from the truth and covering up.

As I walked back to my classroom that day, I thought, *Pattie is such a wonderful person. She would never allow herself to be caught in a situation like this. It's no wonder she's a happy wife and mother—she deserves it. I don't.*

To take your eyes off Me will lead you off the path.

9 decided to talk with my mom. We met at a restaurant in Sacramento and I told her what was going on. I asked for help, advice, whatever she could give me—even though I knew she was going through a lot in her own life. I was desperate to get help—and I was hoping she'd encourage me to move near her. I had been daydreaming of taking some time off from teaching and doing something different—maybe working in a restaurant and going to school. Mainly, I wanted to be close to my mom.

She listened to my story, as I tried to delicately explain to her what was happening. In response she shook her head sadly and said, "Well, Susan, pastors have special needs."

"What?" I thought surely I had misunderstood her.

"I'm not saying it's right or anything, but this is a compli-cated situation. He has no safe outlet for his needs. It's hard to understand why, but maybe God has put you in this situation to meet those. Don't be angry with him."

"Mom, it makes me angry for so many reasons. For one thing, he's not the person he pretends to be. Everyone trusts him; nobody knows what he's really like. Every time he preaches I can't help but think about the way he actually is—needy, whiny, complaining, and manipulative. I'm sorry to say it, Mom, but it's true. I wish I had known what he was doing—I trusted him. Now he's using me." It felt like a breath of fresh air to be able to tell her my feelings.

"All men get that way when their wives aren't paying enough attention to them, Susan. It might be that he's using you, yes, but the important thing is you can't allow yourself to be angry with your pastor. People who become angry or resentful with their pastors have a special punishment, you know."

"And what punishment is that?"

"I don't know exactly. When God calls men to be ministers He honors them in a special way. They are blessed and anointed for His service. You need to be very careful not to stir up trouble for John and his ministry. And don't forget, you need your job."

"I know, I know. I can't walk around telling people about what's going on, but I want so badly to be out of this situation."

"I'm sorry. Do you love him?"

I shook my head. "No. I mean, I love him as a friend and as a pastor—this is so weird, Mom. But as a man? Like, to marry? No. I don't. I can't. He's been so bizarre. He scares me sometimes."

She changed the focus of the conversation. "Ultimately, this is his wife's fault. She hasn't fulfilled her marital responsibility. She should have been meeting his needs and attending church, sitting on the front row every Sunday. I always did. Does she even come to church these days?"

"Not much. Well, she comes on Thanksgiving Sunday. She does the pilgrim service, you know."

"That's not enough."

My mother had been the daughter of an abusive man, also a minister. During the years his five children were growing up, he backslid, left the ministry, and tried farming. They were miserable years for his family. Later he returned to the Lord and to the pastoral ministry. But my mother had always had to tiptoe around her father as if in a minefield. And considering what she also had endured with my father, I guess I should have known better than to ask her for help. We changed the subject and I drove home with tears streaming down my face. I felt more isolated than ever.

Four months later Mom called and with tears choking her voice, said, "Susan, I have been thinking about your, um, your problem. I think John *is* using you. I think you should stop."

"I agree, Mom. I stopped a while ago."

I have given you a conscience. Listen to it.

*W*eeks passed and I began to think, *This church has fourteen full-time staff members. Surely there has to be someone I can talk with about this.*

I went through the list of pastors and analyzed which one would be safest to approach. I finally decided on Erik, the business administrator who had demonstrated an especially deep sensitivity to spiritual things. He was a man of prayer and depth, with a happy family.

I called him one night and was both surprised and relieved when he offered to meet me in his office, which was two doors down from John's. As soon as I sat down, the floodgates opened and I began to weep. This was very unusual behavior for me, and he was shocked, but kind. I was crying from both fear and relief, and I couldn't stop the tears. Every time I tried to get a word out, the tears poured again.

Erik was patient. "Susan, what is wrong? Do you need help?"

"I am so upset about something that is happening, Erik. I

don't know where to begin . . ."

"Just start at the beginning," he suggested.

"Right. Okay, I will. But, first—I have to ask something of you. Please give me your word that you will not tell John Travis that I came to you. It is extremely important—critical, even—that this conversation be confidential."

"Of course. You have my promise."

"Okay, well . . . some things have happened and are happening, and I need help."

"I'm listening. Go ahead."

Something stopped me from telling Erik that night. I was embarrassed and terrified of losing my job.

The fire will come and you will walk through it.

*T*he summer day had come to a full boil; the sky was bleached white with heat. I gripped the door handle of the car as the driver blissfully turned left without checking for oncoming traffic. I squeezed my eyes shut as usual and hoped for the best. When I opened them, he had a broad smile on his face and was calmly reaching for the glass jar balanced beside the gear shift, filled with tea leaves floating in warm water.

I looked at the windshield. There was a tiny statue of Chairman Mao that wobbled its head amiably as we dipped into each pothole. There was something that resembled a Chairman Mao Christmas ornament, swinging from the red looped braid that was hooked onto the dirty rearview mirror. And Chairman Mao smiled down upon us from near the ceiling from a sticker with frayed edges.

"So you like Chairman Mao, I see."

"Of course! I idolize Chairman Mao. He is god."

I had a headache. "He's god? Really?"

"Of course! All Chinese know this." He chuckled.

"But didn't he do many bad things?"

"Of course not. Well, some bad things happened, some people were killed. A few small mistakes."

I thought of the Great Leap Forward, just after Mao ordered all the citizens to collect and melt tools and utensils into steel, using their backyard furnaces. Never mind that the steel was useless; the steel quotas were met, and Chairman Mao was pleased.

Soon thereafter, the Chinese people were ordered to go out and kill every sparrow, as sparrows ate grain seeds, and because Mao was exporting grain to Russia, he wanted the grain quotas to increase. I guess nobody had the nerve to explain to the Great Helmsman that the sparrows ate not only grain seeds but also the insects that fed on the crops. The collective communes were turning out to be colossal errors, too. Farmers lost their motivation to work. It wasn't enough for them to "farm for the good of the whole" and the country was led into one of the worst famines in world history. For three years people starved to death.

Chairman Mao brushed it aside, proclaiming, "Deaths can be good for land. Natural fertilization."

From some of the hardest hit areas came reports of cannibalism. People resorted to eating their own dead family members.

Ouyang had told me about these events referred to as "China's shame." And I had been reading about the atrocities.

Now I gazed at the driver with puzzlement. "So how do you worship your god?" I asked, almost choking on the words.

He didn't catch the sarcasm. "Oh, I have been saving all my money to take my family—my parents and my wife and daughter and my wife's uncle and his family—to Chairman Mao's childhood home."

He seemed almost overcome with emotion at the thought and I pressed, "All your savings will be put into this trip?

"Of course! It's the trip of a lifetime, to Henan Province!"

I shook my head slightly. "Amazing. Simply amazing."

He beamed as he pulled up in front of Mrs. Hua's housing

development. "Yes, it is wonderful. I am very pleased. My lifelong dream is coming true at last."

Sometimes scandal happens because of innocence, sometimes because of ignorance, sometimes because of sin.

The weeping will feel like it's going to last forever, but it won't. There will be joy in the morning—because of My love, My grace.

*F*inally, after sobbing and stalling on my confession in Erik's office, I had told him, "I'm so sorry. I think I need a day or so to feel comfortable with this. Could we try this again sometime soon? Just give me a little time."

The following morning my classroom phone rang in the middle of a spelling test. It was John.

"I cannot believe what I just heard, Susan. Erik was in here and told me what you did last night. You came so close to telling him about us! What the hell do you think you're trying to do?"

I had never before heard John use such language—nor such an angry tone of voice. I was shocked and scared. Erik had betrayed me, in spite of his good intentions. If I had told him how I was being used and manipulated, maybe he would have felt compelled to go the congregational elders. But, instead, I think that he felt obligated to tell John that I had been so visibly upset. I looked at my darling fourth graders, their pencils poised and eyes watching me, waiting for the next dictation sentence.

I muttered, "Um—"

. "I am furious with you. If you ever try something like that again, Susan, I promise you—your job will be gone in a matter of minutes. You will be out of here. So don't even think of meeting with Erik again. Am I making myself perfectly clear?"

Tears stung my eyes. "Yes."

"Everything that happens in this church goes through me,

Susan. You have nowhere to go, nowhere to turn other than me."

"Okay, okay. I get it."

Click.

Now what I had feared was happening. My job was now in jeopardy. I could add blackmail, coercion, anger and profanity to the list of sins that were adding up in John Travis's life. And those were only the ones of which I was aware. How could a supposed godly man function like this? I felt ashamed, manipulated, and defiled. The worst part was that, deep down, I had lost my intimacy with God. My relationship with Him had been on such a comeback following the loss of my marriage. Now I was beginning to feel that my soul was being sucked into hell itself.

That afternoon, as I was heading out to my car, John caught up with me, looking as relaxed as he had been upset earlier.

"Hey, wanna wrestle?" His voice was back to its usual gentle tone. "Hey, Susan, I'm sorry I was so upset this morning. I was afraid you'd go off and do something foolish which would only hurt you in the long run."

"Yeah, I understand, John. I have aerobics in twenty minutes. I need to run."

"And . . ." He raised his voice. "I just got back from the doctor. She gave me another prescription for valium—so I'm relaxed now."

I stopped and looked closely at him. The glazed eyes, the slurred words, the euphoric smiles—I suddenly understood why he was so often in this altered state.

"John, how much valium do you take?"

"A lot. Too much. I know I shouldn't, but I can't go without it now. Paige—she's my doctor—" he winked, "understands me. And, sometimes I take other things." He laughed. "I bet you didn't know your senior pastor was a drug addict, did you?"

I stood staring at him, swallowing hard. "Um, no, I didn't, John. . . . You say Paige, your doctor, understands you? Would you consider her a kindred spirit, too?"

He looked surprised, but offered, "Yeah, Susan, I would. She's a lot like you, in fact. Very giving."

"I see. Does she attend church here?"

"Sometimes she does. I tell you what, I'll introduce you to her. She's a wonderful person; you'd like her."

"Mmm, I bet I would. Well, I gotta run. I don't want to get fat, you know."

He laughed. "No, let's not do that, shall we? I like you just the way you are. Go ahead, babe, sweat your heart out."

I unlocked the car door and climbed in. He leaned down and grabbed my arm. "But seriously, don't ever do that again, Susan. Remember—it's always the woman who gets the axe." He gestured with his hand, pretending to cut off my head, then laughed boyishly.

"But—I promise you, Susan—I will never tell anyone about you. Do you believe me?"

There it was. That question again. I drove off in the dusk, calling out the window, "Yes, John, I believe you."

As I lost myself in aerobics, the realization hit me. "Hey, I was the one in control just now—not John." That simple fact felt like a wave of oxygen, the smallest bit of space that might, just might give me a chance to catch my breath and muster hope.

When I crossed paths with Erik the next day, I stopped him and said, "I trusted you, Erik."

He looked at me with anguish in his eyes. "I know. I'm sorry, Susan. I'm really sorry."

I have never been one to hold a grudge or become angry, but this time I was very upset. I simply looked at him and kept walking without another word. He sighed heavily and continued on to his office.

It was at that point, while still in the midst of my sin and scandal, that I began to pray. I squarely brought it to God. In a posture of prayer, I asked with all my heart that someone would find out what was going on. There was nowhere to turn; nobody I could tell. I was fearful of losing my job—a particularly effective trick Satan was playing on me. Somehow, I was convinced

I would lose my life if I lost my job. But I could not go
on doing this with my pastor. I needed a miracle, I needed
God to intervene and step in and rescue me. I felt trapped. I
felt confused. I would stand on the playground, watching my
students climb the jungle gym or shoot baskets. Then I'd look
up at the hills edging the narrow San Ramon valley and whisper,
"Please help me, Father. No one but You can rescue me."

*Do not venture from My will, child. Doing so will take you into the
pit of despair. It brings one thing—death.*

*E*very morning—just before staff devotions—John either
slipped into the back door of my classroom or called me on the
direct line that ran from his study to my classroom.

"Ask Carol if you can have ten minutes with me today, okay,
Susan?"

Because he was the "boss" he had complete access to my
schedule. Just as recess was beginning, he'd call, reminding me to
"stop by" for a visit.

Carol was always gracious and professional, and as John
sauntered into her office at the precisely arranged moment, his
face registering surprise at my "request" to see him, he'd smile
and lean over her desk, asking winsomely, "Carol, I can spare a
little time, can't I?"

One day, however, Carol lost her cool and spoke sharply.
"Susan, John does have to preach on Sunday, you know."

I said, "This isn't my idea, believe me—" but before I could
finish the sentence, she turned to gaze silently out her window.

That day I asked John about Carol. "What does Carol think,
John? Have you considered how this might look to her?"

He laughed in his confident, casual manner. "Oh, no worries.
I tell her you are really screwed up and need lots of counseling."

"John, I've known Carol longer than I've known you. I don't think it's fair of you to tell her that."

He progressed into his speech about our being "kindred spirits" and "safe friends." I simply, yet bitterly, and with anger seething through me went ahead with the routine, sexually servicing my pastor, but realizing that poor Carol was actually being used to unknowingly guard our scandalous privacy.

My child, someday you will see that the world is far bigger than you understand it to be. I will become larger as you mature and you will return to Me. Then you will honor Me in your thoughts and in all you do. I will help you. I will be with you.

The Christmas holidays passed in a blur. In addition to my new "responsibility" of servicing the senior pastor's sexual needs, I had purchased a townhouse that needed painting, wallpapering, and tiling. (My father had taught me through the years how to work on houses. He had owned over thirty homes and my two brothers and I were pretty good at hunkering down to do whatever needed to be done.) I also wanted to date someone, someone sincere and honest, without any baggage as I couldn't handle anything else but a nice, low-pressure friendship.

"John, I'm single and time is ticking by. I need to date good Christian men and get married while I can still have a child."

He was quiet, his head silently shaking no.

I fidgeted with the book I held. "So, you understand, right?"

"Who did you have in mind, Susan?"

"Well, you do know Bill Tyndall?"

He laughed. "Of course I know Bill. I'm his pastor."

"Yeah, right. Well, he asked me to have dinner on Saturday night, and I—"

"And you want to go?" John bit his lip and burrowed back

into the cushions of his favorite sofa.

"Well, yes, I do. I think he's a nice man. Don't you?"

"Susan, look, I knew this day would come sooner or later.
And I can't supervise every date you go on. I also can't try to stop
you from seeing other men, but when a concern arises, I would
be remiss—as your spiritual shepherd—not to warn you."

I sighed. "So, what is it, John? Is there something about Bill I
don't know? He just seems like a really nice guy."

He took his time telling me his concerns. Apparently, Bill
had been living with a woman until just a few months earlier.
She had dumped him when he lost his business, and he was on
the rebound.

"John, I'm not saying I want to marry Bill. He's talking about
a date to San Francisco—dinner at an Italian restaurant, followed
by one of the best plays out right now. It sounds like fun. When
you're spending the weekends with your family, I am home alone,
you know."

He nodded sympathetically. "I know, and I wish things
were different. But you need to be careful. You could easily
fall in love. You're very vulnerable right now. I worry about
you all the time, Susan. You need to marry a strong spiritual
leader. Do you honestly see Bill Tyndall being that for you? A
spiritual leader?"

I was thinking, *And do you feel you exemplify strong spiritual
leadership, John?* But I sighed and said, "Well, maybe not. At least
not at this stage. I mean, I've barely said hello to him."

"Susan, let's make a deal. You can feel free to go out with
anyone you want to, but promise me one thing. Okay?"

"Okay. What?"

"Do you promise me that you will tell me about every single
man you date? Even if it's only one date?"

Bill and I had a great time that Saturday night. He was a
complete gentleman, and continued to be so for the next six or
so dates. He was also hungry to know God, loved church, and
respected and admired Dr. John Travis.

One night we met after work for dinner and he was beaming from ear to ear. "Susan, you'll never guess who phoned me today! Dr. Travis!"

In a church of almost twenty-two hundred members, getting a personal phone call from the senior pastor wasn't an everyday event. Bill was amazed. I braced myself and muttered, "Uh-huh."

His green eyes were bright. "And guess what?"

"I can't imagine. Tell me."

"He wants to go on a double-date. He and his wife—what's her name? Denise? Karen?"

"Nancy." Since she so rarely came to church, most people had no idea who she was.

"Yeah. Well, anyway, I went ahead and agreed because I know you and the Travis family are great friends. So we're going to a movie tomorrow night; is that okay with you?"

I nodded. "Sure, Bill. That's fine."

He watched me pick at my Caesar salad and asked, "What's wrong? Did I do the wrong thing?"

"No, nothing's wrong, Bill. It's fine—perfect. Let's talk about something else for a while, okay?"

We did go to a mediocre movie the next evening and out to dinner, but the conversation between the four of us was forced and strained. As Bill dropped me off, he said, "That was a very strange evening, Susan. I expected it to be different, you know? Socializing with such a fantastic, rather famous person and all. But Dr. John is very protective of you, isn't he?"

I sighed. "Yes, he appears to be, Bill. I'm sorry you didn't have a great time."

He didn't ask me out again, of course.

The heart is deceitful above all things and beyond cure. Who can understand it?

$\mathcal{A}$s the months in China slowly passed, I began realizing that, though I came to Asia to teach, it was I who was being taught. The lessons were plentiful, commencing every time I stepped outside the Peace Apartments and continuing until I laid my head on my pillow to sleep at night. There was an entire world of new friends to share and teach me all they knew.

One friend, named Apple, was a special gift to me in China, a sister in the faith, young enough to be my daughter. For six years we shared dreams, heartaches, and stories. Apple had grown up in a close-knit, loving family in the most populous city in the world. When Apple's parents realized they were expecting their second child, her mother was forced to hide within their humble home during her pregnancy. Her father, a traditional herbalist, was forced to undergo sterilization.

Before she died of tuberculosis, Apple's mother had sewn all her clothes by hand, and even made her shoes from thick layers of bamboo. There wasn't much money in their household, but there was usually enough to buy food. Her favorite meal was eggs, tomatoes and green peppers or sliced eggplant stir-fried in ginger, garlic and oil.

Apple and her friends played outside together every day after school, simple games in the dirt with sticks and small rocks.

Both of her grandmothers had bound feet and Apple remembers them spending two hours each day on their feet—unwrapping, bathing, peeling and scraping off dead skin, then rewrapping. The women had become accustomed to the pain of feet that had been broken many times over again, since they were eight years old, the bones literally folded over to resemble "golden lilies" and to give them a "marriageable" status. By the time they were old, they welcomed the warmth their tightly-bound feet provided in cold winters. They weren't able to walk—but neither could most women in China at that time. They stumbled—limping and swaying precariously—and stayed close to the home.

Apple grew up and moved to the big city to be near her

older brother. There she learned English on her own—without taking one formal class—and later became fluent in both French and Italian. These days she's learning Spanish from the BBC language site via her home computer. She's also started to take piano lessons and has bought a traditional Chinese instrument to learn her own way—on her own.

She rises early in the morning to join the ballroom dancers that meet in the park across the street. Nothing seems to stop her—nothing discourages her. She keeps her brain busy and challenged, meeting friends for coffee, babysitting her niece, and going to anything interesting around the city—museum openings, flower shows, rock concerts. She has very little in terms of material possessions, preferring to save her money for travel and study. She flew to France for a summer a few years ago—with money saved from giving massages to expatriates (with whom she practices languages).

I asked her, "Apple, how did you manage to find your way around France?"

She laughed and explained in her thick, Sichaun accent, "Well, I was usually studying, but one day I had some free time in Nice. I prayed, 'God, what should I do with this time?' I listened to God and I then knew in my heart that I should get on this bus. So I did. And I prayed, 'Dear Lord, please let me know when to get off the bus.' And after a while, I could feel God telling me it was the right time to get off the bus. So I did. I looked around and right across the street was a little shop that sold only Bibles! So I ran across the street and I looked for a Bible in French. But they were all too expensive. I was so sad. The store person said, 'You are the first customer I've had from China, so I will give you a Bible. Pick any Bible you choose.' I said, 'Oh, no, I cannot possibly accept such a gift.' But he said he knew God wanted him to give me a Bible. And then he gave me two Bibles. One very big French Bible to have in my home and a small one to keep with me all the time. I praised God, because now I can share the love of the Lord with my French clients and all my clients!"

I wondered silently how she felt as the plane landed back in a gray city, murky with pollution. After her summer in France, she returned to Guangzhou with a tan from the French Riviera and dreams of sunlit days on perfect beaches. But after a time she adjusted to the life she once knew and was glad to be home.

When Apple comes to my home, she brings sunshine inside. She breezes in and exclaims, "It's a beautiful day! Look at all that God has given us!" She never complains. She never criticizes or speaks negatively of anyone.

She is grateful for all she has, ensconced as she is in a humble sixth-floor flat. As she smoothes out my tensions, she shares her life and laughter with me. We have tea, listen to music, and pray together.

My child, turn your heart to Me. I know you intimately and love you.

Each February, when the air was still cold enough to sting and the mountain ridge was dark, our church hosted a New Life Conference. That particular year the topic was—not coincidentally, I believe—sin. I slunk into the services each night, as far from John as I could get. He was in his place near the front, wearing his casual sweaters, clapping his hands to the music and taking detailed notes during the messages—nodding vigorously in agreement with the speaker. John was such a dominant presence wherever he went; his broad shoulders and athletic build presented a picture of discipline. He liked to maintain this image for several reasons, mostly because he thought it indicated his spiritual desire to keep the faith, to hang in when things got tough. People everywhere looked up to him, impressed with the grand image he had carefully honed—the all-American, Iowa-born farm boy that everyone loved and trusted. He wanted to be a big kid—casual, fun-loving and supremely at ease in all situations. He had worked with a personal promotion agency to fine tune his speaking and physical appearances. Nothing about Dr. John Travis was haphazard or unplanned.

I did not want to miss a single night of the conference. It was a relief to hear another person present God's Word; my heart was hungry. This time I wouldn't have to sit "at John's feet" listening to his smooth, rehearsed style and act as if I was spiritually moved.

The New Life Conference speaker wasn't smooth—he was rough and simple. His words weren't rehearsed, his gestures weren't programmed, and his voice was grating, even gravelly.

He said, "Sin is awful. It makes the whole earth groan. Every time we sin, we hurt not only ourselves, but the entire world. It is not to be overlooked or taken lightly, people. Sin causes serious damage."

I sat alone, my Bible opened, and as this gifted professor from a Christian university taught us, I was moving from one passage to the next, as if the Holy Spirit was seated beside me, guiding my thoughts and opening my ears to His still, small voice.

Something was clicking. God was working and it was like sitting in the arms of my best friend again. I shed silent tears, watching them splash onto the pages of my old, worn Bible. The truth was being spoken and it wasn't particularly comfortable hearing it, but I was hanging on every word and God was helping me to match each point up with Scripture. I could suddenly see that, in only three short months, my life had become a scandal of awful proportions.

After four evenings of simple teaching from a humble profes-sor with smudged glasses and scuffed shoes, it was clear to me: I had to permanently stop sneaking around with John—squeezing moments here and there, trying to gratify his needs and keep him happy. I could see that it was not my job, not my responsibility to gratify my pastor's "needs." In fact, I could see that it was in blatant defiance against God. In spite of John's assurances, I knew without a doubt that what we were doing was ignoring God's laws. I had learned that all sin had a ripple effect that was already hard at work within the life of this church and that it wouldn't stop until it had destroyed people's lives and marriages.

There was no question about it—John and I would have to stop sinning. The conference ended, and the next time I was summoned to John's office, I was prepared to deal with the problem once and for all. I was through being used and manipulated—made the victim of his desires.

I sat down. "John, I am actually glad you called me in today because I really need to talk with you."

He looked at me with sincerity. "Go ahead, Susan. You know you can tell me anything. I'm all ears."

"Well, I am teaching my students about heaven right now and all I can think about is: What will God, my Judge, say to me someday?"

He smiled calmly and leaned back into the plump cushions. "Susan, He'll say, 'Come in, come in. . . .' Susan, would I try to lead you astray? Think about it. You are one of my lambs. I have been entrusted as your Shepherd. I would never try to harm your spiritual walk with Christ—you know that."

I sat upright. "John, um . . . thank you for your kind words, but we can't do this anymore. It is wrong. I can't do it anymore. It's unfair to me, to you, to your family, and to this church. It is sin. We are breaking God's commandment."

He smiled sleepily. "Susan, I'm so proud of you. You are such a passionate woman. In fact, you amaze me with your heart for God." He leaned over and touched my face. "And that's why I'm in love with you."

We had used our bit of time in conversation, and I needed to collect my class from recess. I left feeling frustrated and angry.

The next time, I brought notes written out on index cards. "John, okay. Please listen to me. I need to talk with you about something that's really bothering me. Have you thought about the fact that you are the only one of us that is receiving pleasure from this relationship? I mean, I have spent three months basically meeting your needs . . . and, well, frankly, it is a very one-sided relationship."

This new concept seemed to stump him.

He sat back, momentarily speechless and then slowly said, "I know, I know. It's hard to be patient, isn't it? I understand that better than anyone, Susan. We'll do more someday, I promise . . . when we're married." He seemed to have found a solution to the problem and he sat up once again, strengthened by the thought. "We will get married and then there will be nothing we can't do, nothing to stop us. As long as you promise to keep giving to me so unselfishly . . . can you promise me that?"

"But John, when do you think we will be able to get married? I mean, do you even love me in that way?"

His eyes widened in disbelief. "Love you? Of course I love you! Would I be allowing you to give to me if I didn't love you?"

"But . . . but—"

"Look, Susan. I can't control the actions of God. The way Nancy eats, I think she may kill herself with food. Maybe then we can get married."

This was ridiculous and I knew it. I didn't want anyone to die so that I could then marry their husband. I added, "Another thing: What if someone should walk in here, while we're . . . while I'm—"

"Won't happen." He reached over to stroke my hair. "I will always check to make sure the door is locked, Susan. Now, can we please stop this nonsense and get back to having some fun? I am so tense today."

"Not yet, John. Another thing I have to discuss is the fact that what we're doing is sinful."

"Sinful?" He laughed. "I think I might know just a tad more about theology than you. Of course, I only have a doctorate from Oxford, and you took . . . well, let me think . . . what was that course? Old Testament 101?"

He was clearly very amused and I was exasperated.

"Okay, John, I know what you say about God's unconditional mercy and extravagant grace, but that doesn't mean that we can go through life doing exactly as we please."

"Susan, listen to me. We are only human beings. It is not our place to try to step into God's shoes and figure these things out. Only God understands His divine grace and it's a useless exercise for us to try to depend on our limited comprehension." John's voice had suddenly taken on his more authoritative tone.

I hung my head, struggling to find the words I needed so badly. John moved closer to me, speaking in a softer manner. "Susan. You have enough on your shoulders as it is. You have your parents to worry about. You told me yourself your mother is living in a renovated chicken coop, isn't that right? And your dad lives with rats in a ghetto basement."

Tears began to seep out the corners of my eyes. "Yes, that is true. All of that is true."

"And your job is critical to your survival, to your parents' survival. Without your job, how could you help your parents?"

I looked up, clumsily wiping my nose. "My job?"

He smiled tenderly. "Yes. You really need this job, don't you?"

"Of course I need it. You know that. But I wasn't talking about my job."

"Susan, everything about us is about your job. Isn't it?" He moved closer and kissed the corner of my mouth, whispering, "I'll see you at morning recess tomorrow, teacher."

No matter what happens, I am with you. You may not sense My holy presence, but I am there.

Near the end of the day on a sweltering June afternoon in Asia I wore a thin cotton sundress because my air conditioning was only marginally functioning. I was fantasizing about Thanksgiving . . . about antique china, starched and pressed damask, creamy linen napkins fitted through sprigs of dried Eucalyptus leaves. In my mind I saw the buttered turkey, I mixed my special dressing with apricots, raisins, and pecans, roasted red and yellow peppers on the grill, mashed potatoes with chopped garlic.

I imagined the crisp autumn colors in Northern California—the golds and burnt creams with dashes of peacock and tangerine. I remembered the sweetness of blowing out the last candle after the guests had reluctantly left for the evening or had retired to the guest bedrooms. I could picture myself sinking into my sofa and gazing at the last flickers of flame in the fireplace, still crackling out a story of the day.

I wanted Thanksgiving. I wanted seasons with falling leaves, mint green hills, and clear skies dotted with cotton-wool clouds.

Since I was not in America on that hot summer afternoon in Asia, I walked to the small park across the street. Under shade trees older women were sitting and chatting. I wondered what secrets they were telling and what secrets they weren't telling. They were the age of those who survived the Cultural Revolution; memories must have haunted their dreams. The past had etched its story into their eyes and their faces were carved with a horrifying history. I wanted to ask them if they had almost starved during the Great Famine of 1958-1961 and how they managed to feed their children during the three and a half years of collective kitchens. I wanted to ask them how the long stretch of eerie isolation had taken its toll on their families and education and personal goals. But I didn't. I silently wished them peace and health. I spoke short, kind phrases when I passed them, nodding slightly in respect. The sight of them always cheered me.

I had my daydreams; they had theirs. We lived under the same polluted skies, and for that short time our lives intersected. Although I would not be in Asia forever, part of me would always remain here, and my being had absorbed much of their thinking, their history.

All this made me wonder at the mystery of life . . . on that sweltering June afternoon, while I wished I could be making a Thanksgiving feast for friends and family.

'Jesus loves you, children,' our Sunday school teacher told us. 'He desires to speak to you and guide you. It is important to listen, no matter how loud the world around you becomes.'

John's personality was changing. Besides being more demanding than ever, he thought almost obsessively about his upcoming sabbatical. His thoughts were rambling, running from his list of financial donors to his upcoming hair transplant. Emotionally, he was covering the gamut—moving from elation as he studied brochures on health resorts in foreign countries to agitation with his staff. He was nervous about his booking as the featured speaker at Chuck Swindoll's church family camp; and he was consumed with his newest book, to be published by a large Christian publishing house. He was making plans to sign books at the annual Christian Bookseller's Convention in Orlando and was also writing reviews of other authors' books. Things couldn't be going better for him and the possibility that he would become famous was paramount in his mind.

'Only trust Him. Only trust Him. Trust in Jesus now. He will save you, He will help you. Only trust Him now.'

Not long after the New Life Conference and my attempts to explain my conviction of sin, John called me on the phone to ask me to stop by.

I said no.

Within ten minutes he was standing in the back of my classroom, temporarily empty of students who were playing basketball in the gym. His face was a boiled tomato.

"What did you mean by that, Susan?"

I looked up from writing on the whiteboard and said, "I meant what I said. No."

"But what am I going to do?"

"I don't know, John. I only know I can no longer engage in that particular activity. Three months of that was three months too long."

The tomato was beginning to steam, ready to burst as he thought for a moment. Then he tried a different approach. "Well, okay, but you'll have to make up for it tomorrow, Susan."

I began to notice a few things in the people around me. I was standing outside supervising my students at recess one day and noticed Diana—a lovely young mother and brand-new Christian—waiting outside John's balcony area. She was pacing back and forth, staring up at his windows, which were covered by blinds. Occasionally, she stood on tip-toes, trying to peer inside the windows. It was uncharacteristic behavior for her.

The next Sunday morning I glanced at her during the worship service, which was easy to do from my place at the piano. She was sobbing.

Another morning I pulled into the church parking lot before 5:30 a.m. and was surprised to see John's office lights on. I waited in the car a few moments and was even more surprised to see Jodi—an elder in the church—come out of the front office with him. She was laughing and holding his hand. As I watched, John reached over to kiss her cheek and wave good-bye. Then I saw shock register on his face when he turned and saw me.

"What are you doing here so early, Susan?" His voice was thin and shaky.

"I have a few things to get caught up on. Are you seeing Jodi, too, John?"

"Of course not. Well, not in the same way as seeing you,

that is. She is a leader in the church, as you know, and we have a lot to discuss."

"I see." I tried to make my voice sound nonchalant. But I wondered just how many other "kindred spirits" John had.

John's anticipated sabbatical was rapidly approaching. Wealthy church members were contacted and asked for generous contributions, an enormous banquet was being planned, and John was busily making reservations and plans. He continued to ask me to visit his study—not nearly as often as before—but I continued to decline. And he was becoming furious with me, to the point where daily routine became almost agonizing.

I had a hard time sleeping at night, due to his inevitable phone calls. He wanted to discuss my "attitude problem." Once he had the operator break in on my phone conversation, pleased with his cleverness. "I told her I was your pastor and there was an emergency," he boasted, "and guess what the emergency is?"

Another time I was returning home from a dinner out with my brother and he was waiting for me at my townhouse complex. When he saw me driving in, he went to a phone booth and called just as I unlocked the door, using some of the foulest language I had ever heard in my life.

"First, I wait for two _____ hours, driving around and around your stupid parking lot. I don't even know which apartment is yours. What the _____ are you trying to do to me? Where have you been, anyway?"

"Out with my brother Steve."

"I doubt it. You probably had a date or maybe you had another meeting with Erik."

"John, that's ridiculous. Please leave me alone. I haven't been on a date and I certainly haven't been talking to Erik."

He had recently preached a sermon about being a "three a.m. Christian," meaning the type of friend someone could call at three o'clock in the morning, with any sort of problem, a person to encourage someone in the middle of the night. The sermon had been well received, as all of them were, and people had begun using the phrase, "three a.m. Christian."

I was expected, of course, to be John's special "three a.m. Christian," particularly when he ran out of his medication. His behavior changed then, and he regularly insulted me in nightly phone calls. After my repeated promises "not to tell," he calmed down, ending with the inevitable sequence of questions.

"What's my special word for you, Susan?"

By this time I'd be half asleep, barely listening, and the answer was automatic, "Gorgeous."

"That's right, Susan. Do you believe me?"

Again, the robotic response: "Yes."

"Are you sure you believe me?"

"Yes." I knew then that the conversation was finally reaching its end and he'd have a burst of sudden energy, his voice returning to his pastoral warmth. "Okay. Good night, Susan. Have a good sleep."

I'd hang up the phone, glance at the alarm clock, and groan. And as his sabbatical drew closer, the phone calls kept increasing—coming every thirty minutes or so. He seemed terrified he would lose control over me; that I would ruin his sabbatical and "tell" someone.

Finally, one night I asked him, "John, why do you think I'm going to tell someone about this?"

"Well, you aren't giving to me anymore, for one thing. That makes me nervous. And your recent behavior reminds me of Skye. You remember Skye, right?"

I thought quickly, then said, "You mean Skye Miller?" A vivid visual memory of Skye Miller sitting on the third row in church came to mind. I could see her clearly—sobbing every Sunday morning, her face red and swollen.

John said, "Yes, Skye Miller."

I cried, "She is just a teenager, isn't she? Didn't she just go to college last year?"

"Yes, and when she arrived she told her college counselor some things about me."

I suddenly felt pity for that poor girl. "What kind of things?"

"Oh, things about me. Things that happened. Nothing like what has happened between you and me, though. Just a little kiss here and there. No big deal."

I remembered having seen her sitting in her mother's car in the church parking lot, crying and hunched over the steering wheel. "Did she fall in love with you?"

"Yeah, she did. But women fall in love with me all the time. I'm irresistible, you know." He laughed.

"Mmm . . . I wonder how she's doing now . . . Skye?"

"Fine, I suppose. She's young. She'll get over it. The point is, Susan, it almost ruined my life! The counselor called me and I had to promise her I wouldn't do it again."

"I see."

I am the Helper, the Counselor, and always will be.

The Friendship Store was four blocks from the Peace Apartments. When I had traveled through China in 1980, we had shopped in Friendship Stores under dim fluorescent lighting, buying tea sets, silk, and chopsticks. In 1997, the Tianjin Friendship Store was in a six-story complex and carried electronics, Japanese goods, and exquisite Chinese artwork. I'd go there on Sunday afternoons, along with hundreds of Chinese families enjoying their day off. The first-floor lounge had a concert grand piano where students of classical music performed on weekends. I often sat at a table with my journal and a cup of "white" coffee.

At that time, finding deodorant in Tianjin was impossible. I decided to search for it at the Friendship Store—they'd carry it, if any store did. I paced along the entire wall of skin-whitening creams, shampoos and conditioners. The clerks must have wondered what I could be looking for.

One clerk approached me. "Madam, please to help you?"

I thought about it. This would be a difficult concept to explain, but I decided to take my chances. "I am looking for deodorant."

Her thin, penciled eyebrows pressed together quizzically. "Deodorant? What deodorant?"

I tried to explain using words, then reverted to the usual game of charades. I mimicked the act of applying roll-on deodorant to my underarms, as her eyes widened.

"Oh, you talk about something, some product which you put on your body before you shower?" she asked.

I sighed. "Not really. It goes on after a shower."

Her eyes scrunched together in deep thought. "And after shower you wash off, yes?"

"No, actually, you leave it on all day, until the next shower."

She was quiet, trying to digest these strange Western habits. "Why? Why leave on?"

"Because," I said, slightly embarrassed, "of the smell. You know that smell on the underarm area? The deodorant stops the bad smell."

Her eyes widened further. "Oh, *that* smell. Yes, I know the foxy odor smell. But, I only have a little smell."

I smiled reassuringly. "I'm sure you have only a little smell, nothing to worry about."

She sniffed the air around us both. "You no have foxy smell, Madam."

"That's because I use deodorant product after every shower."

She lifted one of her thin arms, revealing a mass of black hair, and sniffed, then smiled. "Only very little foxy smell."

I laughed with her. "Don't worry about it. Many Americans like to use deodorant to prevent—to stop—the foxy smells from coming."

She nodded thoughtfully. "I see. But, I think . . ." here she dipped her head closer to my own armpit. "I don't smell any bad smell on you, either, Madam."

"That's because I use deodorant. Does your store plan to carry such a product?" I asked again hopefully, now that we both understood the issue at hand. She lowered her eyes and shook her head. "No such thing in China. But maybe someday!"

Indeed, the product wasn't available at the time but in three years would be found on shelves throughout China. And even seven years later, there were continuous television commercials, teaching the Chinese citizens exactly how to apply deodorant products. The little clerk was right—the product wasn't available at the time, but it certainly would be at a later time.

When I checked out that day, she shyly asked me, "Madam, when you get some deodorant from America, would you get me some? For my little foxy smell."

I promised I'd bring her some deodorant soon . . . and I did.

Lies in the dark; secrets echo off the hidden corridors leading to hell.

"*W*hy are you here?"

I was sipping fragrant green tea. "Huh? Why am I here?"

Ouyang chuckled. "Yes, that is my question. Why did you come to China?"

We had stepped into a small restaurant on a corner where we often walked. It was located at the top of a poorly-lit stairwell, with an aluminum Christmas tree perched precariously on the squat wooden box next to the door. Across from the Christmas tree was a fat, white chicken living in a too-small cage. Beside that was a tank crammed full with clumps of long, slimy-looking eels. The dining room was the size of a bedroom in America, with six tables, three lined up on either side. The waitress brought the beef and onions I ordered. Ouyang ordered an enormous meal: eels sautéed with eggplant, braised beef with potatoes, sour green beans stir-fried in spicy chili oil, steamed spare ribs wrapped in lotus leaves, and bitter melon and rice.

I ignored his question. "You are the only person I've met in Tianjin who eats with their mouth closed, Ouyang."

He swallowed then laughed. "Is that a compliment?"

I widened my eyes in exaggerated response. "Most definitely."

"So, why are you here? I mean, you don't really like the manners of the Chinese people. You hate the spitting and the dirt and the stands selling donkey private parts. You want to be married someday, but you know that China is not a good place for you to find a partner. The cultures are too different."

I bit my lower lip. "Yes, they are different. Probably too different. But I'm not quite ready to be married anyway."

He stared at me for a moment. "You better hurry up and get ready! Your life is halfway over and you still don't have a husband or a baby."

I grimaced. "I know. I need to start getting more serious about that, I suppose. I came here to . . . well, I came to teach."

My friend knew me too well. "No, you didn't."

"Well, partly. I mean, without the teaching job I wouldn't have come, right?"

"Right. But, you enjoy life in California, don't you? It's clean. The air is not such a grimy dust bowl like Tianjin."

I laughed. "Yes, it is beautiful. I love California, especially San Francisco."

He leaned closer over the food. "So why did you come? Really, why do you think you are here in this exotic, dirty place?"

I stopped and stared at my plate. "I think . . . Well, I guess you could say I am running away."

The waitresses smiled at me—four of them for six small tables. I neurotically imagined that they had understood my English and suddenly felt vulnerable.

Ouyang fished for a hot red chili buried in the beans. "Yes, you are right. You are running away."

I attempted to change the subject. "Ouyang, this beef is so

fatty. It's probably forty percent meat and sixty percent fat."

He nodded. "Tianjin people like to eat fat. They think it is delicious. And Chairman Mao declared fat to be healthy. He told Chinese people to eat more fat. There wasn't enough food and many people starved. Better to eat fat than to eat a child."

"Mmm . . . I should have known. Chairman Mao's unsurpassed wisdom." I used my chopstick as a knife and sliced off a big piece of glistening, oily fat and pushed it to the side of my plate. "No wonder I'm getting so fat myself."

Ouyang smiled. "It's not that you're fat; it is your body density. You are dense."

I agreed. "Yes, I am very dense. You are correct. And not just dense in the physical sense, either. In many areas, I have been dense. Like mentally. I made some very bad choices in California. Things I haven't told you."

"Really? These mistakes, these bad choices, Susan. They don't matter now, do they? The Chinese don't think about such things. We think about what happens today, not yesterday. Believe me, if we thought so much about past mistakes, we'd all go mad."

I shifted my gaze out the window and watched an elderly woman wandering down the street. She wore a short pink dress and matching ribbons in her gray pig tails. She was skipping, as a young girl might do. "Look at her," I said. "Poor thing, she must have dimentia."

Ouyang watched her skipping through the heavy traffic. "Very sad. When Chairman Mao took away the personal possessions of everyone and forced them to live in communes, the old people were put into Happiness Homes. But they were anything but happy, as you can imagine."

"That lady looks very happy."

"Yes. She is living with her daughter or daughter-in-law, and has had her hair brushed carefully. Someone loves her very much. Caring for one's parents until they die is the Chinese way."

"She does look happy and carefree, doesn't she?"

"Maybe *you* should wear a pink dress and play in the street,

Susan. Maybe that is what your brain needs." He smiled.

"You are probably right, my friend. But I am not very good at not thinking, Ouyang. I'm slightly neurotic, as you may have noticed. It was easy when I first got here in Tianjin. Every day was an adventure. But now—I feel like I'm getting back to real life. I need to think through and figure out some things."

He asked, "And what should you figure out? Be happy and live your life, Susan. The past does not matter. In China the past plays very little importance to a person. Everyone must go on and do their best to forget the bad things. It does not matter."

"Ouyang, it matters to me. I am having trouble forgetting. It makes me quite miserable sometimes. In fact, if it wasn't for my core belief in God, I don't know what I would do."

"I do not believe in your God. I believe only in science and logical thinking."

We watched through the window as a middle-aged woman came running up to the old lady in the pink outfit. She gently wrapped her in a hug and the woman willingly went with her. I murmured, "Apparently she *is* loved and cared for."

On the walk home, Ouyang asked softly, " Susan, when will your God help you?"

I brushed away a tear. "Soon. He will help me soon. I need to trust Him, you see."

"Is there a special offering you must give first? Is there a punishment to endure before He will give you help?"

I stopped in my tracks and stared at my friend. "No, there isn't, Ouyang. His help is unmerited. It's completely undeserved."

He smiled. 'Well, there you go! Now you won't have to worry anymore."

Tears took away any further words but I reached over and squeezed his hand.

*If you will ask Me, you will know where to turn. To the right, to the
left—I will guide your pathways that clearly.*

My mother took me shopping for an Easter dress when
I was five. Until then my grandmother had sewn my Easter
dresses—blue smocked frocks edged in lace, or yellow dotted-
Swiss that made me feel I was floating. The first dress I chose for
myself was the color of pink cotton candy, with matching tights,
patent leather shoes, and gloves. My mother bought me a hat
with an elastic band that wrapped beneath my chin and a small
purse to carry my Sunday school offering. My brothers wore suits
and ties. Mom herself wore a suit, gloves, and high heels.

Dad recruited volunteers to prepare Easter gift bags for the
children at church—pastel-colored bags wrapped in pink or
yellow cellophane. He ordered a corsage for my mother and a
boutonniere for himself, which waited in the refrigerator—safe
inside its small, transparent box—until Easter morning.

There were picnics in the park with Easter egg hunts, and we
cooked and colored hard-boiled eggs in our kitchen. The church
was decorated with lilies, though Mom was allergic to them.

The church was always full on Easter. There was special
music and the colorful bulletin covers depicted rays of light
streaming from the cross through stained-glass windows.

I am your Home, the only home that will stand firm forever.

I had told Mrs. Hua I wanted to go to church on Easter
Sunday, and she convinced Ouyang to take me. His mother, Dr.
Liu, asked to come along. He called the night before to remind
me, "Susan, tomorrow we go to see the god. Go to sleep early."

It was easy to have a new dress sewn—the fabric markets

in Tianjin were known throughout the world as offering some of the best-quality materials. I found a four-ply silk the color of pistachios. Mrs. Zhang made a dress copied after a photo in a Vogue magazine and I felt very "Easterish" as I rode the Peace Apartments elevator down to the ground floor.

As I stepped out of the lobby, Dr. Liu looked dismayed. "Susan, this dress is beautiful. But you must go upstairs and change into something appropriate."

"Something appropriate? It's Easter."

Ouyang laughed heartily. "Oh, my impractical American friend! Once again you forget you're in China, not America! This is the season of severe dust storms blowing down from the Gobi Desert. This is not a good time to wear an elegant dress."

I whined, "I love this dress. It'll be fine, you'll see."

He waved his hand in frustration. "Okay, okay. We do it your way and you will discover that your green dress turns to an ugly gray color by the end of the day."

His mother simply stared at my high heeled shoes and stockings from Beijing. I followed behind them as we picked our way through the pot holes out to the crumbling streets to hail a taxi.

On the drive, Ouyang explained that his father had attended church here, but before he died he had stopped out of fear that it might endanger his family. We drove through a maze of streets in the old hutong neighborhoods. Then, sandwiched between heaps of garbage and roadside vegetable stands, a church rose before us: enormous, white, with steeple and stained-glass windows.

"Ouyang, this is lovely!"

My dear friend smiled with pleasure. "Yes, indeed it is. Now you stand here while I find the people." He was back in a few moments. "The Easter party is upstairs," he announced.

We followed the strains of organ music and were soon searching for three seats together in the packed sanctuary. Ouyang's mother ended up sitting just behind us, but as we watched later arrivals unable to find any seats, we felt fortunate.

Ouyang was talking with a woman, then turned to me and

said, "She is a Christ. She tells me that most of the people here have been waiting for an hour. They are afraid there won't be any seats available if they are too late."

The people were not concerned with a brand new Easter outfit. They were wearing the same clothes they would have worn to a wedding or to the store. It was always the same. Buttoned wool blazers over shapeless trousers and sensible shoes. I shivered and felt ridiculous, just as Ouyang had warned.

The service began with a choral anthem sung by an impressive choir of seventy-five voices, all donned in blue robes with white stoles. Their rich voices were well trained and rehearsed.

Hundreds of children filed in quietly and sat on the floor around the children's pastor. After the chorus "Into My Heart," the children's sermon was given—a lively telling of Jesus' victory over death and the miracle of the empty tomb. All was quiet in the sanctuary as people strained forward to hear every word.

Next came a baptismal service. The pastor and an assistant slowly baptized at least eighty new Christians. Many of the new converts wept for joy; others were solemn or shy.

We sang "Up From the Grave He Arose," "Because He Lives," and "I Serve a Risen Savior." My singing in English seemed to annoy the woman on my right. Ouyang whispered that I should try singing in Chinese.

Then came the main message. We had already been sitting for over an hour but nobody looked concerned about time. The woman beside me let out a belch. I turned to Ouyang, giggling, and whispered behind a bulletin. "Oh, my goodness."

He chuckled. "I guess that doesn't happen in American churches very often."

I laughed. "No, not as a rule."

The message was delivered by the senior pastor, a woman wearing trousers beneath her clerical robe. She spoke eloquently of how the resurrection is not about magic; Christianity is not a method of finding luck, but of faith, obedience and a relationship with Jesus Christ. Tears rolled down my face.

Ouyang whispered, "What's wrong?"

I wrote a note: "Nothing is wrong. This is the best Easter service I've ever been to."

The worship service lasted until one o'clock in the afternoon. As soon as the last strain of the choral benediction was sung, Ouyang and I were surrounded by people shaking our hands, asking for my name and address. I was busy chatting with people and whenever I glanced up at my friend, I could see him writing out addresses of people who had children or relatives in America. As he listened attentively to first one person, then another, I thought he had never seemed so dear.

We hopped into another taxi and drove to a restaurant for lunch. I explained, "I want to buy both of you lunch because in America, lunch after church is a special time."

Later, as we filled thin pancakes with duck meat and skin, Ouyang asked me, "This Jesus, you believe He rose from the dead? All those people believe He rose from the dead?"

I bit into a juicy bit of duck, thinly-sliced cucumber and thick Hoisin sauce and smiled. "Oh, absolutely. I believe it and they believe it, Ouyang. Mmm, this is so unbelievably delicious."

His mother spoke up quietly. "I am Buddhist. I no believe Jesus. I no believe in cross. But I have happy time at church party."

Ouyang was muttering to himself, "I am a nuclear physicist and a rich businessman in China. I do not believe such rubbish. Miracles? This does not happen."

Some time later, Ouyang invited me to meet his middle-school classmates, Lawyer Yu, and his wife, Professor Liang. They had gone to graduate school in the states—at Harvard—where they met, and were now living in housing provided for university professors. Professor Liang taught Spanish and Latin American studies and was preparing to move to Ecuador in a month. We took a series of busses to Nankai University where we were graciously welcomed to the dorm-style room the couple shared with their eight-year-old daughter, Ye Ji. I was disappointed to hear that I wouldn't be meeting their daughter; her grandmother had taken her to a piano class.

I watched as Lawyer Yu converted the bedroom into a dining room, pulling out the tiny folding cardboard table from the space between the bed and the stacks of thin paperback books against the cement wall. I wondered how they could see well enough to read, study and mark papers in the dim light of the bulb that dangled from the cracked ceiling.

His wife, a petite, round woman with shoulder-length, curly hair was cooking in the community kitchen used by all the professors and families on this particular floor. The fluorescent light was positioned too far from the cook stove. The wall behind the fire was thick with black grime. Professor Liang explained that eight families shared the kitchen. I chatted with her as she sautéed chicken cubes in the sizzling wok, stirring them constantly with a large metal spoon. When each piece had been thoroughly cooked to pale perfection, she added minced scallions, slivered ginger, chopped red chili, minced red pepper, and chopped cucumber. She reached for the bowl of glossy peanuts and mixed them into the dish, then poured in soy sauce, rice wine and sesame oil. Lawyer Yu set out white rice, chopsticks and small bowls.

The four of us laughed and conversed with ease, the sense of friendship immediate. Ouyang told them how I had reacted when I began understanding a few of the Chinese phrases being hurled at me—and Mr. Yu and Professor Liang laughed until tears streamed down their faces.

Professor Liang removed her glasses and wiped her eyes, still chuckling. "I am sorry this happened to you, but it happens to every foreigner—most just don't know what the words mean. China is a very different from America. What might be insulting in America is not a big deal here."

I grimaced. "I noticed."

"I have tried to tell her the same thing but she is not such a good listener," said Ouyang with a teasing smile.

Professor Liang continued, "And beneath those derogatory remarks is extreme respect."

I nodded. "I sense that. I have met the most wonderful people here."

"And they will be your friends for life, Susan."

Lawyer Yu said, "The Chinese are dealing with some incorrect perceptions about Americans. This sometimes causes problems for foreigners."

I said, "May I ask you, what are these perceptions?"

He cast a quick glance at Ouyang who shrugged his broad shoulders and said, "She likes to know the truth, my friends. I do not know why."

The tall, large-boned lawyer cleared his throat. "Well, China suffered often from invasions by Foreign Devils, a term that has been used for centuries in reference to people from other countries. So the basis for mistrust and misperception was built long ago. And then during the years China was closed to the world, we were taught that America had fallen apart. We were told that everyone was suffering from famine in the USA, that there had been an economic depression and people had lost their homes and were living on the streets. The official word in China was that America had digressed to a very backward country. These were total lies, of course; but when all contact with the outside world had been shut down, the Chinese believed what they were told by their government."

Ouyang groaned. "The result of allowing a farmer to become the god of this country! Do you see how clever the Chinese people are?"

Lawyer Yu shook his head. "Yes, we had been taught to believe many lies. Once the doors in and out of China at last opened—around the time Richard Nixon came to Peking—the reality flooded in: America had not become a backward country at all. It had leapt far forward, in fact. We had been duped by our leaders. America, the enemy, was now our leader in technology, education, medicine, and modern thought. The Chinese were forced to become the student."

His wife nodded. "We are still struggling to catch up with what we missed during those years of isolation."

Lawyer Yu sighed. "Thus, we have needed America's experts to come to China and train the people: Scientists, doctors, teachers, businessmen, inventors—"

"And suddenly the Chinese were under the impression that Americans had become very rich," said Professor Liang as she served fragrant, soothing tea.

"Fat cats," added Lawyer Tan.

Ouyang elaborated, "They believe that all Americans are as rich as Rockefellers."

Now I laughed. "You're kidding me!"

They all nodded and Professor Liang said, "Seriously, this is what they think. The Rockefellers, the Vanderbilts, the Astors. The Astor Hotel here in Tianjin is the oldest Western hotel in China—these are family names that the Chinese know well."

I said, "We are definitely not rich. Most of us, that is."

"We know. But we are not the typical Chinese," said Ouyang. "Your school, Susan, is on one of the streets in the old English concession. The homes there are mansions. The old generation here were kept out of those neighborhoods. There were signs on the streets: *No Chinese and No Dogs.*"

Professor Liang added, "Unless you were one of the servants who worked for a foreign family."

I said, "No wonder there is some resentment out there."

Mr. Yu continued, "That resentment is mixed with embarrassment and anger at how far we regressed in the recent past, Susan. When you hear a rude insult, listen for the humiliation and self-depracation within the remark."

His wife said, "There is always much more inside the words. The Chinese are a complex people. In China, nothing is what it seems to be."

Ouyang changed the tone of the conversation. "And they think that all Americans look alike, too."

I laughed. "But, Americans are from every race."

"Yes, of course—the great melting pot, right? This is difficult for the average Chinese person to comprehend."

Mr. Yu added, "And they think Hollywood movies show the actual American life. I cannot emphasize how deeply this concept has been ingrained into the Chinese mind."

I looked at my three friends squeezed around the lopsided table in the stuffy room, and it hit me as frightening that the Chinese would believe our film industry accurately portrays American life.

"Surely they must realize that it's simply acting. How could it be real?"

Professor Liang smiled sadly. "How can it *not* be real to them? And now they are thinking, 'I am jealous that you have so much. I deserve what you have and I have no hope of ever getting it.'"

The subject changed to the fact that Professor Liang would soon be moving to South America to teach in a large university.

"You must hate leaving little Yi Jie," I said.

Her eyes flashed. "Not really. I love my daughter, of course, but I have worked very hard for this assignment. It has taken me twelve years to accomplish what needed to be done. I am excited about living in South America."

Lawyer Yu smiled. "Chinese families have to do many things that American families would not think of doing. We rely upon our extended families to help raise our children so we can travel and work. It's part of what you say in America—'getting ahead.'"

Professor Liang agreed, "We are pragmatic, practical; we roll up our sleeves and get the job done."

Ouyang winked at me from across the table.

I smiled. "So I've heard."

As we walked along the path toward the bus stop, Ouyang asked, "So are you happy you know more about the Chinese feelings toward you?"

"Happy? No, I can't say that I am. It's mind boggling."

"Mind boggling? Is that similar to juggling?"

I looked at my friend's round face shining in the glow of the street lantern. "Not really. Well, perhaps; juggling ideas around in one's brain, letting go of one idea, then catching the other. And having to do it all again until you find a balance somehow."

He shook his head. "Such a struggle to understand. You, the curious American, always asking questions and wanting to know the whole truth. In my opinion, you'd be much happier if you thought less. Just accept life without needing to understand it all, Susan. Knowing too much brings much heartache. Don't forget—curiosity kills the cat."

"I can't help but ask questions and think about things, my friend."

He laughed. "But thinking about useless matters is almost like a hobby for you. Some people play mah jong and other people raise crickets. You? You think and ask difficult questions."

"You're teasing me."

"Half joking, half serious. I know you. You will never change. However, I advise you to try. Learn to live without needing to know everything. Do you think most of the people you know here could have survived if they had tried to know everything? I assure you, no. They would have died in frustration."

The campus was quiet, the walking trail plowed with moon-light. I sighed contentedly. "Ouyang, I am very happy in China. In spite of the cultural differences and misguided notions, I feel very peaceful here. I have met some dear people, intelligent and kind. I greatly admire the Chinese people."

He smiled and motioned toward a bus that had squeaked to a stop. We climbed aboard, found seats and became part of the grinding traffic. It was crowded and stank of garlic and cigarettes, in spite of the open window letting in a wedge of air. After a few blocks, we could see the Peace Apartments loom above the grim shacks. Beyond that was the river, a smelly smear of black ink. Surprisingly, I was happy to be here—this had become home.

Sometime later I was invited to participate in a teachers' conference in Chongquing—the landlocked, polluted city that has the distinction of being the most populous city in the world. Maybe that's because of all the displaced families moving there from the banks of the Yangtze River. As I booked air tickets to Sichaun Province, Ouyang decided to meet me in Yunnan Province after the meetings were concluded. He had always desired to see Guilin and Yangshou, popular tourist destinations for both the Chinese people and the expatriate community.

Chinese cities are almost all the same—at least it can appear that way to a foreigner. But Chongqing is vastly different from Tianjin's flat terrain. The gray metropolis choking with swirling dust and black fumes was built on rocky cliffs that appeared suddenly whenever I peeked out from my speeding, swerving, horn-blowing taxi. The steep stairs that led from ancient sidewalks were crumbling and appeared to lead nowhere—just straight up, past the emaciated men and frail children selling flowers, and grandmothers holding babies above the concrete as streams of yellow pee joined all the other mysterious liquid rivulets.

My taxi slowed down and passed through an intricate iron gate that opened to park-like conference grounds. Immediately the sounds and grime of the city were forgotten in verdant expanses of flourishing grass lawns, walking trails and wooded areas. I wondered briefly where Chongqing had vanished to and then decided not to fret. I could get used to this idyllic oasis.

The accommodations were lovely, as well: clean rooms with heavy cotton bed sheets, puffy comforters, and stacks of white towels. Shuttered windows opened to shaded patios. There was even cable television and room service. This was not what I had expected, but I was happy.

After I checked in, I went to the opening ceremonies, which lasted three hours, consisting of dignitary after dignitary shrieking out the same words of welcome, one after the other: "Please to welcome our foreign guests! Wish you long and happy lives! Please to open the beautiful and historical city of Chongqing to our most esteemed guests."

I attended workshops on teaching strategies. And as I offered ideas for blending drama into a music program, the Chinese music teachers took copious notes and asked many questions. I explained that when my students are studying the works of Beethoven, Mr. Ludwig V. Beethoven comes to visit for a day. Their eyes widened in curiosity and I showed them photographs of the middle-school student who had dressed up like Beethoven and portrayed him in a short drama.

One of the teachers raised her hand. "Excuse me, how did you learn to think of ideas like these? Did you study drama in university?"

"No, not at all. I learned to create these ideas by watching my mother. She was a wonderful storyteller and teacher who used the magic of drama in her lessons." Thus, the influence of my extraordinary mother with her spontaneity and origi-nality—before a high-school Sunday school class or a public-school class of fourth graders—reached all the way to China.

These meetings were punctuated with tea breaks, and each evening banquets were served. Among the other delicacies, we were served chicken feet, pig hooves and pig tongue. And judging by the reactions of the Chinese teachers at my table, the pièce de résistance was the turtle soup. Servers came around to each table and fiercely pounded on the turtles floating in the enormous soup tureen until they were broken into pieces.

On the last night, I noticed a flyer advertising massages. I thought, *What a perfect way to end a nice weekend away.* When I found the tiny massage parlor, it was locked. The sign on the door explained that the establishment was open from 11:00 p.m. to 5:00 a.m. It was conveniently positioned across the hallway from the cocktail lounge. I shook my head, thinking what a lucrative business this is in China. And I couldn't help but remember the fourteen-year-old I had met in Tianjin.

All else eventually passes away, but I endure for all eternity.

*W*hen my dad's brother, Jack, returned from the front
lines of France in 1946, he met and married the daughter
of his boss, Audrey, a striking brunette with creamy skin and
hair that matched her flashing black eyes. Audrey had a strong
personality—witty, outgoing and confident. She exuded elegance
and natural sophistication. Her appearance was glamorous. Visits
to her walk-in closet were thrilling journeys for me as a young
girl. There were designer suits, handbags, gloves, and French
perfumes. There were fur coats and stoles, and leather shoes
in colorful chaotic tumbles. And across from her turquoise,
triangular-shaped bathtub, resting on her heirloom dressing table,
her velvet-lined jewelry box spilled pearls, diamonds and antique
brooches.

But in spite of the Cadillacs and a sprawling home, Audrey
had not led an easy life. Her mother had committed suicide when
Audrey was eleven, and her two consecutive stepmothers had
been cold and aloof. After giving birth to a beautiful baby girl,
Kathleen, she had Christine, an infant who would never develop
beyond the age of a seven month old. She was diagnosed with
Phenylketonuria, a rare inherited disease for which there was not
yet treatment. It broke Jack's and Audrey's hearts. Additionally,
after decades of success in the restaurant business, their diner
was struggling to the point where they eventually, when I was in
college, sold the sprawling ranch home in the Sunnyside Country
Club and moved into a small condominium until they could
gather the resources to buy another house.

Both Jack and Audrey were well acquainted with pain, grief,
and dealing with a good dose of reality. Audrey, who was known
as a strong and savvy leader in their downtown Presbyterian
church, and had served on the search committee that had origi-
nally brought Dr. Travis from Minnesota, was one of the most
loving and oftentimes, most straightforward persons I knew.

A few weeks after John's sabbatical was in progress, she

surprised me with a phone call. "Susan—I just heard some distressing news about John."

I gulped. "Um, what news, Aunt Audrey?"

She had a reputation for carefully guarding confidences. "Well, I can't really say right now. I just want to ask you to be very careful with him and make good choices."

"I hope I can, Aunt Audrey."

"Promise me you'll make wise decisions, okay, sweetheart?"

She died of a brain aneurism that week and it wasn't until John returned from sabbatical that I discovered what she had heard about her former pastor.

All I have promised you— My joy, My presence, My grace—is yours.

*F*rom Chongqing, I flew to Yangshou, near Guilin, where I met up with Ouyang, who had concluded a short business trip to Guangdong Province. We got adjacent rooms in a hotel that had entertained both Richard Nixon and Bill Clinton. We walked up and down the cobblestone streets and I bought small gifts for my niece, nephew and Dr. Liu, Ouyang's mother. We ate at outdoor cafes that featured Western food—lasagna, beef stew and apple pie with ice cream. We floated down the Li River on a bamboo raft in the afternoon sun, feeling as if we were directly beneath the karst peaks, the magnificent rounded mountains that tower over the farmlands. These are depicted everywhere as representational of China, gracing silkscreen and traditional watercolor paintings, souvenirs and even red, five-yuan notes.

"Susan, these mountains were made when the acidic water collided with the bedrock—the limestone."

"They're magnificent!"

"And the weather? You like it, yes?"

"Ouyang, it's absolutely perfect!"

The next day, he convinced me to attempt bicycle riding again. I was terrified of riding in traffic, after my disastrous Flying Pigeon accident, but I decided to give it another try. On the way out of the city, I almost crashed into some children walking to school; but eventually we found ourselves on a quiet, narrow dirt path between terraced fields, where oxen were pulling wagons and farmers were turning brown in the sun. Fragranced with oranges and pomelos, the plains were dotted with tiny villages and solitary farmhouses, meandering streams and laughing children.

We rode past Moon Hill and the Black Buddha Caves and stopped at a small house to use the "bathroom"—a gap dug out in the earth directly over a pen of snorting, hungry pigs eagerly anticipating what we had to offer them. I squeezed my eyes shut and tried not to breathe as I did my business, crying out to Ouyang who was guarding my privacy, "I HATE this! I really SO HATE this!"

He laughed. "Again, you forget you are in China, Susan."

"I'm not kidding. This is a sad, miserable moment in my life, Ouyang. These pigs are going to bite my rear end off."

"Stop talking and focus. Your misery will soon be over!"

"Just make sure nobody tries to come in. I have too many other things to worry about."

"Susan, there is no person around. Just chickens. Many, many chickens all walking around in different directions. I think they're kind of crazy chickens."

The lady of the house was a rough-skinned peasant woman who invited us to have lunch—for a small fee. Grateful for the rest on the patio underneath large shade trees, we gladly paid her ten yuan apiece for the meal of garden vegetables and white rice. Her mother was husking corn and smoking a cigarette at the same time, squatting on a scarred wooden bench. She looked up on occasion to stare at me—the big-nosed foreigner—and to laugh with the northern businessman. Her husband was building something from wood a few yards from the dark, smoky kitchen, also working with a cigarette sandwiched between his lips. I asked if I could look inside the one-room home and the woman shrugged her shoulders, then nodded. Inside was a sagging double bed, three small chests of drawers, and a bamboo ladder leaning against a narrow, wooden bench. The cement floor had no rug. Conspicuously, a beautiful new television sat in the corner, on a smaller table. Near the ceiling hung a large calendar with a traditional Chinese watercolor print, doing its best to brighten the tiny room with a bare cement floor.

After lunch, we continued our journey to a river guesthouse, where we stopped and rented two small rooms that offered hot showers, bunk beds and fishing poles. I took a short nap before dinner while Ouyang went fishing in a small boat on the river.

I slept like a rock after all the bike riding and was awakened by the peppery, smoky aroma of an outdoor grill. My hair still damp and tangled from my shower, I pulled on blue jeans, zipped a sweatshirt, and wandered outside. There Ouyang was engaged in lively conversation with several other Chinese men who were here to fish and swim in the sparkling river that splashed and swayed around the shiny boulders on its banks. Ouyang was proud of his catch, which we were soon devouring with gusto, along with rice, abundant vegetables, and bar-bequed beef.

He ate the opaque eyes of the fish and then dug inside the head with his chopsticks. "The Chinese believe the cheeks are the best part of the fish, Susan. Here, try some."

I frowned. "No, Ouyang. I can't eat fish cheeks. Nor can I eat fish eyes."

He lifted the entire head—fragrant and flaking—up to his mouth. Then someone brought a large platter of snails into which Ouyang dived enthusiastically. "Mmm, snails. Delicious."

I rolled my eyes. "Are you kidding me, Ouyang?

He was surprised. "The French eat snails, don't they?" He hungrily sucked out the snail flesh.

I nodded. "Yes, I guess they do."

We were sitting at one of many long picnic tables on the guesthouse deck overlooking the river. Fat white ducks waddled contentedly in and out of the water, while cats napped on windowsills. The sun was beginning to pale, and the spring air cooled to an autumn-like crispness. A fire had been started in the outdoor stone fireplace and the flames snapped and popped, joining the cicadas in a symphony that reminded me of being at camp as a young girl. I grew quiet, thinking back to sweet summertime memories as a girl in the Santa Cruz mountains.

One of the kitchen staff set down two large mugs of coffee, one black and one "white," as they referred to it in China. I motioned toward one mug and said to Ouyang, "It's white, just the way you like it."

He grinned and thanked the waiter. "And yours is black, as usual. Your coffee is so strong it could get up and walk around by itself, Susan! Do all Americans drink their coffee so black?"

I laughed. "No. I just like it this way. Espresso is my favorite."

He nodded. "Espresso. . . . They serve that to me when I go to Italy for business."

I thought a moment. "I guess it was invented there. Did you know that many people think spaghetti was invented in Italy?"

"Spaghetti? You're talking about noodles?"

"Yes."

He laughed. "Surely everyone in the world realizes the Chinese invented noodles. The explorers loved them and took them to Europe."

I shook my head. "No, I don't think everyone realizes that." Then, as the sun set behind the karst mounds, I added, "I am really liking this place. How did you know about it?"

"You ask crazy questions sometimes. How do you think I know about this place? I am Chinese and this is China."

I sipped the hot coffee. "I know, but this place is . . . different from most Chinese places. It's charming and wonderful. I am more relaxed here than in most places in China. This feels kind of like America. Well, except for the fish cheeks and snails."

"Really? Mmm, that's interesting. The Chinese would not think that. They would think that a shopping mall with a Starbucks is more like America."

"Well, those are like America, too, yes. But, so is this—sitting by a campfire under the trees next to a beautiful river."

Ouyang said, "You are very quiet and relaxed tonight. What are you thinking about?"

"Oh, I'm remembering summers in Santa Cruz. My parents directed a camp for teenagers and even before I was old enough to enroll as a camper, I went along with them to the camps every year. My brothers and I had so much fun."

"Camping? Did you sleep in a tent? That does not sound fun for a Chinese."

"No, we slept in cabins at that campground. But other times we slept in tents and loved it!"

He rolled his eyes. "Oh, terrible."

"What? You don't like to camp?"

Ouyang scoffed at my question. "Of course not! The Chinese have done too much forced 'camping'—labor camps in the remote countryside, sleeping on the ground. These are not things Chinese do for fun. They are necessities."

Again, I was reminded of the great chasm between our cultures and between our respective childhoods. "Yes, I understand."

His almond-shaped eyes glittered with curiosity. "In America, camping is considered to be good? Fun?"

"Oh, yeah! People spend a lot of money to buy tents and camping gear. They travel to beautiful parks and places with natural, scenic wonders, and enjoy the outdoors for a few days."

He shook his head and said bitterly, "You can tell your American colleagues they should try camping for a few years, not for a few days. Or try a few decades!"

"Not so fun, I guess."

"No, not so fun. Believe me."

"I do believe you, Ouyang."

He waved toward the guesthouse, now glowing with

dancing, yellow lamplight. "This is okay kind of camping. This is not so ordinary."

I smiled. "Yes, it's very special, my friend. Thank you for bringing me here."

He raised his wine glass and clinked it against my coffee mug, "Cheers. Here's to camping the American way."

When you accept My divine life and salvation, you will be My own child.

*I*ndeed, some of the happiest memories of my early life revolved around camp. Our church was part of a large district of churches who gathered for two weeks of campmeeting, a blissful time for children and teenagers. We attended church services each evening, followed by campfire sing-alongs, and the days were filled with youth services, sports competitions, choir practices, eating in the dining hall, and socializing. Later in the summer, we returned for a week of youth camp, directed by my parents.

My father had first attended campmeeting years earlier as a teenager. It was during one of the evening services that he accepted the Lord as his Savior. He was, as people phrased it in those days, "gloriously saved." It was a time of much joy for his eldest brother and praying mother; and he soon headed off to college to prepare for a life in the pastoral ministry.

In recent years I often studied my dad's photographs on the pages of his college yearbooks, and I wondered how such a vibrant prayer warrior and minister could change so drastically. I believed the words of Scripture: "For nothing can separate us from God's love"—but I wondered and worried.

Indeed, nothing can separate you from My love.

The next morning, out by the river, Ouyang and I breakfasted on porridge—a bowl of watery rice—topped with preserved duck eggs. Once again the proprietors of the guesthouse served strong, black coffee and we chatted lazily—the day stretched ahead with no demanding schedule and we were basking in the awareness that there was nothing we had to do.

"Tell me more about camping when you were young."

"Well, it was fabulous, Ouyang. We had an expansive mountain playground to run around in all day. Nothing could have been more fun for three kids. We imagined we were in Africa and went on safaris, hunting lions and tigers. We hiked down to the creek and sat on big rocks in the sun. We dangled our toes in the water and balanced on fallen, moss-covered logs. We pretended the biggest log across the river was a high tightrope at the circus and took turns trying to walk across. The water below wasn't deep, but to us it felt like the scariest walk in the world!"

"It sounds idyllic."

"It was. I can still smell that hike. The fresh air—the scent of the redwood trees—it was intoxicating."

"And then when you were older, did you still go down to the creek?"

"We were busier then. There were lots of planned activities for us. Like volleyball, softball and musical rehearsals."

Ouyang smiled. "Your life sounds like a party to me."

I laughed. "It was a bit like a party most of the time. We had no idea how lucky and blessed we were."

He grew quieter. "My childhood was lived in fear. I wanted to go outside and play, but my parents had to force me to stay indoors all the time. I wanted to have pets, to run and explore, but I could not."

"And you were hungry?"

"My parents made sure I had enough to eat, but I never knew how it felt to be full, to be satisfied."

"Ouyang, I feel so guilty about that sometimes. I mean, there is nothing I could have done; but just knowing that, at the very moment you were almost starving, my family had more food than we knew what to do with. Big bowls heaping with salads and mashed potatoes and fresh vegetables. Breakfasts of eggs, bacon and pancakes, orange juice and glass after glass of milk."

He looked away. "You were very lucky in America."

"Yes, we were."

Later that night we were back in Yangshou. We had purchased tickets to ride a boat down the Li River at night, to watch the cormorants do night fishing. We were fascinated with the way the fishermen sent the shiny black birds down into the water, then when the birds returned to the surface, collected all the fish they had caught in their mouths. There were colored lights like sparkling jewels set into the karst mountains; and the river changed into a night fairy land in the moon's blue glow.

"This is beautiful, Ouyang!" I said.

He was quiet as he gazed at the water.

"We prayed for you, you know. Before we ate the big meals in America, we took time to thank God, and sometimes we prayed for 'all the starving children in China.'"

He turned to look into my eyes with a combination of resentment and amusement. "You prayed for us right before you indulged in your nightly banquets?"

"Yes, sometimes we did. We were not able to imagine how it felt to always be hungry."

He closed his eyes. "And I'm sure that the thirty-three million Chinese who died during those years greatly appreciate your prayers." He burst into incredulous laughter.

"I can understand how this must sound, and I'm sorry. It wasn't fair. Life is not fair. Some people have too much, while most of the world's people have so little. Maybe I shouldn't tell you about the abundance of my American upbringing."

"Of course you should tell me. It is the story of your life, the story of you. It certainly isn't your fault that we had a miserable life in China. The risk of becoming close friends with someone from a different culture is that there will be times I feel jealous of your continual party life. Tell me more about the American camps. Were there many Christs [his word for Christians] there?"

As we walked along, the restaurants and bars lining the charming street filled with tourists from all over the world. We found a table to have dessert and coffee.

"Yes, it was a Christian camp that we experienced every summer. So we had worship services, yes. There were choirs and lots of good music. Well-known preachers came to speak. Those were unusually powerful services."

"Powerful? This means—?"

"Powerful because the presence of God was there."

"His presence was there more than most places?"

"Well, yeah. It was, I guess. I don't think I ever thought about that before."

"Why was it more powerful at the camp? Because you were in the mountains and mountains are higher up?"

I smiled. The Chinese culture was big on making distinctions between heights, and buildings had entryways that signified higher or lower class or position. "Well, maybe that was part of it, a little bit. But I think it was more about the fact that so many people were gathered together, all at once and their hearts were united in prayer—all at once."

He nodded. "Ah, yes, I understand. A mass movement."

"Yeah, I guess you could call it that."

His voice lifted slightly. "A mass uprising of the people."

I looked at him. "I don't think it's quite like that, Ouyang, but I understand what you're saying."

He went on. "Mass movements of the people are very powerful, indeed. Our government leaders fear that more than anything else. If the people rise up in revolution, it can be the demise of the Communist government. So the people must be controlled."

"Wow, that's kind of scary, isn't it?"

Ouyang winced. "Very scary. My mother is very afraid of the Chinese."

"She's afraid of her own people?"

"Yes. Throughout the Cultural Revolution no one could trust anyone, not even their neighbors. Children turned in their own parents to be tortured and killed. This is what Chairman Mao taught them to do."

"It's unbelievable, Ouyang, that one man could have that much power, that much control."

"And then when Chairman Mao became paranoid of his own staff he arranged to have them all murdered. One by one, they disappeared. His own comrades!"

"Really? Is this true?"

He shook his head and gazed into his coffee cup. "Yes, it is true. And it is China's shame."

We were spent from the long day. As we walked back through town toward the hotel rooms near the mountain, the lights and life of the town grew dimmer and paler as the mountains—rounded camel's humps—grew closer.

It's about relationship—relationship with Me. One human heart connecting with My divine heart. It is mystery, and it will save you.

I was preparing for the new school year when Daniel strode into my classroom one August evening. I looked up and stared into his Nick Nolte-blue eyes. He wore a pink Oxford-cloth shirt, but he was as white as a sheet.

"Susan, I received a shocking telephone call today. I need to talk with you. Have you had dinner?"

I hadn't, so we drove to Denny's. After ordering salads, he

told me, "Susan, three women in Fresno filed charges of sexual misconduct against John last May. Apparently, he has been a home wrecker for years now."

So this was what Aunt Audrey had heard.

"Susan, I need to ask you an important question. Have you been involved with John?"

I hung my head. "Yes," I confessed.

Daniel frowned. "This is very bad."

I stared at my salad. "Yes, it is pretty bad. . . . Daniel, I am destroyed on the inside. I don't know how I will ever recover. Every time he wanted to see me, it was under the guise of helping me; but too late I discovered he was controlling me. He even threatened to fire me if I didn't do what he demanded. Every time I was with him he was able to make me cry with just a few well-chosen words. He worked my emotions into a frazzle. It was awful. I don't blame you if you want to stop seeing me. I am ashamed to tell you this, and after all that you have done for me. If you don't ever want to see me again, even as a friend, that would be understandable."

"I didn't say I wanted that, Susan. I need to think this through, but I will do everything I can to help you. You do realize that you may have to leave your job—?"

"I love my job, Daniel. . . . Who knows about this? Do they know about me?"

"No, not yet, I don't think. So far, no woman from our church has come forward and everyone's hoping nobody does. We'd hoped this was something that happened only in his Fresno church, but apparently it's a repetitive pattern."

"Apparently."

The following day, on the first day of school, I looked up and there stood John—back from his sabbatical, wearing a bright yellow Polo shirt and glowing with a suntan, his new hair sprouting where his hairline had been receding. His hands were visibly shaking and he motioned me to come and speak with him.

"Susan, it's all up to you now."

"What are you talking about, John?"

"My entire career. My twenty-five years in the pastoral ministry," he enunciated each word carefully. "My life and the lives of my children depend on you."

I glanced at the students working so diligently at their desks. Fortunately, the classroom was enormous and my quiet conversation with John was being held at the open back doorway.

I turned back to John. "And how is all of that responsibility on my shoulders?"

"If you say one word—just one word—it all goes down the toilet, Susan."

"John, it's already on its way down the toilet, I'm afraid. The word is getting around about the three women in Fresno. And, I just know there are many others."

His eyes burned into mine while one of his hands fiercely grabbed my elbow.

"John, I'm teaching. It's the first day of school. Don't do this to me, and don't do this to my students." I was angry and spoke deliberately. "Please leave my classroom and don't come back."

His eyes flamed. "You can't say that to me; I'm still your boss."

"Good-bye, John." I shut the door. Those were the last words I ever spoke to Dr. John Travis.

You will live in a distant land, My child.
'No, please, Father. I cannot live in Africa or China—please!'
You will find Me wherever you go. Wherever you turn, there will
I be.

Clarke and Felicia had been my students for six years. They had a lot in common: both were from Taiwan, both were excellent stage performers, and both had made significant progress in their acting, singing and dancing skills. They were both graduating in two weeks and had been accepted into a prestigious university in California. They were also in love and apparently both in dire need of spectacles. But neither of their families would let them wear glasses.

One afternoon that fall, during a break in a rehearsal, the three of us talked about their desire and need for glasses. Both explained their parents' refusal. "Our parents don't like to think of how we would look in glasses."

Later, I happened to run into them in the cafeteria. Clarke was happily sporting what looked to be a strong prescription for eyeglasses. I congratulated him and he smiled. "My parents finally gave in and got them for me because I'm going to college."

I asked Felicia if she would be allowed to wear glasses, too, and she answered, "I think so. I've been telling my parents that in college the lecture rooms are big and I won't be able to see what the professors write on the board. In high school, I've been able to request a front row seat, but I won't have that luxury in the university. And I'm getting bad headaches every day now."

I was happy for them; they were able to see what they previously couldn't. I had a similar problem—not seeing with my eyes, but with my heart.

The need to see things as they are, to walk straight into life—I think of this on mornings in China when I see thousands of older Chinese out walking. Some of them walk backwards. No, they're not confused; it's a purposeful way of maintaining balance and poise, of keeping the mind sharp, and it's supposed to be good exercise.

This is one of many things I am still trying to get accustomed to in China. I try walking backwards and wonder what good it could possibly do for my body. I can't bring myself to spit out fish bones onto the floor. And I struggle with using squat toilets.

Then, just when I think I have something in this culture figured out, I find I'm dead wrong or misinformed. To live abroad is to allow one's mind to be stretched beyond what seemed possible. Preconceptions will be shattered and the illusory world one knows and loves will surely crumble. A professor in Austria once said, "Education is risky. The more you know, the more thoughtfully uncertain you will become."

A professor in China told me that being in this country for a long period of time has its own way of unraveling what you thought you knew or understood. She told me of a visitor who came for one month and promptly wrote an entire book. She then told me of someone who came for three months and wrote a thoughtful article. Finally, she told me of someone who lived here for three years and couldn't write anything at all—her mind was too boggled with all she had learned.

Even after a decade of living in China, I have only unraveled a few pieces of the enigma that continues to be revealed the moment I step outside each morning. Most days my opinions and conclusions have to be readjusted and altered, for this is a country that is changing every day.

The darkness will rise up on all sides, and you will be thirsty and parched in a dry place.

It was October 1991. The blue sweep of clear California sky transformed into thick darkness and ash. In Oakland, across from where we watched in helplessness, there burned a fire that took everything in its path, including almost four-thousand homes.

On that same Sunday morning, just twenty miles or so through the tunnel and over the hill, the church where I had been a member for almost fifteen years was hit by a fire of a different kind. It was this day when Dr. Travis resigned from his congregation of over two-thousand members. He shook visibly in the pulpit that morning as he said, "I am just under so much stress." And as an invisible heat of disbelief and disappointment

moved through the pews, it burned into the souls of people—
some who had finally trusted in someone. It consumed some who
had just begun to hope in something for the first time.

There were a few women scattered throughout the crowd
that day who knew exactly why the pastor was sweating profusely
in his exquisitely tailored suit. Some were weeping, others were
stone-faced with denial, and at least one was already charting her
course of litigation. Many more had already moved out of the
state and were living in other cities across the country, struggling
to rebuild their lives and families. Church elders and leaders were
stunned by the rapid chain of events that had led up to this
moment, reflecting on the secrets that had taken place behind
closed doors—right under their noses.

As fire-ravaged, blackened rubble and the remnants of
peoples' lives were bulldozed off the Oakland hills and new
foundations were poured, the long work of piecing together the
rubble of broken lives and homes would now begin. Fundamen-
tal beliefs would be challenged as pillars of faith—some perhaps
hastily or shoddily erected in the first place—would have to
be reconstructed, brick by brick, board by board. Unspeakable
things had happened in the pastor's study and the past twenty-
five years in this minister's career was peeling away and falling off
in chunks. Lives were being destroyed, disintegrated by shame,
degradation, and lies.

The next evening after the fire, as I was having a bite to eat
with a friend in Oakland, an eery darkness seemed to reach its
long fingers through the crowd. There was an unusually-lengthy
waiting list for tables, the small foyer crammed with sad-looking
people and fussy children. There was a silence that hovered in
dark patches and few words were uttered, mostly used in quick
phrases to comfort hungry little ones. I looked at my companion
and we mouthed the word, "Fire."

As architects went to their drafting tables and contractors
scrambled for bids, homes were gradually put back together.
Perhaps structures were built better this time, but it was

impossible to replace the lost heirlooms, photographs, and memories.

Similarly, once a church is hit with a firestorm of this magnitude the devastation is enormous. A house of worship should be a safe place of refuge for the broken and defiled. There are programs to educate churches and pastors which are more available now. There are seminars, parachurch groups, and even graduate programs in existence now that deal with clergy abuse, sexual misconduct, and pastoral recovery. There are resources for ministering to people who are struggling to recover from the damage that flattens lives and smashes faith. But fear and loss of trust are difficult and a sophisticated problems to treat; and when coupled with debilitating early childhood experiences, these issues can be almost impossible to touch without the very hand of God reaching right into the mess, right into the pain.

In *Rumors of Another World,* Philip Yancey writes, "We experience the highest realities through the lowest."

As I grappled with the lowest realities that at times had me in a crypt, through the long season of rebuilding the inner structure of my faith, I felt as if I was slithering along the ground in an effort to keep moving. I felt that heaven was strangely absent, or that it was a personal place impossible for me to reach. This feeling was not confined to a day, a week, a month or a year; but it reached on indefinitely into my future. It seemed that the process of healing was a slow one as I lumbered my way through the business of getting through pain, sometimes staggering in the dark. I stumbled and ached for God. The stony coldness was a shock. I was unprepared for this, for this cold slumber that enveloped any hint of life within me. My fallenness had tripped me up; I felt devoid of the warm, spiritual vitality that I had known for most of my life. Sin and scandal steal your soul—and during those dark days, I wasn't sure where mine had gone.

I'm dead. I sinned, and now I'm dead. The death is coming from my heart and it's slowly consuming all health and life.

I was taking a taxi to meet Ouyang for a quick lunch before an afternoon at the Tianjin Natural History Museum. After shouting out my destination to the twenty or so people standing around, the driver took off in a cloud of dust for the opposite end of the city. There were many taxi drivers, of course, but this man was one of the more pleasant of the lot. He never failed to smile, even on miserable snowy mornings or in the midst of stinging dust storms. On impulse I invited him to come and share lunch with us. The driver seemed speechless; he just beamed from ear to ear.

When Ouyang arrived at the restaurant, he was obviously irritated. He managed to keep his feelings under wraps through the lunch of stewed chicken, scrambled eggs with tomatoes and scallions, and fried rice with vegetables. But then the lunch came to an end, and the driver left in his yellow taxi, still looking dazed at the unusual turn his day had taken. Ouyang and I began walking toward the museum, and then his feelings came out.

"Susan, never invite a cab driver to have lunch with you. Never do that again."

"Why? He has been driving me around for almost three years, Ouyang. I thought it was a good time to show appreciation in a small way."

He stopped and glared at me. "Susan, you are being a ridiculous American again. We do not do this in China. A cabbie, a driver, is lower than you. To invite someone of this low stature to have a meal with you is not done in China. He is a worker. You are a teacher. The two do not mix."

I was flabbergasted. "Ouyang, I don't understand. That man has been kind to me and has taken me everywhere. He is a good person and should not be thought of as a lesser sort."

He nodded. "I know he is a good person. But that is not the

point. You embarrass me by forcing me to have lunch with this man. You are the sister I never had, my older sister, but you do not treat me as your younger brother today. On the contrary, you humiliate me. From this day forth, every time that cabbie sees me, he will think, 'I had lunch with that businessman. Now, I am someone special—he is on my level.' But I—I have lost face. I have lost respect. That is very important for a Chinese man, Susan."

Ouyang uttered an abrupt good-bye, then began walking in the opposite direction. I sighed. This culture seemed more puzzling by the year. I spent the afternoon exploring the six halls of the museum alone.

I have come to live within you and teach you all things.

As children, my two brothers and I would often play "church," a natural game for preacher's kids to play. We'd fashion a pulpit from a cardboard box, pull out the "choir robes" and line up all my dolls and stuffed animals in the "pews." We tried forcing the cats and kittens to learn the basic principles of worship, but it didn't work out very well. The guinea pig was great at church, though. We positioned his cage near the pulpit and he'd listen attentively, as long as he had a leaf of lettuce on which to nibble during the service. I'd type up an order of worship and play the piano, then either Steve or Paul would deliver a riveting sermon. While one of them preached, the other would shout, "Amen, Brother!" and "Preach it!" or "Hallelujah!" at timely intervals. When our grandmother visited, she attended our little services and commented, "You boys are going to be real preachers someday; I just know it."

The dolls would eventually come to the altar to pray through to victory, while we sang several rousing choruses of "Just as I

Am" or "Almost Persuaded." We weren't sure what the guinea pig, who had appropriately been named "Fatty," thought of the messages. He seemed mostly concerned with eating as much lettuce as his fat little cheeks could contain. My Chatty Cathy doll had a string that could be pulled at critical moments in the testimony services; but for the most part, our faithful congregation wasn't much for speaking up.

In many ways, there is a temptation to treat the real church of today in a similar way, to play church. We can be seduced into treating the church as a sociological phenomenon, or a nice club, with a nice guy telling a bunch of nice people to be nicer. There is this tendency to develop a kind of a culture of "niceness"—rather than the sometimes scruffy, tattered people of God embracing a holy Savior with confession and passion. As adults, though, even while we play with serious choices that determine our eternal destinies, the tendency to "play church" just gets smoother and more refined, more expensive and certainly more complicated.

Scott Peck states, in *Further Along the Road Less Traveled*, that the first stage of spirituality is the "chaotic antisocial." He states that, in general, this is a stage of absent spirituality and the people at this stage are utterly unprincipled. While they are capable of pretending to be loving, actually all of their relationships with their fellow human beings are self-serving and covertly, if not overtly, manipulative. Chaotic because, being unprincipled, they have no mechanism that might govern them other than their own will. Since the unharnessed will can go this way one day, and that way the next, their being is consequently chaotic. The people in this stage will frequently be found in trouble or difficulty, often in jails or hospitals, or out on the street. Some of them, however, may be quite self-disciplined in the service of their ambition and may rise to positions of considerable prestige and power. They may even become presidents or famous preachers.

Things are not what they seem, My child. I work in a different, holy realm.

I took time off during college to travel in a semi-professional, Christian musical troupe. Just days before I turned nineteen, I flew to the east coast for rehearsal camp. We learned and polished several shows, had numerous costume fittings and photo shoots. We made TV commercials, attended classes in makeup and social skills, and had our hair professionally done. There were records to make and speaking lines to memorize.

One day, the choreographer sat the girls down and explained, "Girls, what we need here is a sort of mix, if you will. A little down-home, girl-next-door kind of wholesomeness combined with . . . frankly, girls, what we need is some good old-fashioned sex appeal. It's amazing what it takes to sell tapes and records these days!" He laughed. "Er, uh, just kidding, of course."

But he wasn't kidding. We all knew that selling records was serious business. So we crisscrossed the country in sequined costumes, portraying an intriguing brand of Hollywood glamour coupled with a fresh, all-American appeal. We worked hard to keep our curls from sagging and our mascara from running—even under hot lights on sauna-like stages where the air conditioning broke down in 100-degree weather. We were expected to skip meals and lug our suitcases from hotel to hotel, all the while keeping our lipstick fresh and our smiles frozen. We performed at the Super Bowl and state fairs, amusement parks and country clubs, civic halls and churches. We entertained for women's groups, conferences, and men's clubs. We lived on few hours of sleep and gallons of black coffee in Styrofoam take-out cups.

People loved us, and they bought stacks of records and eight-track cassettes. Good and lovely people said they were moved by our shows, by our brand of show business. People would weep, give us hugs and ask for our autographs. Once our customized leather bags were hung on mobile racks and car assignments were checked, we sped off into the night to the next city, snoozing a little, while driving fast on dark highways, to get to the next performances.

Before our nightly church concerts, we'd gather in a prayer circle and ask God to bless the performance. Then the director or the assistant producer would tease, "Make 'em weep tonight!" And we did. The words of my little grandmother would ring in my ears: "Through a tear we see God clear"; and I figured it was a good thing when people cried. I felt we were doing something worthwhile and spiritual.

But some of the other things we had to do—well, I was nineteen and it was my first exposure to famous, driven people. I was beginning to see how the marriage of sensuality and religion played a powerful role in drawing out the vulnerabilities of church people. They come prepared to trust the feelings aroused in them by the "religious presentation." They feel safe and protected, within the church, from all that is false; and their emotional doors are opened wide to sometimes unprincipled people. Their trust can easily be exploited.

For a while, after the traumatic events in the Danville church and after the wave upon wave of devastating ripples caused by my own father's choices, I was afraid to attend church. It seemed a bit too much, like the church games my brothers and I used to play in our living room. I didn't know who to trust in church. It just seemed as if too many were using church as a venue for abusing people who were too weak to understand what was happening. I still believed in God, my Heavenly Father, who had been so intimate within me since the tender age of four; but for that time in my life, the church somehow seemed to be very, very different from who God was, Himself.

Pastor and author Jack Hayford wrote, "Beware the god your mind invents, for you'll inevitably worship and become like him; however wretched, however false."

The documentary film *Not in My Church* portrays a woman

drowning in what appears to be a large baptistry. With exquisite stained glass windows in the background and stirring pipe-organ music resonating off the walls in an expansive sanctuary, she finds herself unable to stay above the water—she is choking and begging for help. A minister, dressed in a snowy-white clerical robe, smiles compassionately down at her. He reaches his hand into the water, apparently to give her a hand up, but instead he pushes her further into its depths—until at last, she apparently ceases the struggle. The water becomes perfectly calm and undisturbed, bringing a peaceful death administered by the church "not so triumphant."

That is exactly how it felt to be "involved" with my pastor.

My breadth and depth, My creativity stretches farther than you can possibly think or dream.

*L*ong ago, loggers in mountainous regions would slick down hills of snow with water until they had turned to icy "conveyor belts." These could easily transport massive logs from the mountains to the rivers below. Known as "skid rows," they were powerful and swift. Once a log had begun its downhill slide, there could be no changing its course or turning it back until the "row" or furrow began to level or drop off into the ocean-bound stream.

Early in his ministry my father pastored a congregation in southern California. Occasionally he preached at the "skid row" mission in downtown Los Angeles. He and my mother packed the three of us children (all under the age of five) into the car, and off we'd go into the most dangerous part of the city. Mom would grab our hands and tell us not to stare at the drunks huddled on stained bits of newspaper on the sidewalks.

Dad preached with gusto and sang duets with Mom, while we sat on the front row fidgeting and studying the fuzzy-faced men who sat and mostly stared at Mom. I don't think they were accustomed to a woman who resembled Sophia Loren or Jackie Kennedy visiting their mission.

Many years later, as my life seemed to be sliding faster and faster down an icy, unfamiliar skid row, making a swift tumble to frightening depths, I could almost hear Dr. Travis's voice—from a safe spot on the banks of the river—accusing, "You have done so many stupid things, Susan. Look at what you made me do!"

And I would call back into the wind, "But, John—it was your idea, remember?"

I imagined his grin growing broader and more relaxed as I slid further and further away.

After I was released from that destructive relationship, my life remained almost the same for about two years, but the undeniable effects of sin continued to impact me. One of the first things I noticed and tried to ignore, was that my singing was not the same anymore. The freedom I had once felt, the joy in singing with abandonment no longer existed. My voice felt tight, every note and interval was a struggle.

Music had been a key ingredient to my self esteem, to what defined me as a person who could contribute something to my church and community. And it had been one of the many pieces of the scaffold to which I clung. But, perhaps being busy singing about God had been an excuse to keep from knowing Him more intimately.

I was learning that ministry—even volunteer ministry—can have a way of drying you up on the inside if you don't nurture your soul. Effective ministers are "givers" who sometimes "give until it hurts." When you are giving of yourself all the time, it takes purposeful focus to keep being renewed daily in Christ. Among other things, my "doing" had gotten in the way of my "being." I had been so busy "doing" the "good" things of ministry, it was actually keeping me away from the best of God. Many people fail to nurture their souls and are tempted to minister in the power of their own strength and personality. It is a trap that Satan uses to pull us away from God and spiritual vitality.

The Bible says, 'For the wages of sin is death,' and that is what's happening to me. Little by little, the death is working its way through my cells and tissue and soon I will be completely dead. I will feel nothing then.

For our first annual winter program in Tianjin, my eighth-grade drama students performed an excerpt from Shakespeare's *Macbeth*. We faced challenges, producing the show on the stage of a rented movie theatre with a Chinese-speaking crew. But as school programs have a way of doing, everything came together beautifully. Like students anywhere in the world, our students were breathless with excitement as they changed costumes, moved sets around, and performed flawlessly for their parents—who were like parents anywhere in the world, flushed with pride, cameras in hand.

One of the highlights in the show was the sleepwalking scene. Brooke, from Toronto, was convincing as Lady Macbeth, sleepwalking by the light of a flickering candle. Wearing my flowing white nightgown, she glided up the splintery staircase, her golden hair tumbling over her shoulders, and—much to her teacher's pleasure—a look of terror in her luminous green eyes.

As Marco (the doctor) and Jaleh (the gentlewoman) looked on, elegant in their midnight-blue velvet costumes, Brooke held the audience captive. Her inner depth gave an indescribable vulnerability to her haunted character as she said, "Look, here's a spot" then rubbed her hands, consumed with guilt.

In his Costa Rican accent, Marco pleaded for forgiveness: "Good God, forgive us all. I think, but dare not speak."

Then, as Jaleh wrung her hands, Brooke floated off the stage, a tragic Lady Macbeth slipping into a world created out of her pain and choices.

And here I was, in a country far from my own, walking around in a deep slumber, with the flimsy scaffolding upon which I had been standing broken into pieces—crashed completely. I was walking without my American "crutches" and had to learn how to live in a different way.

I know you forgive me, Father, but I can't get the knowledge from my head to my heart. Please help me.

I was elated, on one hand, that the daily, continual pressure from John was gone from my life. I loved being able to pour myself into my teaching again. But deep within I was lacking so much. Where there had once been an intensity of purpose and joy, there was only spiritual and emotional deadness. I was making blatant decisions that were unwise, wrong and even selfish. Some of these would cause years of anguish and regret. I was a sad replica of the vibrant woman I had once been.

Everything about the scandal was out in the open in the community. The church leaders did their best to find all the women who had been "victimized" by Dr. Travis and offered initial funds for a year's worth of therapy. But in their well-intentioned efforts not to cause additional emotional pain for us, they somehow neglected to reach out in more personal ways.

Jodi, one of the most visible of the victims, was an elder in the church. She was tough and had the full support of her insightful husband and family. She was back to serving communion within a few months. I was astounded at her resiliency—she seemed to grasp the concept of power abuse immediately and in spite of the fact that she had been deeply involved with Dr. Travis for five years, she bounced right back, filing a lawsuit against her former senior pastor. Her picture was splashed across the front pages of the local newspapers and she calmly gave articulate interviews to reporters.

She started an internet support group for victims of clergy abuse. Until God led her into other areas of leadership and service, she was in contact with several women around the country who had been violated by Dr. Travis.

"Susan, you need to either file a lawsuit as an individual or go in with some of the others," she advised. My therapist also encouraged this, though at the time, all I wanted was to live in peace and try to pretend it hadn't happened. Jodi's matter-of-fact, confident outspokenness made me tense with fear. I wasn't ready to join the lawsuits that were beginning to be filed.

Dr. Travis was moved into a cozy accountability group, whose ultimate goal was his restoration to the pastoral ministry. Many supporters stood beside him loyally. From time to time, there were rumors that they were trying to start up a new church, with John as pastor.

No accountability group was formed for the women. Looking back, I believe it would have been beneficial to meet with a safe group of wise, godly women who might be able to see beyond the immediate crisis and personal failure to offer the benefit of prayerful support.

I was in therapy with Bonnie, the same therapist who had worked with my former husband and me. But it was slow going. I was in a state of shock and denial, once again pretending, a skill I had learned so early in my life. Bonnie reminded me that both John and his wife had made a solemn agreement to keep the names of the women confidential. That helped some, but it didn't begin to address the shame and fear I felt inside. I was withdrawing instead of advancing. I was hiding instead of emerging. I was running away instead of walking toward healing.

No matter what you do or where you go, I will be there.

One day I was at the Friendship Store near my apartment building, shopping for a reading lamp for my bedroom. The glass shelves had been stacked with fragile, breakable items—covering every inch of space—and, while looking for the price tag on a lamp, I accidentally knocked a vase off the shelf. The two attendants monitoring the department rushed over and assured me, "No problem. Don't worry. You don't have to pay for the vase." I apologized and suggested that they take a few of the fragile pieces off the shelves, to avoid other accidents.

A week later I was back to buy the lamp. Just as I began to ask the sales clerk if the tacky red tassels could be removed from the lamp, I heard a loud crash and looked over to see a young Chinese couple cowering against each other, obviously wishing they could disappear into a hole in the floor. The girl was beginning to cry from fear, and both of them were shaking.

The sales clerks rushed over, just as they had done a week ago, but their words were very different. "You must pay for this valuable, expensive piece. Please come with us."

The girl began to whimper, and her husband said, "Please, please. We do not have this much money. This is more money than we make in six months' time."

"That is not our problem. You should have thought about that before you touched it."

The husband cried, "But we didn't touch it! I do not know how it fell."

I moved closer and said, "It fell because it was only halfway on the shelf. It would have fallen at the slightest movement."

The couple looked at me gratefully.

"Please, do not make them pay for this item," I continued. "I broke one just like it last week and you did not make me pay for it."

The girl reached out like a frightened animal and held on to my hand.

The two sales clerks looked at each other and one of them spat out the words, "All right. You don't have to pay this time. But don't come here again."

I stood with the couple until the clerks walked away and then I offered to buy them a coffee downstairs in the lounge. The husband looked at his wife then sadly shook his head. "I'm afraid we cannot do that. My wife is very upset and frightened. We will go home now."

A few moments after that, I was descending on the escalator and was stunned to see a group of people—adults—following a man in a wheelchair. They were laughing openly, pointing fingers at him, and calling others to "come and look." The poor man in the wheelchair had a hunted expression in his eyes, and yet he appeared to be sadly resigned to such attention.

Later that night I told Mrs. Hua about the incidents as we worked on a puzzle. She shook her head. "The Chinese do not treat one another well. They have different rules for foreigners. There has been much cruelty in China."

I mused, "Well, America's history isn't as old. Compared to China, we are in our infancy. But it wasn't so long ago that African Americans were tormented and segregated from restaurants, public toilets, busses, schools and churches. It's hard to believe that happened such a short time ago."

She sighed heavily and tucked her arm inside the crook of mine. "Susan, until we are with Jesus in heaven, we have to bear many problems. Many social situations which are tragic, yes? Terrible things. Experiences which make us feel insane. But someday we will be in a perfect place. We will be with Jesus and the difficulties on earth will be forgotten forever."

I smiled at her and thought of all she had been through in her lifetime. Life had not been predictable for Mrs. Hua but she had kept her gaze on Jesus, her Savior. Her hope remained steady no matter what her circumstances.

The next day was a holiday from school, so rather than take the long taxi ride back into the city, I stayed in the guest bedroom. I always enjoyed sleeping there, in the room across from Mrs. Hua's. There was a single bed and a large desk that displayed old photographs under the glass blotter. I sat there and studied all the pictures. Mrs. Hua had been beautiful as a young woman, well-dressed in smart clothes—cashmere sweaters, pearls, high heels and seamed silk stockings. Her husband had been a banker who owned many businesses and spoke French—a man who knew literature and loved opera, fine imported wines and European travel. To think of them sleeping on flea-ridden mattresses for five years in a labor camp, feeding pigs, bending over crops in the field, frantically memorizing pointless passages from Chairman Mao's *Little Red Book*. Life had been insane for my beloved Mrs. Hua, yet here she was serene and hopeful, unpretentious and speaking of forgiveness.

I lay in bed that night listening to Mrs. Hua's soft snores and the occasional splashes from the large fish that was swimming in the bathtub. I felt at peace and very much at home.

You cannot get away from My Love.

The church was navigating its own deep waters. They did far more than most churches had ever done to inform and provide opportunity for healing. They offered well-attended workshops to teach what power abuse was all about and were adamant in their stance that their former pastor had been a "predator." They also insisted that each of the women had been pursued in a calculated manner for lengthy periods of time. It was obvious that most of the people who opened their minds and hearts began to understand that the victims weren't the kind of people to just walk into their senior pastor's office and offer themselves to him.

I sat watching and listening, appreciating the efforts and intentions of the wonderful people at my church. But I was lost in a new complicated system of pathways—created partly by the abusive behavior of an ill person but also of my own weaknesses; my own desires had built a tangled labyrinth of deep, personal shame. And all I could think about was getting through each day, one at a time, while I pretended to be healthy and strong.

Dr. Travis began attending a church of a different denomination, known for its basic Bible teaching and grace-filled messages. Their music minister called me one day and invited me to be the guest soloist one Sunday morning. I agreed, but received a phone call on the Friday night before the scheduled services.

"Susan, the pastor said he can't let you sing at church on Sunday. He said it was something about your behavior."

That was an awkward moment of searching silence, heavy with unspoken curiosity, but I firmly thanked him for calling and explained I would talk with the pastor himself. I stopped in at the church office the next day, which was Saturday. "May I ask why you requested I not sing tomorrow morning?"

He was uncomfortable with my directness—which was certainly understandable—and muttered, "It's your relationship with John, Susan. He attends our church and I don't want him to feel uncomfortable."

"I understand," I said. "But what confuses me is, John has promised not to divulge any of our names to the community."

The pastor sighed, removed his glasses and rubbed his eyes wearily. "Well, Susan, the reality is that he does talk about it. He talks about all of you."

In spite of my church's efforts to keep us from additional emotional and spiritual damage, the circumstances were difficult to control. Each of the women—including Jodi later down the road—finally gave up trying to "belong" to the church. The fact was Dr. John Travis was still very much a part of the community, and he was ignoring his promise to honor confidentialities. And, apparently, according to this new pastor, his wife was talking to everyone she knew and met, giving our names and as many details as she could. It was becoming obvious that wounded people wound people.

As I sat in the pastor's office on that rainy morning, I asked him, "Pastor, why is it that John is surrounded with grace and support and the women have nothing like that? Our church helped us with a year's worth of therapy, but as far as support from other peers, we are basically alone. We are trying to make sense of this painful time. If we talk, we will lose our jobs, our friends, and some of us might even lose our families."

He slowly nodded. "Yes, I can see how this is very difficult for you." He thought for a moment, then held out his hands and gestured in an indication of helplessness. "That's the way it usually is, Susan. Throughout history, it's the women who have committed adultery that have had to suffer the most."

I sighed. "And I don't think there is anyone who knows what the adulterous relationship really consisted of. Except John and the women, of course."

He didn't say anything, this good man, sincerely trying to offer some truth. I thanked him, shook his hand, and said good-bye, but not without asking him to please speak with John and ask for some sensitivity and to keep our names out of conversations, as he had promised.

The pastor said he would talk with John. However, I feared that somehow it wouldn't make any difference.

Wherever you go, My child, I am your Home.

*O*ne Sunday night I was due at Mrs. Hua's for dinner. On the way to her apartment, the taxi cab had a problem—the transmission literally fell out of the bottom while we were stopped at a traffic light. I fumbled around in my bag for the fare, hopped out and hailed another taxi, arriving just a little late.

Mrs. Hua greeted guests to her home with a standing ovation. She clapped her hands in welcome, as is the Chinese custom. Then she wrapped her arms around me and gathered me close for a tight hug and a kiss on my cheek. Her tiny white poodle, Mary, yelped excitedly and I was ushered into the house where many people—including little Amber, the preteen daughter of a book salesman and his professor wife—had gathered for a delicious meal.

"Come in, sit down, Susan," she said, and to the others in the sitting room she called, "Susan's here!"

Someone took my coat and a few others squeezed closer on one of the two plaid sofas. I sat down and accepted the offer of hot tea served by Mrs. Hua's housekeeper.

"What are we watching tonight?" I asked.

"We're watching *Gone with the Wind*," said Amber's father.

"I love this movie!" I said as I reached for a handful of the walnuts and the nutcracker.

Mrs. Hua smiled. "Me too, Susan. I love it very much!"

Amber told me about the two-week training camp she had just attended, where she and other twelve year olds had practiced marching and shooting. They used cardboard targets showing people with Western features. She was dutifully working on homework, using a TV tray as her desk, and her mother occasionally checked for accuracy over her shoulder.

I felt as if I was with family and, as always, images of my home in America flashed across my mind. A sudden wave of homesickness swept over me. How I longed to be having dinner with my own parents, with them together again. The sadness and confusion of the past still rested upon me like a solid weight. It never lifted, and this was one of those rare times I became fully conscious of its hold on my heart.

My Chinese mother knew me well. Mrs. Hua leaned over and held my face in her strong hands. "What is it, Susan? Something is making you sad tonight."

I looked at her, unable to speak. Her sensitivity caught me off guard.

"You are among your own Chinese family here, my dear," she said.

A few faces in the room turned our direction, but most concentrated on the movie. Mrs. Hua pulled me closer to her and rested her arm around my shoulders. "Now, now. Tonight is a time for happiness and togetherness. This is your adopted country and your adopted family, yes?"

I looked at her with tears in my eyes. How I loved this Chinese woman.

We were called into the dining room and *Gone With the Wind* was put on pause. I sat to the left of Mrs. Hua and she served me from her own chopsticks the choicest morsels of meat and vegetables. All good Chinese hosts did this, reaching their own chopsticks into the various dishes and carefully placing the best bites of food on the plates of their guests. Her housekeeper had prepared pickled cucumbers in chili oil, crab dumplings with hot, peppery garlic, braised beef with onions, diced chicken cooked with crunchy peanuts, and a whole fish that just an hour ago had been swimming happily in the toilet.

"So good . . . so delicious," exclaimed the guest, eating with voracious appetites.

Mrs. Hua kept shouting, "Eat more! More!"

Ouyang was away on a business trip to Prague and his dear mother sat across from me, her eyes twinkling happily.

I looked from person to person, around the table, and thought anew how each of the eight friends in the room had become so important in my life. They were distinguished people, fine individuals of human dignity and character, and they had embraced me, welcoming me into their intimate lives.

I raised my glass and offered a toast, something I knew Mrs. Hua appreciated. "I propose a toast to my Chinese friends. I have been strengthened and deepened by knowing each one of you."

Mrs. Hua sang out, "Here! Here!" I smiled, thinking she

must have learned that phrase from an American movie.

Amber's father held up a hand and interrupted. "If I may break in with one correction, Susan. We are far more than your Chinese friends. We are your Chinese family, yes?"

Everyone squealed and laughed, clapping their hands. We all lifted our glasses. "Here! Here!"

I said, "I came to China to teach and to help. But I am the one who has been helped. I am the one who has been taught."

Mrs. Hua clapped her hands in delight and said, "Marvelous! Isn't that grand? She thought she'd come to help the poor Chinese, but we are the ones who helped her—our American daughter, our American sister. And she's a little homesick tonight."

Tears began seeping from the corners of my eyes and I gazed at the table with gratitude. These people had endured horrendous circumstances in their lives. They had lost so much and had so little. And yet—around the black sandalwood table from off the coast of Africa—there could not have been greater joy found anywhere in the world, of that I was convinced.

All the earth and everything on it is Mine. There is no corner where you can go that is without Me. I am everywhere.

*T*he message from the pulpit at my church continued to focus on grace. But the stories were flying back and forth with such exaggeration and inaccuracy, it was getting harder and harder to attend the services. Little by little, my involvement there dwindled and I began to see that the journey of healing would be a long road to travel. I continued teaching at the school and in all, I taught there for a total of twelve years. But I was asked to stop playing the piano on Sunday mornings. That made sense to me—I had been playing too long, anyway. I was in such a longtime habit of rising early on Sunday mornings, however, that I kept doing so; but as my depression began to dig its talons deeply into my being, I just wore my sweats and track shoes. I parked in the back, climbed the stairs up to my classroom and did a little schoolwork long before worshippers began to arrive for services. Sometimes I'd sneak downstairs and watch the services on one of the television monitors mounted in the fellowship hall, sipping coffee and trying to be as invisible as I could.

When Daniel was in town, I dressed up and sat with him in church. He continued to be supportive and patient. He surprised me by finding a wonderful vocal coach in San Francisco and arranged to pay for private lessons. The teacher indeed lived up to his reputation and was planning to prepare me for a little recital for family and friends—but I couldn't imagine who I would invite. My mother was living with my youngest brother and his family in Los Angeles; my father might attend, but I imagined an auditorium with just Daniel and my dad sitting there. I quit the lessons and told Daniel to save his money for something else.

Every time I played the piano for something—as a guest at another church, or for a wedding, a funeral, a school event— Daniel managed to be there, sitting on the front row. He said he loved the way I "attacked the piano." He seemed determined to see me through this "cold slumber." After a while, after the initial counseling funds were long depleted, Daniel took me to see a psychologist, saying, "Susan's just not Susan yet. She's not coming back. Can you help her?"

After several sessions, I was diagnosed with Post Traumatic Stress Disorder and began taking medication, but it didn't stop my terrifying downward slide. I could feel myself slipping and made attempts to grab onto temporary handholds, crutches, and quick fixes. But I was caught in the downward spiral—twisting, turning and falling on the inside. I wondered when I would hit bottom.

It's been said that the best lies always have an element of truth within them. And maybe that is what made Dr. John Travis such an effective liar during those days. He mixed in a lot of truth—some of it straight from the Bible—into everything he said. And sometimes, even though my head and intellect knew better, my heart started to agree with the lies.

As John talked about the scandal wherever he went, he was shooting himself in the foot while he was trying to defend his own actions and destroy his victims. New pieces of information found their way to me at every turn. Someone who worked at a grocery store had been cornered by a woman, a friend of Nancy's, and told all sorts of things that simply were not true. Both John and his wife were chatting freely every chance they got—at swim meets, basketball games, church picnics and aerobics classes.

I called his pastor again. "May I please have a chance to dialogue with Dr. Travis in your presence? Or in anyone's presence? I don't really care who is in the room—it can be a bunch of people, in fact, but I would like to ask him about the stories I continue to hear that he is spreading."

He said, "No, Susan. I don't want John to go through any more pressure than he's already under."

"Well, I thought it might be worth a try. Thank you for taking my call." He could have ignored my phone calls, which went through his secretary; I was impressed that he at least answered.

I was asked to play the piano one Sunday in a neighboring church. After the service a woman made her way to the platform. I watched her squeeze through the pews, her purse bouncing into people as she interrupted conversations in an all-out struggle to reach the front of the church. I waited. She huffed, "Aren't you the woman who used to play piano in the Danville church?"

My heart sank but I held out my hand and responded robotically, "Yes, I am, and you're—?" Ignoring my hand, she literally recoiled in a posture of horror, her hand clapped to her mouth. "Oh, you're the one!"

I averted my eyes and packed up my music, as she hurried off down the middle aisle. I began to feel like I couldn't go anywhere without shame and scandal following and haunting me.

As stories continued to float back to me, I called Dr. Travis's pastor two more times. I presented my request as being biblical. According to the instruction given in Matthew 18, if one has an issue with another Christian, it was imperative to meet with godly counsel to solve it. He listened politely, but continued to turn me down.

One Sunday afternoon I was invited to the home of some church members for lunch. As the lunch progressed, there was an uncharacteristic, stony silence. As dessert was served, the husband took out a yellow legal pad, checked his notes, and cleared his voice.

"Susan, we heard some very disturbing news about you."

I looked up in surprise.

He thumbed through his notes. "Some people have shared information with us about you."

"Information?" I inwardly cringed as I sipped my coffee.

"It appears that you once dated . . ." He looked at me darkly, barely choking out the words, "a black man."

I smiled. "Yes, that was Charlie, the minister of music at our church many years ago, before you two came." A talented, committed Christian. A true gentleman whose skin color happened to be black. We enjoyed a pure relationship, mostly attending social events hosted by the music ministry division of the church.

"Well, Susan, as you know, it is against God's laws to marry outside one's race."

I almost laughed, but instead explained, "Oh, Charlie and I weren't even close to marriage. And if we had been, the colors of our skin would not have been an issue with either of us." I swallowed some coffee, then hoping to diffuse the tension, added, "I understand, however, that it is an issue with some people."

They looked at each other in meaningful silence. His wife nodded in agreement as he continued with his prepared list of sins I had committed:

1. I had been one of the women involved with Dr. Travis.

2. I was wearing skirts that were too short for the—in their words—"pianist of a large church." (I was briefly tempted here to inquire whether it was permissible to wear short skirts if one was the pianist of a small or mid-sized church.)

3. I had supposedly "had an affair with a janitor."

4. I had supposedly "had six lovers."

5. I was divorced.

6. My parents were divorced.

They had many more "facts" about me that they were carefully guarding but wouldn't be able to share with me at the present time. I asked, "And from whom did you receive this 'information'?"

They insisted they couldn't divulge their sources. As they made slow progress through the part of the list they had prayerfully decided to tell me about, I reflected on the dinner they had hosted just six months earlier, on Christmas Eve. It had been a disturbing evening for me. The meal was delicious—the most savory of chicken wings—but there had also been a lengthy list of "informative stories" being presented, one after the other. From the head usher's personal dating life to the affair their best friend was having with his neighbor, each "fact" was discussed, analyzed, and picked over.

His wife had said, "My husband has a sixth sense about these things. He can simply look at a person and knows whether or not they're an adulterer. It's one of his many spiritual gifts."

The grand finale of that evening's conversation had been the fact that our church's music ministry was in big trouble. I was imagining his wife and children breaking into song, "Trouble, trouble, trouble . . . right here in River City."

This time I spoke up, once they had closed their notebook and reached for the family Bible.

"I did go out for a while with a good Christian man whose skin color was black. And some of my skirts are perhaps too short for church, yes. Fortunately, I usually wear dresses that graze my ankles. I have been divorced, yes. And my parents are, sadly, divorced, which has broken my heart. I have dated many men throughout college and afterwards. But I have certainly not had an affair with a janitor. What happened with Dr. Travis did happen, but it was not the sort of situation you may be imagining. It was not a mutual sort of thing that is depicted in movies or soap operas. It was a relationship where one powerful person intimidated and used another person, and who was discovered by his church leadership to have been notoriously manipulative. There have been many areas in my life which have been lacking," I added, embarrassed. "And out of that lack I admit I have made a few wrong choices for which I am deeply sorry. Please pray for me as I try to rebuild my faith and my life."

The husband read a chapter from the Old Testament, his wife nodding vigorously. After he led us in a lengthy prayer, they followed me to the front door. "Oh, and because of these acts on your part, you are no longer welcome in our home."

That was really quite all right with me. Their belief system had become so twisted, that I failed to recognize we were reading out of the same Holy Book. To me, they had become modern-day Pharisees—weary servants of the impossible, wounding people already stomped on by sins and destruction.

Through the years, I have often visualized people like this, trotting around in their Sunday best, lugging big, fat ledgers of other people's sins and meeting for "pie and coffee" to discuss the failings of others under the guise of Christian concern.

I can imagine hearing their loud voices echoing in a canyon down below somewhere, completely stuck and so immersed in themselves and their detailed agendas, they are unaware of a much wider space all around them. There is such a higher plain on which to live, a space that is alive and gentle with God's very breath. It is grace-filled and quite opposite from the chaos that commences below in the canyons of confusion. The tattered and ragged ones that have chosen to rise above the turmoil have a destination that is good and grand, and they are aware of God's deep love for them. But there are those who are so hunched over their comprehensive lists detailing the mistakes of others, that they completely miss the gladness of God. At the same time they don't hear the crying, and they don't see the bleeding, of those who have been wounded by their harshness. In their insecurity and meanness they keep kicking those who are hurting. They want them out of the way somewhere, anywhere, just as long as these broken people don't sit on their sleek and polished pews.

Lord, I don't deserve Your grace. I don't deserve Your healing touch. But, please, help me.

Ouyang was educated to be a nuclear scientist in the most prestigious university in Beijing. He was also a successful businessman who lived—as most unmarried Chinese men do—with his mother. He condensed a lifetime of history education into three years for me, and together we lamented over the ancient and lovely traditions that are now being replaced by modern, more Westernized ways. His mother, Dr. Liu, often cooked for me, and I spent many peaceful evenings with them in their apartment, sitting at their Thai rosewood table, discussing life and Chinese art, laughing at silly jokes. At the same time part of my heart was far away across the Pacific Ocean, wondering what my own family was doing.

One evening Dr. Liu and I looked up from our watercolor painting and there stood Ouyang holding his violin.

"Ouyang! You're going to play for us?" I was delighted, as I'd been asking to hear his music for a couple of years.

His mother and I put away our calligraphy inkstones, leaving the thin sheets of paper to dry, and settled down with cups of chrysanthemum tea, while Ouyang tuned his instrument. Soon we were enveloped in the warm mellow melodies he had learned as a child, taking violin lessons in secret: Beethoven, Mozart, and Mongolian shepherd songs. The sun descended and the house grew dark, but nobody wanted to break the magical mood to get up and turn on a light. So we sat in the dark, moved and stunned by the perfectly-played music.

Finally the last note was played. Ouyang set his bow down and put the violin back into its case. His mother and I clapped.

"Brava, brava. That was beautiful, my friend. But how did you remember it all? Do you practice?"

His mother laughed. "He never practices. This is the first time he's picked up his violin in years."

Ouyang smiled at us. "I will not forget that music. I learned it as a child and it became . . ." He looked around, as if searching for the appropriate words. "It became part of who I am, part of my cells and blood and tissue."

"I do understand that, yes." I nodded, thinking of a different sort of music that early in my life had become "part of me."

His mother said, "Oh, it was difficult getting Ouyang to learn the violin, Susan. We had to close the windows of the house whenever he practiced. If any of the Red Guards had heard the music, we might have been sent to prison or to the countryside."

"What a tremendous risk you took to make music a part of his life."

"We had to. I could not allow my only son to grow up without knowing music. It was my duty as his mother."

Ouyang smiled tenderly at his mother. "And my parents did not have the money to pay for the lessons. So they gave food to my teacher—eggs, rice, oil and flour."

I looked at her. "You must have gone to bed hungry many nights because of the way you sacrificed for him."

"I did, I did. But it was worth it! The hunger lasted for a little while, but the music lasts forever, yes?"

"Yes," I agreed.

Ouyang, refilling the teapot with hot water, called out from the kitchen. "One can't forget the music of one's childhood."

Sing them over again to me, wonderful words of life. Let me more of their beauty see, wonderful words of life.

After school one day, an angry parent who was a close friend of John's stood in the parking lot, handing out letters to parents. It was an account of my involvement with John—filled with half-truths and complete lies. Some parents demanded a meeting to ask why I was allowed to continue teaching in the school. I had to admit: if I had been a parent who didn't know how abusive Dr. Travis had been, how he had threatened my job, or how there were over twenty-two women all over the country who had been in the same position, I would have been upset as well. Though I received a huge amount of support from many families, I could understand that people simply couldn't believe their beloved pastor, with his charming and winsome personality, would have chosen to do something so terrible. During this time, I tried to listen, to reply in gentle tones, to counter a question with a question, for the purpose of understanding and peace. But I became accustomed to—and even tried to prepare emotionally for—people showing up in my classroom or apartment to "talk" with me about it.

My therapist, an attorney, and Jodi—the elder who had vigorously pursued a litigation of her own—all advised me to file charges. So I called John's long-suffering pastor once again, to be certain. "Please, I am asking one more time to have the opportunity for dialogue with Dr. Travis and to ask him in the presence of his pastor to please stop talking about what happened."

Again I received a flat refusal.

I wanted the abuse to stop. It had changed in nature now,

but I wanted to be able to say, "Okay, it's really over. This man can't hurt me anymore."

The assistant pastor told Jodi, "I just want to take a big piece of tape and put it across John's mouth and then put another one across Nancy's mouth." The gossip was really becoming a problem, and not just for me.

The most difficult part of filing formal charges was the fact that the newspapers only printed parts of the story. For example, they took the fact that Dr. Travis had been the pastor of the church for six years to indicate that I had been involved with him for six years. I was stunned at how confused the reporters seemed to be and how words in print are so easily believed.

It was a civil suit, since what happened wasn't a crime under the law.

I am your Salvation. Only through Me will you be healed.

*B*efore the Cultural Revolution, Ouyang's father had been the head surgeon at the largest hospital in Tianjin. As an intellectual, he was released from his position and asked to "go home," with a meager monthly salary, a fraction of what he had once earned. His wife, a nurse at the time, was also "sent home to stay." They were fortunate that they weren't sent to a remote, primitive location, as most educated individuals were.

Ouyang's father doggedly continued his medical research and contributed to professional journals, but the rest of the time was spent in studying and simply absorbing the Bible. For he was a Christian believer.

Many years earlier, Ouyang's father had been a guest professor in Toronto and, while staying in a hotel room, had found two books in the top drawer of the bedside table—the Book of Mormon and a Gideon Bible.

Assuming they were both amenities to be taken home, he packed both into his luggage, along with the tiny bars of soap. When he returned home, he put the Bible and the Book of Mormon away on a shelf in his study.

With all the time he had on his hands after his forced resignation, he studied both of the books methodically, approaching them as a scholar. He eventually arrived at the conclusion that it was the Bible that was speaking directly to him. There, alone in far-away China, without any biblical commentary, evangelist or pastor, he quietly accepted Jesus Christ as his personal Savior.

And so, during the long days of the Cultural Revolution, as he was not allowed to step outside his tiny home, Ouyang's father developed a deep, strong faith as he grew in knowledge of the Scriptures.

His son, Ouyang, was raised in the Communist schools, and by his Buddhist mother, not to believe in God, but to put his faith in science and nature.

Before he died of cancer, Ouyang's father told his son that it was God, and only God, who sustained him during those difficult and almost unbearable years of house arrest. He asked his son to consider the teachings of the Bible. But—with all due respect—Ouyang rejected his father's request. He explained that he could not consider the truth that might be discovered within the pages of this strange book his father had brought back from a far and distant land. He was a scientist and had been raised in a Communist society.

I write My words into your heart, My child. My life will neither wax nor wane. I am always the same. And I am calling you.

*D*eciding to pursue litigation was another bad choice, one of many that were heaping up in my life, rising like an impenetrable Great Wall blocking me from the gladness of God's presence. I was being told different things: Some people gently told me that I would be lifting the final vestige of shame by asking for restitution. Others asserted that I would cause incurable damage to myself, the church, and any hope of my salvation would be lost. I wasn't sure what to believe, but it was easier to listen to caring and kind words, rather than harsh and judgmental ones.

The actual experience in the judicial system was not difficult. It seemed to be permeated with a sense of fairness on all sides. The representatives from the insurance company had been through the same process several times with Dr. Travis and were familiar with the story—almost the same in each case. The judge, who was the mediator, was firm yet gentle and clearly outraged by the behavior of this man. At one point, she sent Dr. Travis across the street to sit in a café because he kept staring at me, his head turned completely to the side to burn a gaze into me.

During a lunch break, John's attorney commented to my attorney, "But so many other women were happy while they were with John. Why wasn't Susan happy too?"

After a year and a half, the settlement was agreed upon and it paid some bills. John had been sued so many times, he declared bankruptcy; but the church's insurance was satisfactory. Did I make the right decision? Absolutely not! I would never advise a man or woman in the same situation to seek litigation.

What I needed and wanted was to be able to be a member of the church and continue to be restored in my Christian walk. I wanted a return to integrity and spirituality more than any financial remuneration. Something so profound would have been best accomplished by a small, committed group of wise women.

Some days were like looking into a mirror and I could clearly see my areas of weakness for the first time in my life. I could see that there was nothing said to me or about me that I hadn't said or thought about someone else at another point in time. I thought about the saying, "Everything comes full circle."

Outwardly, I remained strong and calm, but inwardly I was regressing into a cocoon of shame. I was agreeing with people about what they were saying, for the most part, but I couldn't admit it. That was one of the biggest problems with the formal litigation: it limited and confined my growth at a time when I desperately needed to be in prayerful fellowship with others.

At the conclusion of a particularly emotional encounter, I came home and simply fell on my knees, praying, "Father, I miss you so much. I don't deserve You at all—I just miss You. I need You. I've done all the wrong things. The lawsuit is wrong, and I'm so sorry. Everyone hates me. I need to hear from You, Father."

It was one of the most amazing moments in my life. I reached for my Bible and it opened to Isaiah. My eyes scanned the page and stopped at the silent urging of the Spirit of God at the ninth verse of chapter 41. I read and highlighted the entire passage, marking the date. I was filled with a hope that could not have come from any other source. And, all through the next several years, the words of this passage (verses 9-13) have touched me. Here is what they say:

I took you from the ends of the earth, from its farthest corners
I called you. I said, 'You are my servant'; I have chosen you
and have not rejected you. So do not fear, for I am with you;
do not be dismayed, for I am your God. I will strengthen
you and help you; I will uphold you with my righteous
right hand. All who rage against you will surely be ashamed
and disgraced; those who oppose you will be as nothing and
perish. Though you search for your enemies, you will not find
them. Those who wage war against you will be as nothing
at all. For I am the Lord, your God, who takes hold of your
right hand and says to you, Do not fear; I will help you.

The day finally came in the mediation room when the kind judge said, "All of us around this table feel you deserve an enormous amount of money—if it were available."

I was grateful for the confidential settlement; it was enough for what needed to be paid.

Interestingly, it was stated in the records that I be allowed the rights to write the story of what happened.

My ways are a mystery to you, but when you hear My voice, you can rest and trust in Me.

As our brother-sister relationship deepened, Ouyang began to ask more questions about the Bible plainly displayed on my coffee table. One night he started in again: "Even though you feel very guilty about your behavior in the past, you continue to read the Bible, Susan?"

I flipped off the television with the remote and looked at my friend. "Yes, I do. I have to read it."

"You have to? You mean, you agreed once to read and study it every day, like Chairman Mao's *Little Red Book*?"

"No, no. Not like that at all. I have to read it because . . . I can't imagine trying to live without it."

"Does it contain a list of rules?"

"No, it's more of a book about love—God's love. It explains the relationship He wants to have with us and how He made a way for that to happen."

Ouyang frowned. "Do you do all the things it tells you to do, then?"

I shook my head. "No, I don't. I wish I did. I think someday I will be more mature in my faith and better able to do what it tells me to do. But I have been very foolish."

His voice grew softer. "You are a human being. You are not perfect."

"Yes, but—I knew better. I knew what to do, and I failed. For that, I will be forever sorry."

He tilted his head, processing the information. "And for that you must now pay the price?"

"Oh, Ouyang, you have such a way of helping me to focus on the things I believe in: No, I do not have to pay the price. Not now, not ever."

"And this means?"

"This means that the price has already been paid." I gathered my legs underneath me on the couch.

He threw up his hands in relief. "So then! What do you have to worry about, Susan?

"Nothing! The price has been paid."

He thought a moment. "But how? How was it paid? In fees to the church? Perhaps a fund of some sort? The Communists pay a monthly fee, you know, out of their income. It's only twenty or thirty reminbi. How much was the fine that had to be paid?"

I smiled. "Nothing. It wasn't a monetary fee."

"Then what kind of punishment was it?"

I said softly, "Jesus, the Son of God, bore all the punishment Himself. He gave His life on the cross and because of that sacrifice—there is no debt for sin. No fee, no fine, no punishment."

His eyes widened in amazement. "What? This—this religion is crazy! This I cannot believe."

He picked up the remote and found a movie we had planned to watch. Halfway through the film, he turned off the television. He was agitated. "Susan," he said, "you say you committed a great sin, yes? And for that sin Jesus was killed. But, my father committed no sins. So why did he also become a Christ man?"

I opened my Bible and read aloud Romans 3:23-24: "For all have sinned and fall short of the glory of God, and are justified freely by his grace through the redemption that came by Christ Jesus."

He shook his head stubbornly. "No, Susan. My father was

not a sinner. He was a good person, a wonderful doctor who devoted his life to his patients."

I didn't know how to respond. "I know he was a wonderful person, Ouyang. I can see his life within you, his son, and the dear wife that he left behind. This I believe. But no human being can claim to be without sin, for we are born with sin."

"The Bible's words . . . they are very strong. And you believe them. So did my father."

I smiled. "Yes, they are living words, Ouyang. They have life and breath. They aren't like the words of mere men."

He thought a while. "But what quality is it that makes the words of this book true and the words of other books not true?"

"They're God's words to us, and they are living and breathing and pulsating with life and movement and energy."

"Read more of the words to me." His voice was choking with sadness and grief, yet irresistible curiosity.

Thinking about Ouyang's father suffering through the insanity of the Cultural Revolution, I wanted to choose passages that might help to explain his father's hope. I turned to the eighth chapter of Romans and read, "'For your sake we face death all day long; we are considered as sheep to be slaughtered.' . . . in all these things we are more than conquerors through him who loved us. For I am convinced that neither death nor life, neither angels nor demons, neither the present nor the future, nor any powers, neither height nor depth, nor anything else in all creation, will be able to separate us from the love of God that is in Christ Jesus our Lord."

I looked over at my friend sitting on the rocking chair. He was waiting for more, so I flipped back to Psalm 23 and read, "The Lord is my shepherd, I shall not be in want. He makes me lie down in green pastures, he leads me beside quiet waters, he restores my soul. He guides me in paths of righteousness for his name's sake. Even though I walk through the valley of the shadow of death, I will fear no evil, for you are with me."

He stood up and paced back and forth, thinking.

I continued, "'Your rod and your staff, they comfort me. You prepare a table before me in the presence of my enemies. You anoint my head with oil; my cup overflows. Surely goodness and love will follow me all the days of my life, and I will dwell in the house of the LORD forever.'

"Then, in the book of John, it says, 'For God so loved the world that he gave his one and only Son, that whoever believes in him shall not perish but have eternal life—'"

"Stop," said Ouyang, still walking back and forth.

I looked up. "You want me to stop?"

"Yes, please."

"Why?"

"It's too personal. These are very private words and should not be uttered aloud."

I closed the Bible and looked at him. I said quietly, "These words are indeed intimate. And they are powerful."

"And they are alive," he pronounced.

I smiled. "Yes, they are alive with the very life of Jesus Christ, God's Son."

He thrust his hands into his pockets and shook his head slowly. "This is crazy, Susan. A religion for madmen! In other religions, human beings must strive to become better, do the right things and say the right words. In this religion—the religion of my father—the right words are uttered only by God. This is very different thinking to a Chinese scientist."

I am life. Through Me all things that have life are held together.

I returned to teach in the school where I had been employed prior to the Christian school. It was a private, college-preparatory environment and, while I missed my wonderful colleagues at the church school, I was happy to be working again with the friends

I had taught alongside years before. At first I was embarrassed to
see them again; after all, my name had been in a few newspaper
articles; but the only comment was from one woman who looked
directly into my eyes and said in her southern accent, "You've had
a hard time, haven't you?"

I was teaching fifth-grade history, writing, and drama—a perfect position for me. Now that the entire experience was officially
"over," I expected to bounce back and return to my former,
perky self. But I found that the death—the cold slumber—I had
been experiencing, that had been ushered into my life by the
presence of sin, was more devastating than I ever expected. While
I could still sense God's presence, there wasn't, of course, the
same intimacy and fellowship that I had once known with Him.
I craved a return to my intimacy with God—but He seemed
distant, even aloof, most of the time.

In his book, *The Road Less Travelled,* Scott Peck writes that we
can certainly break the Ten Commandments, but doing so will
only break us. My "breaking apart" was fairly obvious, I think.
I don't know how my teaching managed to be so creative and
strong during this time; in every other area I was falling apart.

My living quarters—in which I had always taken pride—
turned from House & Garden to Condo & Clutter. It didn't
happen overnight, but within a year, I had gone from keeping an
immaculate home to living . . . like a slob.

One day my brother stopped by and looked around. "Where
did all this junk come from?" I was sitting on my blue couch,
in my faded blue flannel nightgown—torn and stained with
coffee—and looked up at him through smudged glasses. I had no
idea where my meaningless mess had come from. I didn't even
know what all the stuff was. Boxes of papers and piles of things
littered the apartment—stacks of bills, letters, magazines, recipes.
There were heaps of clothes I could no longer fit into. I sat there
looking at my feet, wondering whether I would ever be able to
get out of this pit of despair and apathy. I had a huge closet
stuffed with clothes that I couldn't squeeze into, and my passion

for exercise had been replaced with quick runs to sophisticated eating establishments like Carl's Jr. and Taco Bell. I had not touched food like that since college days, but within a few months my body developed a taste for it.

I maintained a degree of professionalism at school, but my home life had become chaotic. Sometimes there were better days when I would get a burst of energy and dump out a box of things to start a massive, impossible project—like organizing photo albums for my entire life. Naturally, I'd get sidetracked with something else and would end up stepping around the stacks of photos, scraps of colored paper and glue sticks. Weeks later I'd throw it all back into an even bigger cardboard box and give up. I wasn't paying my bills on time, and when the phone was disconnected, I decided I liked it better that way. I lived without a telephone for more than a year, going out to the pool area to use the pay phone when I called my family.

I had a new boyfriend during this time, a sound technician at a large East Bay church. We sat on the blue couch and watched television—night after night—until he went home. We ate pretzels, potato chips, beef jerky, hard candy, and ice cream. I allowed myself to gain quite a lot of weight, sitting there on the blue couch munching treats, laughing at the funny things Kevin said, feeling comfortable with his gentle, undemanding ways.

Though you feel it is over, I have plans for your life.

*T*he cranberry-red telephone rang shrilly. I stumbled from the bedroom to the living room to answer it. "Hello?"

"Susan, I feel foolish for asking this, because I do not believe he exists, but please pray to your God. Ask Him to help my mother's cold." *Click.*

The next morning I called Ouyang. "Is your mother better?"

"She's getting better. Thank your God for helping."

"Ouyang, He might appreciate receiving your thanks directly, you know. He would love to talk with you and have a close relationship with you."

He called that night. "Susan, how can I have a close relationship with your God, since He can't possibly exist?"

"That's the mystery of faith, my friend. It comes down to faith. But He gives a peace that convinces us of His presence, so it isn't as difficult as it seems."

Click. (At that time, the people of Tianjin had had telephones in their homes for only three years, and they hadn't yet learned to say good-bye before hanging up.)

The following afternoon Ouyang was waiting on the street outside my school at the end of the work day. His face was swollen like a turnip with layers of bandages and purple bruises.

"Ouyang, what happened?"

"I was riding home last night on my bicycle about ten kilometers from my office. I stopped to have some wine with a friend from middle school, and I had too much, apparently. Look at me!"

"In America, people who drink too much and drive are called drunk drivers. I guess in China that would be drunk riders."

"Yes, I was a drunk rider. This happens often in China."

We walked to a small restaurant that specializes in slow-roasted pork, so tender the meat falls off the bone. We savored each bite of the rich, sweet meat mixed with jasmine rice and green beans sautéed with garlic and red chili peppers.

I said, "So delicious, Ouyang. I sometimes can't believe the food in China."

"It's either wonderful or terrible for you! When it's pig tongue or ox privates, you hate it! When it's pork, beef, or chicken, you love it! The American diet is too boring. You eat only three kinds of meat—beef, chicken and pork!"

I laughed. "Not really, Ouyang. You forgot fish."

"People want to go live in other countries, but many stay just because of the food!" he laughed, then winced at the pain.

"Ouch, it looks like your face hurts. What did your mother say when you got home?"

"She didn't say much. Her anger was too great, I'm afraid."

"I don't blame her!"

I thought back to one Easter Sunday fifteen years earlier.

Ouyang noticed my sudden silence. "What's wrong?"

"Oh, I was remembering something from the past. My father was once arrested for drunk driving and he didn't get home until just before it was time to go to church. And it was Easter."

"Oh, the grand Easter party—I remember. So? That's not a big deal. Everyone drinks too much once in a while."

"Not pastors of churches, Ouyang."

"Is he an alcoholic?"

"No, thankfully. He has only one addiction—gambling."

He smiled. "He is your father. You love him and your God loves him, yes?"

"Yes, I do love him, my friend. And I know for sure that God loves him dearly."

"Then it doesn't matter what he does. I never liked the fact that my father smoked continually. I asked him many times to stop; but he couldn't. Now he's dead, and I wish everyday he was still here smoking. Even the things we dislike about our families become precious when they're gone. We miss their coughing. We miss their grouchiness. We miss their human condition."

On our walk back to the Peace Apartments, we walked through an area of hutongs that always made me acutely aware of the sense of friendly community amongst the old neighborhoods. The people mostly lived outside, underneath strings of lights hung on tree branches. People were brushing their teeth, squatting near the street and spitting into the dirt. Some were sleeping on newspaper and makeshift plywood mattresses. Some shaggy-haired boys were balancing on loose boards tossed aside in dirt; grandmothers were cooking; and the men were smoking, playing games and talking. Ouyang waited while I held a toddler in my arms, a baby I often stopped to play with.

"Susan," he said. "Somehow you must learn to forgive your father for not being perfect. For gambling, for drunk driving, for changing. This you must do, yes? You agree?"

"Yes, I do need to forgive him, my friend. You are correct."

"If you do not forgive, you will die a miserable woman."

For once, I was speechless.

"Your father is not your God. He is a sinner, just like you are. He is a human being."

We walked in silence for a while, both of us thinking our own thoughts. Then Ouyang said, "Now, I want to ask you about your problem, the rest of your problem. The part that you're trying to get away from."

"Oh, that. Yes—my problem."

He stopped and faced me. "Do you think the problem is getting better now? Is your God helping you with it?"

"Yes, He is. All last year I had nightmares about it. I woke up through the nights, unable to forget my failures. And I began reading the Bible more and disciplining myself to simply sit in God's presence, absorbing His love."

He smiled. "Again . . . too intimate for me. Don't forget I am a scientist and a pragmatic Chinese businessman."

"Thanks for reminding me," I teased. "Okay, let me try to explain it another way. I realized I was running from God when I was running from my problems, you see. So I began to change the direction I was running, and I began running towards God. When I made the smallest step toward Him, I realized He had already been walking towards me. Does this make any sense?"

"It makes perfect sense. It sounds like your God knows that you are a human."

I nodded. "Yes, He does and He has provided perfectly for my human weaknesses." My Chinese nuclear-scientist friend had a way of helping me see exactly what I needed to see.

We slowly walked, talking until the twilight blended colors

and shadows and at last there was only a deep blue-black. The flashing neon lights of the city grew dim. We made our way back to the Peace Apartments in thick, still darkness.

The pain, the pain. . . . It's too much. . . . And I want so much. I want, I want.

I was once offered a job in an upscale department store as a personal shopper. The idea was appealing: get to know the wealthier, classier clients, make home visits, and do their shopping for them.

It was during this time of decay in my life that I realized I had my very own Personal Shopper dedicated to my shopping success. During those days when the symptoms of post trauma were slamming into my life, I went shopping nearly five times a week. The incessant chatter of my hardworking Personal Shopper filled up all the emptiness inside. I'd be sitting at my desk when she'd begin: "What time is it? Oh, it's only four o'clock. Well, these papers should be graded, but first—let's get some groceries. You can make a nice, healthy dinner—just green salad and lightly steamed broccoli. Then you'll feel like coming back to work. After all, won't you be more alert after eating a nutritious meal?"

Pleased with myself for coming to some kind of decision, which was extremely difficult to do during those days, I'd continue the conversation all the way out to my car. By the time I had fastened the seatbelt, my Personal Shopper had managed to change the plans.

"Listen, why don't you get groceries tomorrow? You're so hungry right now, and you barely had any lunch, so wouldn't it be easier to go someplace nice and quiet, order a quick bite to eat, and then be done with it? No lugging big bags back home, no dishes to wash. So easy! In fact, it would be fun to swing by the mall, wouldn't it? Granted, it's a bit out of the way but Nordstrom does have such a tasty spinach salad."

Of course, I loved going to Nordstrom, where everyone was cheerful and friendly, and where I could enjoy a quiet dinner. And after eating, they made it so convenient to stop for a cup of fresh coffee to carry around while I wandered through the gleaming, attractive store with all the nice people. (I've learned since, that normal people simply do not go into an expensive department store not needing or intending to buy anything and then exiting with several bulging shopping bags in tow.)

My Personal Shopper got to work. "First, let's just take a little walk through the children's section . . . " She made it so easy. And why did the insertion of that small word "just" strategically placed into a sentence somehow make it all more acceptable?

"Oh, my . . . now, what's this? You didn't see this dress last week, did you? Mmm, the price is high, but it's so cute. Your niece, Lauren, will look adorable in this. I don't know—this pink is a little too peachy. Where is that nice salesgirl? Let's ask her for her opinion—after all, she's the expert here."

A few light, enjoyable conversations with eager and patronizing clerks made life so much more pleasant. They never commented on my weight. They knew nothing about my sinful mistakes. They managed to convince me that they liked me.

My Personal Shopper seemed quite devoted to her task twenty-four hours a day. She was eager to look through mail-order catalogs at a moment's notice and stayed up late to watch the Home Shopping Network with me. Her stamina was amazing! Just when I thought I'd run out of energy, she'd rise to the occasion and pull me through yet another wild shopping expedition. The only breaks she took were during the tense moments at the cash register, when I'd stand—breathlessly wondering whether my card would be accepted. Was it maxed out? Would they have to make a phone call to verify my check? My heart pounded as I smiled at the clerk, marveling at her kindness to me. I'd say weakly, "Wow, I guess I spent a lot today, didn't I?"

My Personal Shopper was nowhere to be found during these times. (Maybe that's when she went to get a refill on her coffee.) The ever-cheerful clerks never let me down, though. They filled the awkward silence as tissue was tucked around each purchase, their words always soothing and logical-sounding: "Well, this way you have these things and . . ." I'd sign the credit card slip while she walked around the counter and handed me the beautifully-wrapped bag, adding in a soft voice, "You'll be ready for any occasion with this in your closet." I'd nod seriously and reflect on her wisdom. "Mmm, yes, that's true."

Just as I was heading out to my car, perhaps several hundred dollars later, my Personal Shopper magically showed up with a few parting words. "Oh, now you didn't see this blouse earlier, did you? Did they just put it out? Maybe it's a new arrival!" I'd stop to finger the blouse. "You know, it reminds me of that top at Laura Ashley. And that reminds me . . . is their mid-winter sale still on? Maybe you should take the time right this minute to walk over and have a look. Think of what you might miss."

My life had become chaotic and lonely, yet packed to the brim with clutter that somehow kept the pain down to a manage-able level. I was filling up all the space that longed for healing and for wholeness with endless decisions about styles, color combina-tions, and accessories. If I kept myself busy enough with "stuff," I might not have to think about what an empty place my soul had become.

Nothing can fill your desires but My loving presence.

Ouyang began calling daily with prayer requests. Would I ask my God to help his friend who was hospitalized with hepatitis?

Would I talk with my God about his girlfriend who was playing violin in the Singapore Symphony? Would I ask my God to put a bit of divine pressure on her to move back to Tianjin?

He asked questions, thinking and wondering as his brilliant mind kept soaking in what I was telling him in simple ways. One day he asked if he might borrow my Bible to read it for himself.

And he did read it. It took several months, but he read it from cover to cover. We continued to talk and share deeply—all through that long white winter. Then one evening, as we were sitting comfortably on my sofa, I accidentally knocked over a glass on the table, creating a domino effect that sent the Bible on a flight across the room, to land on the hardwood floor.

Ouyang shouted, "Be careful, Susan! Remember those words are living words! You can't just throw them around like that. They have their own life."

Stunned, I smiled into his angry black eyes, one slightly smaller than the other. He thought for a moment. Then he stunned me even more.

"I believe now," he said. "I want a relationship with the God who understands humans."

Listen to Me and hear My Voice. For someday all other sounds will fall away and the only sound will be My Voice speaking and reaching and living . . . forever.

*O*ne winter night Ouyang and I had dinner at a German restaurant near my school, about two miles from the Peace Apartments. We appreciated the effort that had gone into attempting Western food, and enjoyed the large bowls of chocolate ice cream that we ate with chopsticks. As we sat at a tiny table near a snow-flaked window, Ouyang said he had something to show me.

We pulled on our heavy snow parkas, another layer over at least four layers altogether, paid the bill and stepped out onto the icy streets. Being with a good friend on a Saturday night was warming and deeply comfortable. Ouyang considered me his gift from God, sent to share the love of the True God, but I felt he was a gift, also. He was sent to teach me, to make me laugh, to show me his country. Most of our times together were intense, complicated, and often filled with delightful hilarity.

Trekking in the snow, we passed through the hutong neighborhoods, close and compact, lit with fluorescent lights. Ouyang helped me avoid stepping on the rats that came out at night. The sounds of the night surrounded us: honks from swerving taxi cabs, squeaks of passing bicycles, and strains of Celine Dion singing "My Heart Will Go On" from every street corner.

We walked even further away from the crowded streets and reached a stretch where the only sound was the soft crunch of snow under our boots. I whispered, "Ouyang, where are we going? Can you give me a clue?"

He motioned to be quiet and whispered in my ear, "Soon. You'll see."

We went around another corner, and just in front of us was a park encircled with intricate iron fencing. Here we stopped. I heard something—the sound of moving feet. The feet were shuffling, stepping, and crunching in the icy snow. And then, as my eyes adjusted to the gloom, I saw the people. There were lots of people, dancing in the silence on an oval cement slab next to the weathered gazebo in the darkness of the park. Though they were bundled in heavy, drab outerwear and chunky boots, their movements were light and graceful. And as I watched I imagined them floating in pastel chiffon or silk that flowed in sync to the imaginary music. Instead of being cushioned in thick layers against the cold, I "saw" the men in Western-style suits with ties and black dancing shoes that caught the moon's glow. And instead of the silence of a snowy evening, I imagined a fantasia orchestra with rich, mellow sound. As my eyes grew accustomed to the darkness, I could see the bliss on their faces—now lined and wrinkled—faces that had seen the violent, bloody Cultural Revolution. It had stolen much from them, but not all.

"Ouyang—" I whispered.

"They've been dancing like this a long time. They kept the dancing alive, secretly, while they were confined to their homes or in prison camps or while being 're-educated' in the countryside."

We watched in respectful, awed silence and I reached for my friend's arm. "Ouyang, it is so beautiful."

"Indeed it is. This is the culture that was stolen and replaced with the culture of nothingness."

"But they kept it alive, what was taken from them. For all those years."

He smiled. "Yes, exactly. The angry mobs could take everything they owned of material value . . . but they weren't able to take what was in their hearts."

I murmured, "Our treasures are not in things that can be taken by thieves or eaten by moths. Our treasures are found in our hearts."

Don't forget My Voice . . . I am always speaking.

The days on the blue couch in my messy house came to an abrupt end. Through a teaching colleague who knew someone with the right connections, I was offered a teaching position in northern China. I was interviewed by telephone twice. Then I traveled to Los Angeles to meet the school director's completely charming wife. She asked, "Are you ready for this? Life will be very different, you know."

It sounded like music to my ears—different I wanted!

I accepted the job, cleaned up the house, threw the blue

couch away, and put everything else into storage. Traveling with six cardboard boxes, my laptop computer, and three suitcases, I arrived in Beijing to teach music and drama in Tianjin, near the Yellow Sea and south of the Gobi Desert.

I didn't know it at the time, but something new was on its way. Out of long seasons of culture shock and intermittent loneliness that stretched before me, would come a healing that could not have happened had I remained in a cycle of escaping into shopping, eating and sleeping. I had to be literally removed from one environment and deposited into another before the destructive routines were broken. And what was left was a raw, festering wound that I strained to hide so cleverly.

And so I landed in a country broken by its own history, a most fitting place for a lost person such as myself. The healing didn't happen all at once; it would take years. There was still so much pain—a gaping, enveloping darkness.

And here I was, in exotic Asia, in Communist China. Everything for me was new and unique. I was experiencing a different culture and language. But I had escaped the junk food and unhealthy magnet of the depressive blue couch.

Life at the Peace Apartments was simple. Almost without thinking I eased back into some of the healthier routines I had adhered to most of my life—exercise, prayer, journal writing. The most important change was that worshipping God became critical and practical to me again.

And these days were critical to the rebuilding of my character. There were no tempting department stores and very little English programming on TV. I didn't have Internet access for the first two years, either, so I spent much of the initial time simply bringing my brokenness before the Lord. There were fleeting moments of spectacular glory, as I quietly began turning to God. There were times when I could almost touch Him—the veil seemed so thin. I could hear His voice penetrating my heart with whispers that sounded familiar and true—words I had once known beyond the shadow of doubt but now needed to hear anew.

There were times of tearful repentance and confession, times I felt unable to believe again for fear of what He would say to me. As time passed and as the dust began to clear and blow away, I saw Who was standing right there beside me. The grime and mess of what I had allowed my life to become made it hard to see at first, but then—after waiting in silence—there He was. Christ Jesus strode through the embers and ashes, looking beyond my weariness and weightiness—right into my soul. He picked me up effortlessly and carried me to a safer place. He stayed close; I began to trust in Him once again, to feel His scarred hands washing away the filth, smoothing the matted hair and unsnarling the tangles in my life. I knew there was no need to hide myself in shame anymore, for He had come to release me from bondage. He brought me into a place swept with fresh winds.

He had not abandoned me! In fact, I was astounded when I realized He still loved me and whispered words of love to my spirit. And it was through His Spirit that He spoke of His desire to heal and rebuild my life for His glory.

My Word does not return to Me void. I accomplish all that I intend and My intention is for your good. Always.

Mrs. Hua's step granddaughter, Meow Meow (a popular name in China!), was preparing to take an oral English test to qualify for a study-abroad program in Canada. She asked Ouyang and me to have dinner with her in Beijing, to give her practice in speaking. We caught the train and, within an hour, we were making our way through the pressing mass of hotels, taxi drivers, and beggars on the square outside the railway station.

Meow Meow had reserved a table for us at a famous Beijing restaurant. Ouyang took one look at the spread and whispered, "Susan, I don't think you will enjoy this Chinese meal."

I looked across the table at Meow Meow, her eyes shining with anticipation. I couldn't be rude and refuse to eat, so I picked up my chopsticks. The meat on my small plate was mostly fat and bones. It was a challenge to find a few slivers of flesh.

Meow Meow noticed I was struggling to eat and asked Ouyang if she should order a different dish. He laughed. "Susan has a hard time eating bones." He looked at her with an expression of mock weariness. "She is the opposite of a Chinese."

I suggested, "Maybe we could ask them for the same dish, just without so many bones?"

Meow Meow looked doubtful, but when the waitress stepped up she asked if they had some leaner meat.

The girl looked surprised and turned to me. "This is dog. If you don't like bones, order beef or donkey."

Dog! I concentrated on not gagging.

Ouyang was obviously suppressing a laugh. "I decided not to tell you it was dog, Susan. Dog isn't always bony or fatty. Sometimes it's delicious, like mutton. But dogs are very complicated animals, and not good, emotionally, for humans to eat, in my opinion. Besides it's not winter. If one eats dog it should be in the winter time."

Meow Meow solved the problem by requesting to see the menu again. Then she read the remaining choices to us:

FRIED DOVE GIZZARD WITH PEPPER
SHREDDED FISH SKIN WITH SAUCE
YAK EAR WITH PICKLED PEPPER
SNOUT WITH SLICED GARLIC
SHEEP MUSCLE MIXED WITH PEPPER
FRIED BEEF OMASUM WITH PEPPER
STICK INSECT MIXED WITH CASHEWS AND CELERY
SPICY ROAST PRAWNS

She pointed to the last offering and I apologized for being unwilling to eat dog. Ouyang asked the manager if I could keep the menu as a keepsake and we went on to practice English.

I want, I want. I still want so much, Father.

I never intended to stay in China so long. One year led
to the next and, after three years, I accepted another music
position in Guangzhou, the first city I had visited on my trip
in 1980. I said good-bye to Mrs. Hua, Ouyang, Dr. Liu, and
all the friends who had become my Chinese family. Asian Tiger
Moving Company trucked down all my belongings, coinciding
their arrival with mine.

It was in Guangzhou, near Hong Kong, that God moved
more deeply in my life than I had ever experienced. There were
secret areas that He desired to touch with His Spirit—layers of
thinking that needed healing and cleansing. There were depths
of childhood pain that rose up when I least expected them to.
There was a deeper work He wanted to accomplish in me. I had
much more to learn.

As I took the train to Hong Kong, I reflected on the differences in the landscape, quite changed, as all things were, from
my first train journey to Hong Kong long ago. Gone were
the verdant plains sweeping right up to the gently rolling hills,
and in their place were factories belching black smoke and tall
dormitories hastily erected to house the workers who labored
within those factories. Neatly-squared apartment buildings stood
evenly spaced, their white-tiled balconies lined with damp clothing. From my seat on the train, they resembled doll-sized clothes.
As the train rumbled into Hong Kong, I reflected on the beauty
of what I had seen long ago on that first July afternoon compared
to what I saw today. Now, row after row of gray skyscrapers made
a colorless pattern against an equally gray sky. And I could imagine the people inside those apartments—whole families stuffed

into tiny, airless rooms, shuffling about in plastic sandals. They were living uncomplaining, as life required them to live. They were trying to breathe through a tiny hole but were gradually suffocating.

I looked at the passengers on the seats around me. Well-groomed businessmen in suits and ties were studying papers held in leather briefcases. Young women in their twenties and thirties, wore strappy sandals and silk dresses. And there were some rougher mainland Chinese women on that train—their skin spotted with sun and age. They were shrieking into cell phones that had Beethoven symphonies as ring tones. They called one another and then dissolved into giggles. One woman shoved a finger into her nose while she fidgeted, opening and shutting the curtains again and again. She was wearing a pink polyester top over pants with a swirling pattern of oranges, burgundy and royal blue. A few of the others turned completely around in their seats to stare at the foreign passengers. After a while, they put their feet on the arm rests of passengers' seats directly in front of them. When the attendant rolled a cart of chicken legs down the aisle, many bought them and things quieted down for a bit. Their concentration now was devoted to chewing the glistening, brown chicken legs, crunching teeth against bone. Finally, most of them managed to get comfortable and calm down enough to fall into deep sleeps resonating with loud, throaty snores.

I tried to move my mind away from the drizzly humidity and the smell of unwashed hair to the white sky pressing down on the buildings outside. I prayed for a kinder and more open heart, then I moved into prayer for these women travelers. My guess is that they were factory workers taking an excursion into Hong Kong. I thought about how the clothes or the things they made were probably the very items that we would buy in Wal-Mart that summer.

I will stop at nothing for your heart, My child. I want your entire heart.

I had been living in Asia for five years. I knew by this time that God had forgiven me completely, but the grieving process continued. And I was still having a hard time forgiving myself.

On the personal level, I was facing major surgery. It was scheduled for the last day of the school year in Hong Kong. Ouyang called to ask about it, then we went on to other topics. He was full of the wonder and joy that a new Christian experiences, learning to walk with Jesus.

"I have decided the Christ faith is a kind of mysterious thing," he announced.

"Yes, I think you are right, my friend."

"And we don't have to solve the mystery to be a Christ."

"Yes, it is impossible to figure out a holy God, isn't it?"

"Very impossible! This is why so many cannot believe in such a God that cannot be scientifically explained."

"And yet once we open up and trust, we find a peace in acceptance."

His joyful laughter was contagious. "Yes, true. Very mysterious kind of peace. Impossible to explain logically!"

"Ouyang, let me ask you something. If you could have a God that was explainable and logical, would He be much of a God, do you think?"

"No. I do not want a god that is a statue I can carry around in my backpack or hang on my wall. Those gods are not real. How can they be? Man has created them to fulfill something in his own imagination. Those kinds of gods are too little."

"Yes, yes, I understand exactly what you're saying, my friend."

"And I don't want a god that I have to travel long miles to visit, one that lives in a temple. I want a God who is everywhere, even though the scientist in me struggles with that idea."

I smiled. "I was just thinking about this last week, Ouyang—about the mystery of God. It never goes away, you know. That sense of mystery and not understanding everything. But the Bible tells us someday we will understand completely."

"Yes! And I believe that, Susan. God has His own way of thinking."

"That is so true, my friend. When I discovered I had to undergo surgery, I was quite angry with God, I am sorry to admit."

"I think we can tell Him all our feelings, Susan. Even your American feelings which are so dramatic."

The week before this conversation, I was writing curriculum plans late into the night in the music office, having spent the day at the doctor in Hong Kong. I had been in Guangzhou for two years, putting in long hours building the music program. And my heart was still heavy with unfulfilled hopes and desires. I was feeling a great deal of self pity. I looked outside at the Southeast Asian spring rainstorm, and decided not to go out until the skies began to quiet down. The heavy rains pounded sideways, pounding into buildings and windows, and I had learned the wisdom of staying put until the inevitable break in the storm came.

I put aside my work and knelt in the darkened office. I prayed, "Father, I do not understand why life has been so difficult. I would have rather died and gone to heaven than to live through the terrible things that I have experienced. Why didn't You help me more? Why didn't you stop some of these things from occurring? Father, I want good things to start happening. I am so tired of all the bad things. Please just don't let it hurt so much anymore."

There was no response. No wondrous voice speaking in my heart. All was silent except the fat drops pelting the windows outside.

"Father, okay. I can't pretend to not believe in You. I know better than that. And You know that I know better. So, I'll move on to the disappointment. I won't complain to others,

but between You and me, Father—it's been too much disappointment. Okay?"

Silence. More tears. I was thinking about the baby I had lost
and the upcoming procedure which would remove, along with
three large tumors, all chances of having a baby. The disappointment came in waves. "Father, I would have been contented with
one baby. Why couldn't I have had just one when others have so
many children?" The tears flowed and the rain poured. "Father,
please speak to me."

Silence.

I spent another hour on my knees, then paced the length of
my office, watching the rain beat fiercely outside. I continued,
"Father, You know what a great wife I would have been. You
created me to love. You know how hard I'd work at it—please,
Lord, let me be a wife to a husband who loves me. Surely there
must be one man out there that I can respect and adore?"

Silence. Tears. Rain.

I fell to my knees again, more subdued this time. "Okay,
Father. I know You are always speaking, even in Your silence. I
know I am prideful. I confess that, and I ask for Your cleansing.
Please, tell me. What else do You want from me? What else has to
happen before I can experience intimacy that is blessed by You?"
The tears were pouring from a seemingly limitless source.

"You want me to serve You, to love You, to continue to give
You my all, I know. Can You please—because I am human and
weak and longing—give me some indication of when my desires
for marriage might be met?"

I pressed my tear-stained face against the window in the
darkness, watching the taxis coming and going on the street
below. From somewhere deep inside the pain, I cried out in
anger, "How dare You ask everything of me without giving me
anything, Father. Please, help me. I don't understand the pain. It's
gone on too long and it's too hard for me."

I waited for an answer with an open heart, but there was
none. I continued in prayer, in this calling out of my pain to my

Heavenly Father for at least two more hours. Finally, just after midnight, I bent in a posture of humility and worship. "All right, I worship You in spite of having to live with such heartache for so long. I give You everything, even if all I have is just this nagging pain. I choose to believe in You, no matter how long my desires go unfulfilled. I will be Yours, no matter what."

I turned off my computer, locked up the office and walked down the four flights of stairs to the lobby, where I nodded good-night to the security guard. I walked the ten minutes through the steamy streets and took a hot shower before crawling into bed with my heart still broken. I fell asleep reflecting on the fact that I was choosing to trust in a Heavenly Father that I could not see and frankly, at this point—could not sense clearly. I was far away from my American culture. I had no crutches on which to lean, and I felt as if I was standing on a cliff, falling in faith to some unknown depth below. What if there was nothing more ahead of me other than more pain and loss? There were no guarantees that life would get happier or easier—and I was scared.

It's been seven years since that rainy night when broken and bent by shattered dreams, I placed my trust into the hands of God completely. He was compelling me, even in His silence, into a deeper place where He was preparing to meet me.

You will go in and out through Me, the Door, to find healing and refreshment, grace and purpose.

Before I left California, I had my fifth-grade classes read Marguerite deAngeli's classic medieval tale, *The Door in the Wall*. Once the students became familiar with the "thees" and the "arensts," they found themselves caught up in the story of a boy, Robin. He was left alone in a great house somewhere outside of London. His father, a knight, was away at war, while his mother was attending to the queen of England. Left to the care of servants who, one by one, fell ill with the plague, Robin himself became the victim of yet another physical malady—one which left him unable to use his legs at all, lying helplessly in bed day after day. He would listen to the other children playing merrily in the street just beyond the walls of his room. Finally, a good-hearted monk was told of the young boy's state and he took the invalid to his monastery in another city.

My fifth graders looked up and asked, "Will he ever walk again?" But as the story unfolded, the question somehow became irrelevant; Robin was learning all kinds of things at the monastery: how to carve wood, play a musical instrument, swim. He became so immersed in living, although differently than he had once hoped, he almost forgot about the things he could not do. And, as the story draws to an end, Robin realizes that even in his crippled condition, with his legs bent "like two sausages" his condition had itself become a door in the damp stone wall that stood between the sick bed and the echoes of laughter in the street.

Years later, while I was lying in the bed at Matilda Hospital in Hong Kong, gazing out the window with a view of the blue bay, I thought back to that story. My hopes for a child were ending in that hospital. To have a baby of my own would then be out of the question—that door was slamming permanently shut.

After the surgery, I lay on the bed without once turning on the television. I watched the ships on the harbor, moving like tiny toys in and out of the bay. I listened to the sounds of the hospital and chatted with nurses in crisp, white uniforms. I thought about how my life was unfolding in Asia, and I remembered the years in America where I had been locked inside a walled prison, reduced to listening to the laughter just on the other side. My imprisonment was mostly of my own choosing, but that fact didn't lessen its agony or sense of isolation. Everything had seemed out of reach, behind a door I couldn't unlock. And as the grace of Jesus slowly unfolded itself in its living, speaking way, life gradually seeped into my legs of stone, causing them to walk and to run and to even leap in joy.

As I healed in the hospital so far from the land of my birth, I sensed Jesus was with me. His own life had become a wider part of the door. I knew, as sad as I was again, that the grief would not disable me this time. I was stronger now, more sure in the heart of Jesus' own heart.

John 10:9 tells us that Jesus is the door and that He offers us a pathway, an entrance in and out. And as a child wanders in blissfulness, finding play and pasture, nourishment and nurture in fields of green as far as the eye can see and even beyond that, I knew I had a gracious invitation to pass through the doors of my own broken dreams. I would never hold my own baby in my arms, but I knew the giver of all life. I might not ever have a lovely home again, but I was at home within the heart of God. I would never receive a Mother's Day card or be able to read bedtime stories to my children. However, I understand the anguish of crushed dreams—and that understanding carves out a deeper path through which I run to God.

And just as Robin in the story discovered, the brokenness and malfunction that was left in the wake of sin was in itself becoming a way of finding God. While He was offering release to me, as I had been huddled in pain, wrapped in smallness, He was also causing unimaginable good to rise out of the rubbish. And I began to hear the strains of His Voice beckoning me to come out from behind the stone wall to a wider place—a place where I could run and dance and laugh—and to leave my crutches behind and climb higher and further than I would have thought possible.

It's not as if I was denying the pain that had been there; I was moving beyond the pain to all that awaited me in a relationship with the Divine.

You can put all your trust in Me, My child. I am committed to caring for you—forever.

*O*n one of my extra-long "commutes" to work—the Trans-Pacific flight I take at the end of each summer—I met a woman scientist from northern California. On the fifteen-hour journey we got acquainted. She explained that she was returning for a visit to her parents' home in Beijing. She had fled China just after the Tiananmen Square Incident in 1989—she had been one of the idealistic university students who had gone on a hunger strike for days, sitting in the hot sun on the People's Square, protesting the government and calling for democracy. Now she lives in Fremont with her scientist husband and seventeen-year-old daughter. They have a stunning four-bedroom home with a family room, home offices, and swimming pool in the backyard. Her American dream has come true.

I asked, "Are you glad you came to America? Has it been all you hoped for?"

She sighed wearily. "I was elated at the beginning. We had good paying jobs . . . and freedom. But now I can't help but think about the simplicity of China. When I visit my parents, I get together with my university classmates and they tell me how easy it has become to make money in Beijing. Of course they don't make the salaries my husband and I make, but they don't suffer from job stress either. Everything, such as housing and food, is cheaper in China. My friends don't have cars—that makes life less complicated. And they have support from friends and family nearby. Their children are less sophisticated but happier. My friends don't have to worry about where their children are—they know they're in the next room, studying. I can barely sleep at night, wondering where my daughter is and what she's doing. She has a car, as do all of her friends. She is rude and belligerent to me. This wouldn't happen in Beijing. Yes, I miss the simplicity of China."

I had to agree with her. When I'm in America, I miss China. People ask, "What is it about China that you find so appealing?" That is a difficult question to answer. Besides being able to teach in outstanding schools that serve children from many countries around the world, I have come to cherish the feeling of China itself: the smells, the density, the trees, the surprises, the smiles, the mystery, the madness, the resentments, the trust. I feel honored to be living in the frayed fringes of some of the most tumultuous history anywhere. The cells of my skin have sloughed and floated off to mingle with those of the Chinese people, and who I am has now become irreversibly intertwined with part of who they are. The air, the thoughts, the expectations and the habits keep popping and exploding like quick jolts and sharp jabs, piercing into my understanding of the way things should be.

While in the States, my mind was on my Chinese friends. Dr. Liu wanted me to bring her an African-American baby doll. Mrs. Hua wanted more Spirulina and American aspirin. I spent days searching Los Angeles for a Charlie Chaplan momento for her.

One summer day, while on my way to a continuing-education course at Cal State Northridge, I stepped into an elevator. A Chinese woman in her twenties was going to the same floor. I asked, "Where are you from, in China?"

She answered, "Tianjin."

I laughed. "You won't believe this, but I teach school in Tianjin!" The world was shrinking.

Memories and reminders of losses loomed larger when I was in California. On each visit, I went through my storage units and boxed up things to give to charity or to needy people: furniture, clothes, shoes, books. Little by little I was letting go of the crutches and junk to which I had once clinged. The emotional grip that material possessions had on me was loosening. The void that I had been struggling to fill up with stuff became more tolerable. I was learning to live with the ambiguity of not knowing what the future holds. I could tolerate times of silence

and grief. I was able to release the pain in tears, as I cried to
think of the tragedies of my marriage and my parents' marriage.
I was no longer afraid to face that pain; I didn't have to hide
it anymore. And as I allowed myself to look directly into the
suffering, there was a sweet tinge of grace that brought me closer
to the aching side of others . . . and to the aching side of Jesus.

In losing your life, you will find life.

I spent the 2005 Christmas holidays in Hong Kong, in one
of my favorite hotels, a mid-priced establishment that edges the
Victoria Harbor, where one can see nightly laser-light extravagan-
zas. There was even a small ship draped with Christmas lights and
the sound of carolers floated by every half hour or so. This was as
close to an American Christmas as I could get.

The first night I awoke with the flu. It was worse the next day
and grew steadily worse as the days passed. I had inattentively left
my medical insurance card in Guangzhou and was determined
to avoid going to the expensive Hong Kong hospitals. The hotel
staff knew me well, as this was the hotel I normally stayed in,
and they kindly replenished my bottled water supply to keep me
hydrated. I spent five long days in bed with a high fever, severe
diarrhea and vomiting.

On the morning of the fifth day, I knew I had to get back
to Guangzhou. I had been tossing and turning the entire five
days on my bed, listening to the sounds of Christmas. With some
help from the hotel staff, I managed to check out and take a
taxi the short distance to the railway station. We had to stop a
few times en route so that I could throw up on the street—as I
apologized profusely.

The driver was certain I'd be unable to make the train trip.
He helped me carry the bags to buy the ticket and then delivered

me to the train attendants, who were clearly not impressed with my odiferous and disheveled state. I had not had a shower in five days and I was a mess. In spite of being so ill, I was embarrassed.

The train attendants in China and Hong Kong don't help you with baggage. I had traveled often on the train and knew this, now wondering how I'd survive the long lines, being jostled about by the rushing crowds. I knew that being sick wouldn't make a difference to these people and I was right—at first.

It took sheer will power to get through customs and immigration, pushing my bags along with my feet, then sitting on top of them whenever I could. By the time I made it to the passenger waiting room, I had collapsed on the floor and was unable to go any further. People stepped around me, muttering, "You should be in the hospital" or "Why are you trying to travel?"

The whistles blew and the crowds ran to the escalators, but I was still lying on the linoleum floor, trying to inch my way along. I had left my bags at that point—they now seemed unimportant compared to my goal of boarding the train. I had to get to Guangzhou and to the hospital.

One of the uniformed attendants reluctantly offered to carry my luggage. I was amazed. He also helped me to my feet and took me to the elevator. I hadn't noticed an elevator before and was thrilled to avoid the escalator, which seemed too tricky in my present condition. He stood behind me in order to steady me on the moving conveyor, otherwise I don't think I would have been able to stand at all. The stench on my clothes and in my hair was revolting, but I was almost too ill to care.

He kept saying, "You are too sick to go on the train. You must go to the hospital now."

I kept shaking my head. "No, I cannot. My insurance is in China. I must go there."

In spite of his reservations, he continued to help me. When we finally got to the entrance of the train, there before us stood the most unusual-looking Chinese man I had ever seen. He was practically a giant and spoke a dialect I had never heard before. The expression in his eyes was—different. He was simply standing there, not collecting ticket stubs or checking passports. When he saw me, he took my face in both his hands and focused his eyes directly into mine.

"Susan, you need to see a doctor."

I nodded. "I will, as soon as I get to Guangzhou. My doctor is there. But I am so sick, I'm afraid I will throw up on the train." I vaguely wondered how he knew my name.

As his eyes kept locked with mine I gradually felt calmer. "I am here to help you," he said.

"Are you a doctor?"

His eyes shifted to one side and he smiled slightly. "No, I am not a doctor."

But by then he had already taken my bags and the task of climbing onto the train seemed easy with his assistance. And as strange as it sounds, he walked behind me down the aisle but I don't remember walking at all. It felt more as if we floated down the aisle. As he showed me my seat, I mumbled something about my bags and he said, "Don't worry about that. I am taking care of them."

I sat and he knelt beside me in the aisle on one knee. I was worried I would begin vomiting again. He kept looking at me directly. He took out a small vial of oil or thick liquid from the inside pocket of his uniform. He poured a small amount onto his hands then pressed it into my temples. I immediately began to feel sleepy.

"I haven't slept in a week," I said.

"I know. Now you will sleep."

With feverish eyes I watched him for a few moments. He wasn't doing any of the usual tasks the attendants did. He wasn't serving coffee, he wasn't selling cigarettes or stamps or liquor. In fact, he wasn't around at all, unless he was directly in front of me. I wondered who he was, as I fell into a deep sleep.

I woke up once when he brought a blanket to wrap around me, tucking in the ends against the cold. I asked again, "Are you a doctor? There's something healing about you, but I can't figure out—"

"No, Susan, I am not a doctor." He smiled, then pressed my forehead back, and once again I fell asleep.

After the two and a half hour journey, I woke up and looked around. He was nowhere to be seen. I stood up, feeling refreshed, and asked a train attendant, "Where is my luggage? Where is the tall man?"

She glared at me sullenly. "I have no idea what you're talking about. Just get off the train, and hurry."

I eased myself off the train onto the platform and there he was again—standing beside my luggage, smiling with the kindest smile I had ever seen. I looked at him and said, "You are an angel, aren't you?" As I uttered the words, my heart lifted up in a kind of joy that caught me by surprise.

He smiled and his eyes danced. "Now you go to the doctor. Right?"

I was still sick, but I felt elated, as if the tall man with healing powers and I were sharing an amazing confidence. "Yes, I'm on my way now. I don't know how to thank you."

His face was radiant. He shook his head and he said quietly, "Go now, then."

I turned toward the escalator, then looked back once more.

He held his large hand in the air and said, "See you later, Susan!"

On the escalator, I turned again to catch one more glimpse of him, but he was not there. I was filled with joyful peace. And even though I started vomiting again as soon as I got into the taxi, there was a certainty that I had met someone who was not of this world. I knew I was not alone. Someone was tenderly watching out for me and somehow the experience on the train had given me a deeper joy than anything I had ever known.

I arrived at the clinic for foreigners, with vomit stuck in my hair and sliding down my jeans, still throwing up even as the elevator doors opened. The nurses rushed up. "How did you get here? You're too sick to travel!" I stayed there for a few days under close watch, but the joy—the unspeakable joy—remained strong and steady. I felt I had been given a small glimpse of the life that exists all around us, and ahead of us—the reality that we can't see with our human eyes. Along with that awareness came deep praise to God, my Heavenly Father.

You are My own child, My delight and joy. I am breathing and living within you. Find your joy and hope in Me and My perfect heart. My intentions toward you are good.

It was still winter my first year in China when the spring Festival preparations began. This celebration of newness was coming in spite of the fact that the streets were blanketed in gray slush and there were no signs of spring anywhere.

Teacher Feng, one of my Mandarin tutors, spent an evening cooking in my small kitchen. She prepared six dumplings, explaining that six was the lucky number for the New Year in China.

I looked up. "Do you really believe that, Teacher Feng?"

"Maybe I do." She shyly turned away to check on the boiling water. I sensed the anticipation in the air, as my friends had proudly explained all the traditions—they were thoroughly cleaning their homes, sweeping away the bad and making room for the good. They set up special offerings of fresh fruit and tasty snacks to the kitchen god in hopes the kitchen god wouldn't remember all the bad things—the harsh words and family arguments—it had heard during the year.

They placed red streamers around their front doors to welcome in good luck. They contacted anyone who owed them money and demanded full payment, as it is bad luck to begin the new year while either owing money or lacking money owed.

Walking around the streets became more enjoyable—people

were wearing new clothes and seemed visibly happier. (Earlier, I had asked Ouyang about the grim expressions on most faces and he had said, "The government is trying to convince the people to smile more, to look happier.") But now behavior had become noticeably softer, gentler. The difference was remarkable; the feeling in the air was one of happiness and peace. On the first day of the New Year, behavior is at an all-time best, for most Chinese believe that one's conduct on the first day of the year will influence their luck for the entire year.

All schools were closed for one month and most businesses were closed for two weeks. Children were elated, expecting new, crisp, lucky money placed in red envelopes. Orange trees were being sold everywhere and I bought one to keep in my home, its fragrance sweet and fresh. My Chinese friends were buying train tickets to travel home and visit their families. Others were expecting relatives and children to return to their homes for delicious food, small gifts, and the precious lucky envelopes.

Fireworks and firecrackers are sold and lit during this time—the loud noises and pops are meant to frighten away bad spirits that might be lurking around. Tianjin is one of the cities that continues to allow fireworks and firecrackers, and a doctor told me that the emergency rooms fill with patients missing fingers or eyes due to careless handling of fireworks. On my walks to and from school, I was continually surprised with unexpected blasts and small explosions around me. From my twelfth-floor apartment for fifteen consecutive nights, sleep was difficult as the strength and volume of the fireworks—a non-stop extravaganza in the sky to rival those in Disneyland or on America's Fourth of July—were deafening and alarmingly close to the tall skyscrapers.

But it was still winter! I wondered how they could talk about spring's arrival while we were still wrapped up in padded layers, wool gloves and Mongolian-style hats with fur ear flaps.

As I was walking with my friend Meili and trying not to slip on the icy street, I asked, "Um, Meili. I have a question—why are we celebrating spring *now*? It's obviously still winter."

She looked at me, her eyes twinkling. "Ahhh . . . just wait, Susan. You'll see."

Finally, the much-anticipated day arrived. And, in spite of my doubts, the temperatures were indeed warming up. The melting snow dripped off the trees, and people began packing away their bulky winter wear in moth balls. Spring was on its glorious way.

I loved my first Chinese New Year celebration and joined in with my friends, traveling around in taxis to the homes of their uncles, aunts, grandparents and even distant relatives. Baskets of oranges and star fruit, mangoes, apples, and papaya were reverently carried in from taxi cabs. The food was special and plentiful; laughter echoed off the walls in tiny, happy homes. With all the people crowded around the tables, it was hard to see the cracks in the walls. There was always room for one more, it seemed, and people sat on beds and desks to partake of the enormous feasts. Stools that had been outside in the snow all winter were wiped off and brought inside. Cup after cup of tea was poured; chopsticks were flying to retrieve delicious morsels of food; laughter was plentiful everywhere we went.

At the end of my first Chinese New Year's Day, I watched yet another fireworks display through my windows, wrapping blankets around myself to keep warm, and I smiled. The day had been every bit as special as Thanksgiving in America, my favorite holiday. There was an intimacy of sharing. There was love expressed in families. This love had humbled and healed me a bit more, somehow.

I brought a cup of tea to bed with me, and I thought and wrote for a while as the brilliance flashed and rumbled in the sky outside the windows.

The pain is slipping away from me. I can feel it going now. I hear traces of laughter riding on the breeze, and the hard beat of sadness walking away from me.

*O*uyang and I were strolling through the streets on a spring
night, my last spring in Tianjin. The cicadas were stilled by that
late hour, and the taxi cabs had quieted for the night. A heaviness
hung in the air, and the strong scents of this Asian world invaded
my senses once again. I was feeling peaceful, at home in my
adopted land.

As we walked along, he said, "Here is a garden."

It was almost imperceptible in the moon's yellow light, but
there, beyond an iron fence, was a garden that stretched for an
entire city block. Growing within the garden park were trees
laden with blossoms, roses, and yellow chrysanthemums mixed
with delicate green vines and trailing leaves. The spiked fence
barricaded the garden from the public, but Ouyang knew where
to find the gate. And, because he began speaking so softly, I had
to lean closer to hear his words. He began telling the story of
a time long ago, when he was a small boy and first stumbled
upon the garden.

It was 1966 and he had seen far too much destruction
from behind his mother's blue Mao trousers. People were being
punished for crimes such as reading a book or carrying flowers, or
singing a phrase from an opera that wasn't one of Madame Mao's
compositions. The message was clear and strangely paradoxical:
anything of beauty was strictly forbidden. That included gardens,
except those sanctioned by the government for the purpose of
raising flowers to be used for national holidays.

The gardener, Mr. Dao, noticed the small boy hiding
amongst the roses. He scolded him for sneaking into the forbidden, fragrant oasis, and then invited him to return the following
day. Little Ouyang began visiting every afternoon and Mr. Dao
taught him how to plant, prune, and fertilize the roses. Many
happy hours were spent there, with one old man teaching one
little boy how to grow beautiful flowers.

Two of Mr. Dao's roses—"Blue Danube" and "Vienna

Charm"—won prizes in the Vienna flower show. Years later he unfortunately became one of over two hundred thousand people killed in the earthquake of 1976. Ouyang still grieves the loss of his friend.

We wandered around the garden, inhaling the lush scents and touching the velvety blooms with the tips of our fingers. I recognized some of them as being identical to some of Ouyang's patio roses. He moved amongst the bushes as if he were greeting beloved friends.

I could almost hear the ranting and screaming that had raged in the streets surrounding this hidden garden. The flowers, in their purity and simplicity, had been shielded from the rampant terror on the other side of the fence. And one small boy, sporting a single pigtail on the side of his head, had been compelled by their beauty and listened to a faithful old man who taught him how to lovingly nurture a secret world of beauty.

When the splendid becomes splintered, and the glorious becomes gauntleted, there will still be a garden filled with astonishing brilliance hidden somewhere. This secret place, with its intoxicating aromas and flowers, will yearn for the sun in the murkiness and shadow of what once was. But the light will pierce through the night, turning the remnants of what has been broken, into a sanctuary.

When the scaffolding that keeps us propped up crashes down, we forget that deep within the collapse are the truths that have been planted by the very breath of God.

I am the source of all Light and I will fill your path with Light so that you will not be lost anymore. 'The light shines in the darkness, but the darkness has not understood it' (John 1:5).

*I*t was my eleventh Chinese New Year. The lobby downstairs

was decorated with spectacular displays of orange trees lit with tiny lights. Living so near Hong Kong was fun, but I missed the north, where China was brand new to me and felt more like living in a small village. I had learned to love the New Year festivities in this enormous city, though. Lights, flower shows, and fruit baskets abounded. Breaths of fresh air seemed to sweep the tired, hazy metropolis.

The winter of my life—my hibernation and hiding—was coming to an end. Jesus Christ was rolling the blanket of shame off of me. He was personally taking away my very sins.

In China, land of a broken people racing to catch up with time lost during the Cultural Revolution, my own heart was awakening after its own dark slumber. I was breathing in new winds of renewal—fresh reminders that God was with me.

What a joy to actually fling apart the heavy veil that had clouded my spiritual vision and to be able to behold the new light of morning, streaming in from the One who is Light Himself.

During ten years of living in China, I flew across the Pacific Ocean forty-five times. I lived through four days of house arrest during the Kosovo crisis in 1999. I lived in the very city where SARS and Avian Flu originated. Once in a while, a wave of fear would rise up and spread through my school community—some teachers and families would pack up and return to their home countries, frightened by terror threats and health epidemics. For me, the wonder of living overseas became diluted and mixed into daily adventures amid a huge sea of cultural differences and those days the expatriates fondly term China Days. But Asia became my second home. It offended, insulted and puzzled me many times, but it became part of me.

Forgiveness and restoration are part of the Spring Festival, and I found myself walking into springtime. I entered a new spiritual era in my life's journey—smiling in the hope of the new beginning that had reached into the distant corner where I had been hiding. There is no place God can't find His children.

You will never be lost to My love.

I've made it through the long journey. The darkness is growing paler now; it's almost sunrise. I'm in the clearing and the
angry voices around me are fading. The internal chatting in my
mind has stopped.

In my imagination I look down and see the white lace
edging on my Sunday school socks, the patent leather Mary Janes
swinging, skimming the church basement floor and I hear my
mother's voice dramatizing the story of the one lost lamb. I hear
the Shepherd's voice calling and calling across the meadow and
through the long years that stretch between. I hear Him calling
through the young pastor's words and my father's eyes. Is it my
pastor or my father? I'm not sure, but there are other pastors too,
lined up in suits and ties, smooth-faced, waiting for me to come
to the altar. Why? I am so ugly, so wrong; so weak and so bloated
and bleeding. I need to get up there, to the front. I need to kneel
and pray but I can't move my legs. Why? Are they broken? What's
wrong with my legs?

Something is bleeding. I look down and see the dark blood
on the lost lamb—the wool is stained and matted. Someone
needs to gently comb out the snarls. Someone needs to straighten
out the broken limbs and to smooth the terrain, covering the
holes so the lamb won't fall into them anymore.

But then there's a slight rustle in the morning breeze and
I see the Shepherd Himself striding through the embers and
ashes of the altar that has now been split apart. The stained glass
windows are getting grimy and murky, the organist is playing the
wrong notes. The pastors are now wearing rags that are worn
and frayed—they are smoking stale cigarettes that are making me
cough, and the smoke is blocking my view of the Shepherd. I
wait on the ground because my legs can't move and there are too

many treacherous holes all around. If I try to get up and walk, surely I will fall again. So I wait. Then, there He is again, the steady, strong Shepherd. He is walking with a large gait that cuts through the smoke and debris, and He is looking directly at me. He doesn't seem to notice the stains and dirt and He is—in words of the heart—telling me He wants to pick me up and clean the open wounds with His kiss. He reaches down to where I am hunkered in the mud and lifts me effortlessly higher and carries me to a safer place. He is whispering words of love and healing, promising that He will never leave me. And while I am recovering He stays near. The snarls and knots are being loosened and there is a fragrant aroma on His breath that enters me and carries out the sadness, more and more of it, every time I exhale.

He begins to remind me of the love we shared in my child-hood. He remembers! And now He's sharing His hopes and designs for my future, for the place He desires to build within me. It is a place where He will abide. It's my heart He's talking about. He is explaining that He has already done all the work to make it perfectly clean and whole, a fitting home for His Spirit. It will be a home that has been through the white-hot fire, transformed and sparkling like crystal. It will be a home filled with light scattering from each hidden corner. He is now laying stones and gathering bricks to rebuild its walls. He mixes the cement Himself and hand selects each beam to make it strong. It will be spacious, with no dark closets. He is filling each room with His own love and His own character. I ask Him, "But what about my sin? I have failed." He looks at me and His eyes burn a holy love right into me. "I have forgiven you." And I marvel that in the leaving of home, I have found my home again—in His heart.

Scandalous love! This love shook the world when it was displayed on a simple cross—the cross of our faith and the symbol of our hope. It was scandalous, the people said. The Son of God nailed to a cross like a common thief? It was seen by both pauper and king to be monumentally inappropriate, outrageously disgraceful, unthinkably contemptible, a stumbling block to many. It was shockingly despicable, but it was scandalously necessary. It was the only way we could be saved, saved from ourselves—a love more "scandalous" than our failures. And there is nothing from which we can't be saved, rescued, redeemed and healed. He is bringing us out of our layers of pain, closets of shame, and rocks under which we've been hiding—to live, play and dance in the sunlight. "Therefore, there is now no condemnation for those who are in Christ Jesus" (Rom. 8:1).

This is the story of my journey. What is your story? Are you living a scandal that is trying to destroy you? Are you afraid to let the self-protective layers peel back, exposing your raw and aching self? Are you living with pain, brokenness and heartache? Come to Jesus. Yes, bring your broken spirit before Him. Plead with Him, argue with Him, crave His presence for your thirsty soul. He was wounded for our transgressions. He was bruised for our iniquities, for the totality of our sins. The punishment of our peace was laid upon Him. By His stripes, by the scars on His back, in His hands, in His feet—we are healed. He was despised and rejected by mankind. He was a man of sorrows and ambitiously acquainted with grief. And for some inexplicable reason, we are incredibly precious to Him.

Are you desperate for healing? Are you hungering for restoration? Bring your hurting heart to God. Open your life to his redemption and your mind to His healing. Confess to Him the scandal of your life and He will replace it with the ultimate scandal of His love.

In the process of my restoration, God chose to take me to China to teach and to minister. Over the past decade, as I have flown back and forth across the world's largest ocean, I have gazed out the window of the airliner at the immense body of water 32,000 feet below, various scriptures have come to mind. The first is found in Psalm 103:11-13, where we are reminded by King David, who had a few scandals of his own: "For as high as the heavens are above the earth, so great is his love for those who fear him; as far as the east is from the west, so far has he removed our transgressions from us."

God has removed our sins, transgressions and scandals much further than we could ever expect. Still gazing upon the silver ocean below, I am reminded that God will "hurl all our iniquities into the depths of the sea" (Micah 7:19). That promise feels exceedingly good to me, way down deep. If God really does that with our sins, there is absolutely no way that I could possibly find the torture of scandal that has been flung into that infinite ocean. Neither can you.

Acknowledgments

This is my first book and would have been impossible to write by myself. I am deeply grateful to my wonderful Cladach editors, Catherine and Hannah, for being prayerful and wise in their work.

To Debra Self, my best friend of forty-four years, who knows my heart inside and out. Thank you for proofreading with your impeccable eye for detail. I love you, Debbie.

To my brothers for your blessing, friendship and hilarious humor that keeps me laughing. Thank you for letting me focus on the message and not have to worry much about other details. You are both exquisitely talented and sensitive men. I love you and am so proud of who you are.

To my spiritual brother, Tom Ross, and his wife, Kathy, for covering me in prayer from their home in Minnesota as I fly around the world.

To Jim Burrill, for sending computers from Colorado on an "as needed basis."

To Corrianne Lasivicious, my South African-turned-Brazilian friend, for sharing her artistic expertise.

To Ouyang Long, still living in Tianjin, for your photographic memory, rapid fire email responses, and deepening heart for God.

To Howard John Ong, for designing the website and sharing ideas over Chinese dinners.

To my friends and family who have encouraged, blessed and prayed along the way. I owe you much more, but all I can say is "thank you": Kathleen Bade, Judy Christy, Jerene Dunn, Balaji Venkatesh, William Stevenson, Michael Skinner, Janet Martin, Richard Marchal, Simona Stefanusca, Kris Miller, Cherie Whitzhunt, Sharon Weik, Kathy England, Barbara Sweeney, Pat Carbonaro, Mitchal Vaughn, Sally Savas, Riete Njeken, Melisa Eyle, and Dr. Dao Shizhen.

And to the good and praying saints at Community Presbyerian Church of Danville, California.

Additional copies of this book are available from the publisher at www.cladach.com, and through bookstores and online retailers.

Visit the author's website at www.susanelainejenkins.com for updates on her journey and to send Ms. Jenkins your comments.

Both the author and the publisher would enjoy hearing from the readers of this book, especially if this story has been a help or encouragement to you.